A Big Wave

It's easier to photograph a sand dune than a wave. This book is, I think, a pretty good picture of a pretty big wave. Bear in mind, though, that the wave is rolling on, and the photograph is blurred in places. A month's more work would have been nice, but a year's work wouldn't have finished the job.

The idea of publishing a book about a standard, which changes every month, less than a year after the standard's first rough draft is a little scary. But it's a very good idea. We are living (and XML was built) in Internet time, but that hasn't changed the fact that a good book is the best way to explain something important to a lot of people.

The way it worked was, I got the chapters by e-mail and hunted down the (few) mistakes and (many) places where the standard had shifted out from under the authors—all to the accompaniment of background shouts from the publishers about "we gotta ship now!" There will be mistakes. They'll be mostly my fault, either because I missed them in the text or because I helped change the standard. But I think that if you read this, you'll have a pretty accurate understanding of what XML is and isn't. I will say, though, that if you're going to sit down and write a computer program to do something with XML—which is not that hard—this book is a good place to start, but you really must read the full specification. It's not fun, but it's free, it's short, and we went to a lot of work trying not only to get it right, but to make it useful.

Low-Hanging Fruit

Building XML was actually pretty easy. The Web had shown, in an unbelievably short time, how much you could do with a few simple tools. The SGML community, by dint of arduous work over a decade, had learned which pieces of the standard were really needed to get things done. The Web was crying out for extensibility, modularity, and reusability. SGML had 'em. All we had to do was leave out a few parts and explain what was left. This has to count as one of the juiciest low-hanging fruits in the history of standards-based computing.

Important: We didn't invent anything. XML's one "new" thing is well-formedness, but a whole lot of computer programs had been doing useful work with this type of text for years. Once again, all we did was observe what actually worked and then wrote it down.

XML's difficulties were in the politics and personalities, not the design work. With almost every feature of SGML that was left out, there were cries of agony from people who really needed that little piece. There were those who worried about XML because it was too simple and Web-oriented, and others who worried because it was too complex and SGML-like. If we hadn't had deft leadership from Jon Bosak, consistent support from Charles Goldfarb, and heroic volumes of work from our committee members and my co-editors (mostly stolen from their "real" jobs), the whole project would quickly have fallen apart. Others without whom XML would not be worth a book: James Clark, for inventing solutions to many of our hairiest problems, including the name *XML*; Eve Maler, for gimlet-eyed editing of dozens of successive nearly identical drafts, improving every one; Jean Paoli, for convincing Microsoft that SGML was not the enemy; Phil Karlton and Lauren Wood, for doing the same at Netscape; Michael Sperberg-McQueen, for Herculean grammar engineering; and Yuri Rubinsky, for building the community that it all grew out of.

What Happens Next?

This book contains predictions about XML's future that I think are pretty astute. But I have one prediction that's even better, guaranteed in fact: By the time you read this, new applications will have come along that are not predicted here.

In 1997 and 1998, I think that metadata will be the XML's "killer app." No library or filing cabinet or document repository is without metadata; but the World Wide Web, and most intranets, have none. This is idiotic, and the need for useful information about information is immense. The metadata problem is not solved, but it is clear that XML will be a part of the solution.

Why XML Is Important

About 10 years ago, working on the *Oxford English Dictionary* project, I first encountered the idea that when you store a document on a computer, you should tell the computer mostly about what its parts are, and leave the decision about what it looks like for later. "Of course," I thought, and wondered why all the world's documents weren't being stored that way.

I still wonder, and now I think it just might happen. Ten years ago, traditionalists could scoff at SGML, saying, "This is not appropriate for secretaries typing memos, nor for knowledge workers typing reports. It's the presentation that matters." They might have been right then, but today those memos are becoming e-mail, and those reports are delivered electronically. I honestly can't think of any important class of documents today—outside of pure marketing—where structure, reusability, and longevity don't matter.

Knowledge, which never comes cheap, is carried by language. Text is language made permanent. Generalized markup preserves text in the face of change and makes it a richer, better knowledge vehicle. XML makes generalized markup easy. That's why it's important.

—Tim Bray, Vancouver, August 1997

> **Tim Bray** *is co-editor of the XML Specification and is principal of Textuality, an independent consulting practice.*

presenting
XML

Richard Light

201 West 103rd Street
Indianapolis, IN 46290

Copyright © 1997 by Sams.net Publishing

FIRST EDITION

International Standard Book Number: 1-57521-334-6

Library of Congress Catalog Card Number: 97-67511

2000   99   98   97   4   3   2   1

Interpretation of the printing code: the rightmost double-digit number is the year of the book's printing; the rightmost single-digit, the number of the book's printing. For example, a printing code of 97-1 shows that the first printing of the book occurred in 1997.

Composed in AGaramond and MCPdigital by Macmillan Computer Publishing

Printed in the United States of America

President   *Richard K. Swadley*

Publisher and Director of Acquisitions   *Jordan Gold*

Director of Product Development   *Dean Miller*

Executive Editor   *Beverly M. Eppink*

Managing Editor   *Brice P. Gosnell*

Indexing Manager   *Johnna L. VanHoose*

Director of Marketing   *Kelli S. Spencer*

Product Marketing Manager   *Kim Margolius*

Associate Product Marketing Manager   *Jennifer Pock*

Marketing Coordinator   *Linda Beckwith*

Acquisitions Editor
Beverly M. Eppink

Development Editor
Bob Correll

Production Editor
Ryan Rader

Copy Editor
Andrew Cupp

Indexer
Kelly Talbot

Technical Reviewer
Tim Bray

Editorial Coordinators
Mandie Rowell
Katie Wise

Technical Edit Coordinator
Lorraine E. Schaffer

Resource Coordinators
Deborah Frisby
Charlotte Clapp

Editorial Assistants
Carol Ackerman
Andi Richter
Rhonda Tinch-Mize
Karen Williams

Cover Designer
Aren Howell

Book Designer
Sandra Schroeder

Copy Writer
David Reichwein

Production Team Supervisor
Brad Chinn

Production
Chris Livengood
Tim Osborn
Gene Redding
Janet Seib

Overview

Contents

Part II   XML in Detail   65

5   The XML Approach   67

Dedication

This book is dedicated to the large number of people in the SGML and W3C communities who have selflessly given their time and expertise to make the idea of XML a reality.

Acknowledgments

I would like to thank my wife, Jacky, for her steady support through the hectic process of writing this book, and my son, Noel, for letting me have enough access to my (his?) computer to actually write it!

Thanks also to Beverly and colleagues at Sams.net for their support and guidance, to Technical Editor Tim Bray for politely pointing out my errors of understanding, and to my contributing authors Simon North and Charles A. Allen. All these people have been a constant source of ideas and enthusiasm for this project.

—*Richard Light*

About the Authors

Lead Author

Richard Light (richard@light.demon.co.uk) is a freelance consultant and software developer, specializing in museum information systems. He has tracked SGML since the late 1980s, and OUP published his "The SGML Tagger" add-on software in 1993. He is currently Treasurer of the International SGML Users' Group. Richard lives in West Sussex, England, with his wife, Jacky, and son, Noel.

Contributing Authors

Simon North (sintac@xs4all.nl) is a languages graduate and is also a qualified avionics engineer. His background includes working as a helicopter repair technician, a software quality assurance engineer, and a technical translator. Simon is an experienced technical writer and is an expert on all forms of technical documentation, specializing in online, multimedia, and interactive delivery methods. He is one of the authors of the Dutch national standard for consumer documentation. He has been involved with SGML since 1989, and he was an active participant in Dutch CALS/SGML standardization activities. Simon is an avid Internet surfer, having built his first intranet in 1993. His latest hobby (since giving up free-fall parachuting) is collecting e-mail accounts: Simon can be contacted at sintac@xs4all.nl. For *Presenting XML*, Simon wrote Chapters 16, 17, and 18 and Appendixes A and B.

Charles A. Allen (charles@webMethods.com) is a cofounder of webMethods, the leader in Web Automation. Prior to joining webMethods, Charles was a founding member of Open Environment Corporation, where he took on senior-level responsibility for business development and strategic sales activities and was instrumental in Open Environment's acquisition of Jarrah Technologies. Prior to Open Environment, Charles worked for Cambridge Technology Group as a consultant specializing in client/server technology. He has also worked as an independent software consultant and a U.S.-based reporter/researcher for Asahi Shimbun. Charles attended Princeton and Yale Universities. Charles wrote Chapter 15 of *Presenting XML*.

Tell Us What You Think!

As a reader, you are the most important critic and commentator of our books. We value your opinion and want to know what we're doing right, what we could do better, what areas you'd like to see us publish in, and any other words of wisdom you're willing to pass our way. You can help us make strong books that meet your needs and give you the computer guidance you require.

Do you have access to the World Wide Web? Then check out our site at `http://www.mcp.com`.

> **Note:** If you have a technical question about this book, call the technical support line at 317-581-3833, or send e-mail to `support@mcp.com`.

As the team leader of the group that created this book, I welcome your comments. You can fax, e-mail, or write me directly to let me know what you did or didn't like about this book—as well as what we can do to make our books stronger. Here's the information:

Fax: 317-581-4669

E-mail: `mset_mgr@sams.mcp.com`

Mail: Beverly M. Eppink
        Comments Department
        Sams Publishing
        201 W. 103rd Street
        Indianapolis, IN 46290

Introduction

In 1996 a group of 80 SGML (Standard Generalized Markup Language) experts spent a hectic 11-week period developing a simplified version of SGML that could be used on the World Wide Web. The aim was to provide Web users with a means of defining their own tags and attributes when they wanted to, instead of being forced to use the HTML tagging scheme. By November 1996, the World Wide Web Consortium SGML working group was ready to announce the first draft of XML—or Extensible Markup Language—at the SGML 96 conference in Boston.

Since then, the XML language draft has been updated twice, and the first draft of the XML linking mechanism has been released. When complete, the XML standard will consist of three parts:

- XML-Lang: The actual language that XML documents use.
- XML-Link: A set of conventions for linking within and between XML documents and other Web resources.
- XS: The XML style sheet language.

Thus, XML will provide a complete, platform-independent and system-independent environment for the authoring and delivery of information resources across the Web. It will support much richer hypertextual linking than HTML offers.

In this book, we offer you an introduction to XML and a review of its main features. We show you some of the ways in which XML can and might be used, both on the Web and within intranets.

Who Should Read This Book?

If you're interested in the future of the World Wide Web, you need to read *Presenting XML!* This book is designed to cater to a range of levels of interest—from strategic overview to technical detail.

At the broadest level, this book aims to give an overview of the potential of the XML technology. This will be relevant to anyone considering how to get more out of the World Wide Web, and anyone who is using Web technology within an intranet. The successful deployment of XML could have a dramatic effect on the way that the Web does its business: the relationship between *clients* and *servers*; the nature of information delivery and commerce on the Web; the whole concept of a *Web site*. As such, XML is a subject that cannot be ignored by anyone who aims to do business, or simply deliver information, on the Web.

At a more detailed level, the book provides a thorough summary of what XML actually is. For anyone who is considering the adoption of an XML strategy, this should be sufficient to gain a clear idea of the areas covered by XML and the capabilities that it offers. To achieve this, we examine the draft XML standard fairly closely and give an overview of what the three parts of the XML specification contain. We also provide examples of XML applications.

Note: The XML specification is very much a moving target, but we are confident that the changes that are made from this point forward (and there will be changes) will not affect the "big picture" in a major way.

Throughout the book, we assume that the reader has some level of familiarity with HTML coding, and we make comparisons between HTML and XML wherever relevant. This should help to establish the differences between XML and HTML, as well as build on existing knowledge. (However, extensive knowledge of HTML is not a requirement to understand the book!)

How This Book Is Organized

Presenting XML is divided into four main parts and two appendixes.

Part I, "Introducing XML," gives a relatively self-contained overview and history of XML. It starts by explaining the concept of *generalized markup*, of which XML is an example. It explains why HTML is unable to fulfill all the demands that are made on it, and the reasons something like XML is needed on the Web. The main advantages of XML are summarized, and the section ends with an outline of the resources that will be required to actually implement XML applications.

Part II, "XML in Detail," contains the technical stuff. In this section, we go through the XML language specification in detail and review its main features.

We then look more briefly at the other two aspects of the XML specification: linking and style sheets. Finally, we review the behavior that is expected of software that processes XML documents.

In Part III, "Using XML," we go back to the broader picture, and see how XML might be put to practical use. This is tackled in a number of ways.

First, we look at a typical HTML page and see what needs to be done to it in order to make it valid as an XML document. The aim here is not to suggest that anyone should be rushing off to convert all their HTML to XML! It is meant to be an opportunity to understand some key differences between HTML and XML, starting from a familiar format.

Next, we tackle a simple potential application of XML—for memos. This covers all the following essentials:

- Writing a memo DTD
- Encoding a memo
- Using XML's powerful linking facilities
- Writing a simple style sheet

After this, we paint a broad-brush picture of the potential role that XML can play in integrating diverse business systems and supporting Web-based commerce. Finally, we examine what effect XML is liable to have for a specific application area, or *vertical market*. The area in question is that of museum information systems. You will learn how XML can help to deliver complex, structured museum information in a flexible and cost-effective manner.

Part IV, "The Future of XML," takes a look at how this new technology is likely to shape up in practice.

We start with a review of the software that is emerging. In addition to XML-specific offerings, we look at packages that have their roots in SGML but are now providing significant functionality for XML applications.

Next, we review the issues that remain to be resolved in the XML specification. This review begins with a discussion of the common heritage that SGML and XML share, and it goes on to review activities that contribute to the completion of the XML specification. Finally, we look at how the existence of XML is causing SGML itself to change and develop, with positive implications for XML.

We conclude with a review of real-world XML applications. Some of these are actually up and running already, while others are still at the planning stage. The applications described give an interesting, even exciting, glimpse of some of the things that can and will be done with XML. No mean feat for a standard that isn't even complete!

The appendixes provide reference and supporting material.

Appendix A summarizes the differences between XML and SGML. This is, in effect, a list of the things that were left out of SGML in order to make XML a viable proposition for the Web.

Appendix B lists references and sources of further information on XML. As with any W3C initiative, it is important to consult online sources for the up-to-date picture. This is particularly true for XML, given its relatively incomplete state at the time of writing.

We have actually put theory into practice, by authoring this book in XML-like SGML, and using its inherent flexibility to deliver the message in a variety of media. The Sams.net Web site that supports this book, which can be found at the URL `http://www.mcp.com/info/1-57521/1-57521-334-6`, contains an HTML version and a browsable SGML version. In addition, the same source text was converted by an XML-like style sheet into Rich Text Format, so that it could take its part in the normal copy-editing cycle at Sams.net and actually appear in printed form!

Conventions Used in This Book

In this book, we use some basic conventions for consistency. When presenting actual XML markup, we use `monospace` type. This type is also used for fuller examples and listings that are given their own space, like this:

```
fuller examples and listings
that are given their own space
```

Beyond this type convention, we use sidebars to pick out important pieces of information. These take the following different forms:

Note: The Note sidebar is used to present an interesting piece of information relating to the current topic.

Warning: The Warning sidebar flags issues and problems of which you should be aware.

Tip: The Tip sidebar contains a handy tip or technique that you might find helpful.

Introducing XML

Markup in Theory and Practice

by Richard Light

This book aims to tell you about XML (*eXtensible Markup Language*). However, in order to understand XML, you need some background.

In this chapter, you start by looking at what the term *markup* means, and then you learn about the idea of *generalized markup*. You'll learn how the *SGML* standard implements these ideas and then see how the *HTML* language can be treated as an SGML application. This chapter covers the jobs that HTML does well, and it highlights some areas where HTML is struggling. By the end of this chapter, you should have a good idea of what XML is and why it is needed.

What Is Markup?

Markup is any additional information that is added to the text of a document. You don't have to go far to find it: Every word processor inserts lots of markup into the documents it creates. This markup is used to control the way the document looks—both on the screen and when it is printed out. It represents things such as

- Font family and font size
- Bold, underlining, and italic
- Page size
- Margins

In addition, the markup used by many word processors can control more so-phisticated aspects of document creation and presentation, such as

- Footnotes
- Bookmarks
- Tables of contents
- Index entries

Although you cause most of this markup to exist (by selecting font and para-graph styles, setting margins, and so on), in a modern word processing envi-ronment you never type it in explicitly, or even see it. You just see its results when your document looks and acts the way you intended.

> Note: The preceding wasn't always the case, because before WYSIWYG (what you see is what you get) systems came along, authors were often faced with the job of inserting markup by hand.

In most cases, the markup is held in a binary format, so it wouldn't make any sense to you even if you could look at it. However, on the journey from its original SGML (XML-like) form to the Word format used by the Sams.net edi-torial process, this book passed through a format called RTF (*Rich Text Format*), which uses ASCII codes to represent the markup. This is the first paragraph of this chapter, encoded in RTF:

```
\keepn\par\pard\sb240\sl-264 \b0\hyphpar0
This book aims to tell you about XML ("eXtensible Markup
Language"). However, in order to understand XML, you need some
background.
```

All RTF control words begin with the \ character. The whole slew of them on the first line tells how the paragraph will be formatted. Here is the meaning of this markup:

- \keepn: Keeps this paragraph with the next paragraph.
- \par: Starts a new paragraph.
- \pard: Restores the default paragraph properties.
- \sb240: Twelve-point space before the paragraph.
- \sl-264: Puts a 13.2-point space between lines. The negative value means that this spacing is used even if it is shorter than the tallest character.
- \b0: Switches bold off.
- \hyphpar0: Switches off automatic hyphenation for the paragraph.

RTF was developed with the aim of making it easier to transfer word processor documents between different hardware platforms and software packages. Its primary role is as an interchange format. RTF markup is clearly documented, as the preceding example shows. Any program that can read RTF files and interpret the markup they contain is known as an *RTF reader*. Such a program doesn't have to be a word processor; it could easily be a read-only browser or a desktop publishing package.

> Note: In this respect, at least, RTF is similar to XML. XML also is designed to allow documents to be interpreted correctly and used by different software on a wide range of hardware platforms.

What Is Generalized Markup?

You just learned that markup is a fact of life—at least in a word processing setting. What is different about *generalized* markup?

The key distinction is that most of the markup in word processor documents is there to help with the presentation of the document. Generalized, or descriptive, markup has a much simpler philosophy: It just indicates the structural significance of a piece of text within the document as a whole. Thus, in the RTF example, the only instruction that counts as generalized markup is \par, which states that the next piece of text is a new paragraph.

If you apply a generalized approach to the RTF example, it immediately simplifies the markup:

```
\par This book aims to tell you about XML: "eXtensible Markup
Language". However, in order to understand XML you need some
background.
```

On the other hand, this means that the document no longer contains any instructions on how to display the paragraph!

In order to display and print documents containing generalized markup, you need some means of providing the formatting information that you have taken out of the documents themselves. This is typically achieved by some sort of *style sheet* mechanism. A style sheet contains information on how each structural object within the document is to be formatted. Style sheets have a couple of advantages over formatting information embedded in the text:

- Consistency: All headings, paragraphs, and so on are formatted in the same way. It is all too easy when using a word processor to decide on a different style for your headings and change them all by hand, only to miss one on the last page. I've done it. Haven't you?

- Flexibility: By associating different style sheets with a document, you can make it look slightly different or totally different. Thus you can easily create, for example, a large print edition of your documents for the visually handicapped in addition to the standard edition, without having to edit the source document at all.

Desktop publishing software frequently uses a style sheet mechanism.

SGML

> Note: Because XML is actually based on the SGML standard, this description of SGML deliberately has been kept short. Only aspects of SGML that help your understanding of the overall situation are described here. Any specific aspect of the SGML standard that also applies to XML will be described in Part II, "XML in Detail."

SGML, or *Standard Generalized Markup Language*, is an example of a generalized markup system. It is an International Standard (ISO 8879:1986), which was first published in 1986. SGML provides a markup scheme that is simple, platform-independent, and extremely flexible. It is widely used for encoding structured documents ranging in size and complexity from aircraft maintenance manuals to haiku.

Note that SGML is not a piece of software. It is simply a way of representing documents. If you want to do something useful with an SGML-encoded document, you need software that understands SGML and does the job you want. Because of the size and complexity of the full SGML standard, such software tends to be relatively expensive.

Structured Documents

SGML introduces the important concept of an *end-tag* to mark the end of a structural element. The initial paragraph of this chapter would look like this when marked up in SGML:

```
<p>This book aims to tell you about XML: "eXtensible Markup
Language". However, in order to understand XML you need some
background.</p>
```

The <p> is a start-tag (replacing the RTF \par code), and the </p> is an end-tag.

In SGML terminology, the paragraph is an *element* within the document, and it has an *element type* of p (which stands for *paragraph*).

The presence of end-tags allows SGML to support a hierarchical view of a document's structure. Thus, the quoted phrase within the paragraph could be marked up in its own right:

```
<p>This book aims to tell you about XML: <q>eXtensible Markup
Language</q>. However, in order to understand XML you need some
background.</p>
```

Now you have a q (*quotation*) element inside your p element. This process can continue upward: You can embed your paragraph inside a section, put that section inside a chapter, and finally put the chapter into the single element that contains the entire book. It also can go downward: Some SGML applications (for example, those involved in linguistic analysis) mark up every single word in each document!

Notice that the quotation marks have vanished from the paragraph. One useful feature of generalized markup is that it can replace specific characters like this. Putting the quotation marks back in can be part of the style sheet's job. This also gives you more flexibility. You can decide to use single quotes ('), double quotes ("), or even French-style chevron (« ») quotation marks when displaying the document.

In a similar way, you can leave out chapter and section numbers and let your style sheet number them for you when the document is displayed. This makes it much easier to rearrange the order of chapters and sections as a book develops. You don't have to renumber. You can even get your style sheet to generate a table of contents for you (with correct page numbers) from the chapter headings in the book itself.

Elements with Added Value: Attributes

Marking up a document's structure is a useful task, but for practical applications, you often need to add more information. For example, this book has several kinds of note boxes: plain notes, warnings, cautions, and tips. Following the principles of generalized markup, you might define a single note element to hold all these different types of note. But if you do that, where and how do you indicate what type of note you have?

Recognizing that you will often want to add value to your structural markup in this way, SGML provides a general facility called *attributes*. These additional pieces of information appear in your start-tags. For example, a warning-type note element would be marked up like this:

```
<note type="warning">In cases of dire emergency ...
```

The <note> start-tag now includes an *attribute specification* for the attribute type.

SGML attributes can take any of 15 types of values, which can broadly be grouped as follows:

- Character data: Any sequence of characters that is valid in SGML.
- Entity names: References to resources outside the SGML document.
- IDs: A unique identifier for this element within the document.
- ID pointers: Cross-references within the SGML document to elements with the IDs quoted.
- Name-type attributes: Attributes whose values, broadly speaking, are limited to one or more words consisting only of SGML *Name* characters (which are letters, digits, and a small number of separator characters).
- Notations: Attributes that specify the notation in which the content of an element is expressed.
- Number-type attributes: Attributes whose values are limited to one or more words consisting only of SGML *Number* characters (which are digits).

Entities

SGML is designed to cope with real-world documents, which typically include things such as illustrations that can't possibly be marked up in SGML. They typically contain nontextual information expressed in binary format. SGML's approach to this problem is to provide the concept of an *entity*, which can be thought of as any sequence of characters or bit patterns that can be treated as a unit. One common example of this is a file, although you probably don't normally think of files that way. Several types of entities are found in SGML, but the type that is relevant for multimedia documents is the *non-SGML data entity*.

You've already seen the attribute types for referring to entities. The following is how you would embed an image file into a `figure` element:

```
<figure entity="figure1">
```

Note that the attribute value `"figure1"` isn't a filename. Somewhere at the start of the document, an *entity declaration* attaches `"figure1"` to a real filename and indicates the *notation* in which the file is encoded:

```
<!ENTITY figure1 SYSTEM "fig1.bmp" NDATA BMP>
```

This says that the entity name `"figure1"` means the file `"fig1.bmp"`, which conforms to the `BMP` notation.

This method of embedding multimedia resources into SGML documents is totally open-ended, because there is no limit on the number of notations that can be declared.

Another use of entities in SGML is to represent characters that are difficult to enter on the keyboard or characters that have a different representation on different platforms. Accented characters are a good example of this, as anyone who has tried to copy a document in French from a PC to a Mac knows. SGML's approach is to use an entity reference to represent the character, as in the following example:

```
Fernand L&eacute;ger
```

In this example, `&eacute;` is an entity reference for the character é. This entity reference is treated as *system data* (`SDATA`), which means that it will be mapped to the correct representation of that character when the SGML document is processed on any platform.

SGML as a Metalanguage

SGML doesn't enforce any particular set of element types on its users. Instead, it empowers users by providing them with a means to declare their own element types. Therefore, SGML is better described as a *metalanguage*—a language for defining markup languages. Each time SGML is used to solve a certain type of problem, that is known as an SGML *application.*

This flexibility is achieved by letting SGML users define what is allowed in each document. This is achieved by providing a set of rules, collectively known as the *document type definition*, or *DTD.* The DTD states (among other things) the following:

- The element types allowed within the document
- The characteristics of each element type, including its allowed attributes and the content it can have
- The notations that can be encountered within the document
- The entities that can be encountered within the document

The DTD is actually part of each SGML document. Part of the DTD (the *external DTD subset*) is normally held in a separate file, but it is still treated as though it forms part of the document. This means that SGML documents are self-describing, because they carry their own structuring rules around with them.

> Note: This doesn't mean that SGML documents contain everything you might ever need to know about them. Some things, such as the semantics of elements and attributes and the conventions for the correct entry of data within certain elements, cannot be expressed within the formal SGML syntax. All you can do is put these rules into SGML comments within the document, or document them separately.

HTML as an SGML Application

Even if you have used HTML coding extensively, many of the concepts in that description of SGML might not be familiar to you. Yet HTML is perhaps the most widely known SGML application that exists. How can this be?

Syntax Conventions

For a start, HTML uses SGML syntax. You have start-tags, end-tags, and at-tribute specifications. The following code, taken from a random Web page, is a fragment of perfectly valid SGML:

```
<body bgcolor="#FFFFFF" text="#000000" link="#054BBB"
vlink="#054BBB" background="/Images/backshadow2.gif">
<a name="top"></a>
<img src="/Images/bump.gif" border=0 width=50 height=5 align=left>
```

DTD Design Approach

Two HTML DTDs are "proper" SGML and are officially supported by W3C: HTML 2.0 and HTML 3.2. These define sets of elements suited to the job that the HTML application was originally designed to support—online display of pages of textual information, interspersed with images, with hyperlinks within and between these pages.

The design of the HTML DTDs has been influenced by the demands of online display. Several of the element types are included purely to support visual features of the resulting Web page, such as the following examples:

- br is a line break.
- hr is a horizontal rule.

Other elements are provided solely as *switches* for the current font style, such as the following examples:

- tt is typewriter text.
- b is bold.
- i is italic.

In each of these elements, the start-tag switches on the feature and the end-tag switches it off again:

```
<b>Very important:</b> switch off before disconnecting.
```

In other words, HTML (in particular HTML 2.0) tends to use the SGML markup to hold full details about the style in which the page is to be presented. As you have already seen, this brings the advantage of self-contained HTML pages (with no need for a separate style sheet) and the disadvantage of inflex-ibility. Each page has a single, predetermined presentation style.

It is also clear that the designers of the HTML DTDs were eager to use SGML's minimization facilities to the full. This is a good strategy because it can greatly reduce the amount of markup you need to add to a Web page. The most obvious example is end-tag omission—the practice of excluding an end-tag and allowing the SGML system to infer its presence. As an example, the p (paragraph) element type is declared as follows in the HTML 2.0 DTD:

```
<!ELEMENT p - O (%text)*>
```

The - O bit of that declaration states that the <p> start-tag has to be provided each time, but the </p> end-tag can be omitted if you like. The (%text)* is a shorthand and states that text and various low-level elements are allowed inside each paragraph. Because paragraphs cannot occur inside paragraphs in this DTD, starting a new paragraph is sufficient to tell an SGML system that the previous one must have come to an end.

Internal and External Hyperlinking

One aspect of HTML that doesn't owe much to SGML is the hyperlinking mechanism. The syntax of the *Uniform Resource Locator* (*URL*) was designed to work with the Web's underlying HTTP protocol. Most URLs in HTML documents appear as the href attribute of the a element type:

```
<A HREF="/cgi-bin/redirect.cgi?location=http%3A%2F%2Fwww%2">
<A HREF="http://www.w3c.org/">
<a href="#top">
```

All attributes in HTML that can contain a URL are of the character data type. No attempt is made to use SGML's ENTITY or ENTITIES attribute type for external hyperlinking. Nor is there any use of the concept of notations, which might have been used to distinguish different image types, video and audio clips, and so on.

Similarly, internal links are implemented by using the name attribute of the a element type to label an a element as the potential target of a link:

```
<a name="top">
```

However, in principle, the SGML ID - IDREF mechanism could just as easily have been used.

The HTML approach to hyperlinking is simpler and requires less formality than the alternatives that SGML might have offered. As you have seen, in SGML external entities are referred to via an entity declaration at the start of the SGML document. So, if the href attribute was of type ENTITY instead of CDATA, the link to W3C's home page would have to start with an entity declaration at the start of the document:

```
<!ENTITY w3c SYSTEM "http://www.w3c.org/">
```

This would then allow the a element to include a reference to the entity "w3c":

```
<a href="w3c">
```

Clearly, this is more work and is easier to get wrong.

ID attribute values must conform to the SGML Name syntax, which limits the characters and symbols they can contain. ID values have to be unique within their document; otherwise, the document is invalid. Similarly, IDREF values must point to an ID that actually exists.

URLs provide a very elegant means of referring to another page and then to a specific point within that page. You only have to concatenate an external reference and an internal one within the href attribute value, and the job is done:

```
<a href="http://www.w3c.org/index.htm#section2">
```

This declaration finds the a element with name equal to "section2" within the page with a URL of "http://www.w3c.org/index.htm".

SGML Conformance

In practice, much of this discussion is pretty academic. Many HTML applications make no attempt to ensure that the pages they produce are valid SGML.

For a start, every valid SGML document needs to start with a *document type declaration*, which specifies the DTD to which it conforms and might look like this:

```
<!DOCTYPE HTML public "-//W3C//DTD HTML 3.2//EN">
```

This is a reference to the standard HTML 3.2 DTD, with no local declarations. Without a document type declaration, you cannot begin to decide whether an HTML page is valid SGML, because you have no idea which type of HTML it is trying to conform to.

This situation is compounded by the approach adopted by most Web browser software, which is to ignore the document type declaration, if provided, and simply skip all markup that the browser doesn't understand. This leads to robust performance because all markup errors in the page being viewed automatically will be ignored. However, it makes things even worse for those who want to use the full power of SGML in their Web pages. SGML has some clever features, such as marked sections and the use of general entities to pull in *boilerplate* text, which are not picked up by Web browsers. Any HTML page that is valid SGML but uses these features actually will be displayed incorrectly.

When a browser vendor provides support for additional element types (for example, for frames), it is by no means certain that the vendor will also provide an updated (unofficial) HTML DTD in which those element types are declared. In this case, it becomes impossible for users to create pages using these extensions that are valid SGML.

It is quite possible, on the other hand, to create HTML pages that are valid SGML. You can use the validation services at `http://www.webtechs.com/html-val-svc/` and `http://ugweb.cs.ualberta.ca/~gerald/validate/` to check any HTML page for validity. A common approach is to use the full power of SGML to manage your pages in-house, and then put them through a normalization program that resolves and removes all the funny SGML things that confuse Web browsers, such as general entity references and marked sections. Only the normalized pages (which are *still* valid SGML) are deployed on the Web.

The Advantages of HTML

Overall, the Web community has ignored the fact that HTML is an SGML application. Or, to paraphrase Paul Simon's song "The Boxer," the Web community "takes what it needs and disregards the rest." This hasn't caused the community any great pain, mainly because HTML is actually very good at the job for which it was designed.

As a means of supporting cross-platform Web page presentation, HTML works well. It uses SGML-style markup to achieve its goal of a reasonably consistent on-screen presentation. In addition to the element types declared in the HTML

DTDs, this markup includes *entity references* for characters that are represented differently on different platforms—another SGML technique. Here are some examples:

- £ is the pound sign.
- ¼ is the symbol for one quarter.
- ¨ is an umlaut.

Adding HTML markup proved to be so straightforward that originally many Web pages were authored using a simple text editor. (The widespread availability of free and cheap WYSIWYG HTML authoring tools and the increasing sophistication of the average Web page have lessened the need for hand-coding.)

As you have seen, the hyperlinking mechanism in HTML makes no use of possible approaches suggested by SGML. Despite this, it has proven to be very effective at linking within and between Web pages. Similarly, multimedia support has been provided without requiring the use of SGML entity references or the concept of notations. Web pages now link in many more information types (video clips, audio clips, and Java applets) than were originally envisaged without any problems.

HTML: Where the Cracks Are Beginning to Show

It could be argued that HTML is starting to be a victim of its own success. As the only show in town when it comes to delivering Web content, HTML is being expected to do the following:

- Display extremely long pages.
- Provide better control over how pages look.
- Support many types of hyperlinks.
- Deliver an increasing variety of information on intranets as well as the Internet.

Let's examine each of those points.

Displaying Extremely Long Pages

Many HTML documents are much too long to be called *pages*. However, the HTML DTDs provide little support for breaking each page into logical sections. The only top-level structural elements are

- head: The title and other front matter for the page
- body: The main body of the page

Within body, HTML 2.0 doesn't provide any means of dividing the body text into smaller sections. HTML 3.2 provides the div element type, which in principle can be used for this purpose.

In order to encode a long text so that it looks sensible on the screen and retains a logical representation of its structure, you need to use HTML 3.2 and carefully align the different levels of headings (h1, h2, and so on) with a set of nested div elements:

```
<body><div><h1>1. The Main Point</h1>
<p> ...
<div><h2>1.1 The first sub-point</h2>
<p> ...
</div> <!-- end of section 1.1 -->
<div><h2>1.2 The second sub-point</h2>
<p> ...
<div><h3>1.2.1 A very small point</h3>
</div></div> <!-- end of section 1.2 -->
<div><h2>1.3 The third sub-point</h2>
<p> ...
</div> <!-- end of section 1.3 -->
</div> <!-- end of section 1 -->
...
```

However, the DTD does very little to help you with this approach. For example, any level of heading can occur anywhere in the text, so it would be all too easy to put an h2 element where you meant to put an h3. This wouldn't be an error as far as the DTD was concerned.

Another way of tackling this problem is to break the long page into a number of linked pages. However, that adds an extra authoring and maintenance overhead to the document. Unless it is done with care, it can make the document less accessible to end users. Frames can help with the presentation of large documents, and are supported by the current HTML 4.0 draft. However, you can be sure that some of your users won't have frames-enabled browsers.

Providing Better Control Over Page Layout

Trying to get a Web page to look correct on any platform and with any browser becomes harder in proportion to the sophistication of the page. Coding tricks such as single-pixel images are now routinely used to achieve the desired layout.

Conversely, as a client with special needs, I might want to make the Web pages I receive look different.

Having the layout information as part of the page markup is proving to be a limitation. The CSS initiative solves part of this problem by providing a separate style sheet mechanism that can be applied by the server site or by the end user.

Supporting Multiple Types of Hyperlinks

The single link type supported by HTML doesn't support the variety of types of relationships that actually occur between pages. If each page is seen as a unit of information, the pages around it can have a variety of roles. Some are "see also" pages giving interesting related information. Others are "part of" pages, which are structurally linked to the current page and form an integral part of a document that has been split up into a number of pages (for the reasons just outlined). Being able to distinguish these different types of links would allow the Web browser to offer better navigation. At a minimum, Up and Down buttons could be used to navigate hierarchically, as well as the ubiquitous Back button.

Delivering Any Type of Information

HTML is most clearly struggling in the area of information delivery. Many applications now hold information in an application-specific format and convert it to HTML for delivery on the Web. In Chapter 14, "Creating an XML Museum Information Application," you will see how museum records have been converted to HTML as a one-off process or on the fly as they are requested.

Converting to HTML at the time of delivery has a number of disadvantages. In general terms, this design means that only the Web server has the full picture. In a database-driven Web site, all conversion (to HTML) must be done by the server. Every time the client wants to make another decision, she has to have another interaction with the server. More HTML has to be downloaded. This adds massively to the load on the server and, indeed, the whole Internet, with a corresponding degradation in response times for everyone.

Also, because the client receives only HTML, she is unable to do more than browse it. The original database records might contain structured information that could be usefully processed on the client's machine, but the conversion to HTML loses this structure.

> Note: The W3C's Document Object Model (DOM) initiative will, when implemented, allow more efficient interaction between clients and servers, including the remote editing of HTML documents. However, there is nothing in the requirements draft for DOM that suggests that it will apply to data formats other than HTML, XML, and CSS (Cascading Style Sheets).

Finally, it is worth pointing out that HTML pages are not really pulling their weight in relation to search and retrieval. The approach adopted by most Web search engines is to ignore the markup and simply treat each page as unstructured free text. The result is that most Web searches generate a very large number of hits, most of them irrelevant to the original inquiry. The only way around this has been to use classical indexing methods by embedding metadata into the Web pages themselves or by setting up parallel resource discovery systems.

Summary

In this chapter, you learned about markup and generalized markup. You then made a whistle-stop tour through the main highlights of Standard Generalized Markup Language (SGML), which is a classic generalized markup scheme.

Next, you turned your attention to the current markup language of the Web, HTML, and looked at it in a new light—as an SGML application. Finally, you saw some areas in which HTML appears to be struggling to meet the demands that the Web is placing on it.

Armed with this background, you can now go on to meet a new markup language—XML.

CHAPTER 2

Enter XML

by Richard Light

In Chapter 1, "Markup in Theory and Practice," I introduced the concept of generalized markup. You learned how the generalized SGML standard has been used as a design basis for the Web's own markup language—HTML. I went on to demonstrate that, sadly, SGML and HTML haven't proven to be compatible in practice, and I discussed some of the reasons. Finally, I discussed areas where HTML itself is struggling to meet Web users' expectations.

In this chapter I introduce the Big New Idea—*XML*, or *Extensible Markup Language*. I discuss its brief history and whether XML is a threat to HTML. Finally, I outline the three major aspects of XML: the language, XML linking mechanisms, and the XML style sheet facility.

The Origin of XML

Where did XML come from? Up until 1996, the SGML community as a whole hadn't taken much of an active interest in Web issues. Helper applications (such as Panorama™) that worked with Web browsers had been developed to allow SGML documents to be delivered over the Web and browsed by clients. It looked as though only two choices were going to be available to information providers on the Web—use full SGML and accept that you can only deliver information to a minority audience that will bother to acquire a specialist helper application, or adopt the universally acceptable medium of HTML, along with its limitations.

The Grand Alliance

In mid-1996, a group of approximately 80 SGML experts joined forces with the World Wide Web Consortium (W3C) to form an SGML Working Group under the chairmanship of Jon Bosak of Sun Microsystems. Their goal was to develop a markup language that had the power and generality of SGML and at the same time was easy to implement on the Web. This markup language had to do the following:

- Support generalized markup on the Web.
- Produce documents that ideally will be valid according to SGML's rule book.
- Provide hyperlinking support that ideally will be upward-compatible with the URL approach.
- Provide a generic, powerful style sheet mechanism.

Their first achievement was to develop an initial language specification for XML, which was announced in November 1996 at the SGML 96 Conference in Boston. A second draft was issued in March 1997.

Warning: The description of the XML language in this book is based on the March 1997 draft, which was the latest one available when I was writing in June 1997. See `http://www.textuality.com/sgml-erb/WD-xml-lang.html` for the latest version. For a more general view of progress, check out `http://www.w3.org/Activity/XML` for the current status of all aspects of the XML specification.

Shortly afterward, in April 1997, the first draft of the XML hyperlinking specification was issued.

On July 1, 1997, these ad hoc working arrangements were formalized along W3C's standard lines. The W3C SGML Editorial Review Board (ERB) took on the mantle of W3C XML Working Group (WG) and now follows W3C working group guidelines. This W3C XML WG is taking on the formalization of the XML standard. On the same date, the current SGML Working Group transferred its work to the XML WG, which renamed itself the W3C XML Special Interest Group. These changes regularize the position of XML as a W3C-approved activity.

What Has the SGML WG Come Up With?

Of course, the SGML Working Group has come up with XML, but what is that exactly? XML is both less than SGML and more than SGML.

Formally, the XML language specification is a *profile* of SGML. Less formally, it's a subset. The SGML Working Group has selected only those features of SGML that it feels are absolutely necessary for the Web. It has thrown the rest of the SGML standard away.

So XML is a lot less than SGML. It is less complex and less loaded with all those clever features (many of them optional) that have proven troublesome for programmers aiming to develop SGML-compliant software. (Believe me, I've experienced these troubles firsthand.)

On the other hand, XML retains the key benefits that SGML offers. With XML you have generalized markup, so now you can invent your own tagsets. You can make your documents self-describing, and you can validate them. (These concepts are described in "Self-Describing Documents" and "Valid and Well-Formed Documents," later in this chapter.) You can break up large documents into manageable chunks, you can deliver complete or partial documents on the Web, and so on. I think of XML as an "80/20 solution": 80% of the benefits of SGML for 20% of its complexity.

Why is XML more than SGML? The answer is found in the other two aspects of the XML specification. In order to be useful on the Web, XML needs to have linking and style capabilities built in. SGML has no style mechanism, and while it provides the tools with which a hyperlinking scheme can be built, it does not actually define a hyperlinking mechanism itself.

In developing these parts of the XML specification, the SGML WG has tried to use both existing standards and current Web practice. An International Standard for hypertext and multimedia linking is called HyTime (ISO 10744). For style sheets, the International Standard is called DSSSL (Document Style and Semantics Specification Language). HyTime and DSSSL are both based on SGML. In both cases, as you will see, ideas taken from these standards have been applied in simplified form and in combination with more pragmatic initiatives. This has produced results that, like the XML language, are simple enough to use, yet powerful enough to be worth using.

XML Versus HTML

If XML is a great new way of marking up information for the Web, does this mean the end of HTML? Will there be a fight to the death between two conflicting markup schemes? Will you have to recode all your existing pages? The answer is a resounding no.

For a start, HTML and XML operate at different levels of generality, so they will not often be in head-to-head competition. As you learned in Chapter 1, HTML is an application of SGML, which means that it provides a specific set of element types, with a particular purpose: online display of Web pages, with hyperlinking. On the other hand, as you just discovered, XML is an SGML profile, which means that it can support an unlimited range of applications. Some of these applications may be HTML-like in their scope, but most will have very different objectives and design.

In a bit more detail, here are the respective roles that XML and HTML might play in the future.

The Role of XML

XML will be most interesting to people and organizations who have information resources that don't fit into the HTML mold and resources that they want to make available over the Web. These are some examples:

- Books
- Financial transactions (EDI)
- Technical manuals

- Chemical formulae
- Medical records
- Museum catalog records
- Chess games
- Encyclopedia entries

XML's role will be maximized in situations where the information resources are of long-term value (since valid XML documents conform to an International Standard—SGML); there are complex relationships within and between them (since XML's hyperlinking facilities allow these relationships to be expressed in a system-independent manner); or if they are to be put to different uses (since it is much easier to repurpose information where it is marked up in a generalized manner). In those circumstances, people will be willing to put in the extra work of setting up an XML application. (It is certainly more work to adopt XML than to use HTML as it stands.)

One interesting possibility is that XML applications might be used to enhance HTML applications. For example, the Meta Content Framework proposal from Netscape et al involves the use of XML-encoded documents to describe and index Web sites. The XML contains a description of each page and a hyperlink to the actual page:

```
<Page id="http://www.acc.com/scorpions.html">
<description>Scorpions in the sun</description>
</Page>
```

A reverse link, from the HTML page to the page description, could be made using the HTML link element.

The Role of HTML

In many cases, using XML won't be worth the effort. For all its limitations, HTML is a ready-to-run application that works "out of the box." There is an enormous range of authoring software for creating HTML pages and links between them, software for managing HTML-based Web sites, and search and index software for information retrieval.

Most Web sites exist primarily to promote an individual or organization, and to inform about their work and products. It is most important that these pages deliver a clear, well-presented message—using the information they contain for other purposes is not a high priority. For this type of site, HTML will probably remain the most appropriate markup scheme.

Another role that HTML plays, and will probably continue to play, is as a delivery format for information from databases and other information sources. Increasingly, software is becoming available that supports dynamic Web sites, where pages are created on the fly. Their content can come partly from prewritten chunks of HTML, and partly from databases. In the future this material might be delivered as XML, especially in situations where the client that receives it wants to be able to do some local processing. But today the delivery format for these dynamic pages is firmly HTML.

> Note: One exercise in this book requires you to take the basic HTML 2.0 DTD and some Web pages, and morph them into XML. (See Chapter 12, "Morphing Existing HTML into XML.") However, the reason for doing this is not to suggest that all existing HTML pages need to be converted to XML. On the contrary, you will find lots of reasons that it is not worth trying to make this conversion, and you will come up with a better understanding of the differences between the HTML and XML approaches.

Browser Wars?

Will a new generation of XML Web browsers come along to do battle with current HTML browsers? I don't think so.

Because the XML language specification is so straightforward, it is quite feasible for existing Web browsers to be upgraded so that they can show XML documents and HTML pages interchangeably. Users need not even be aware whether they are looking at XML or HTML! This process has already started— Internet Explorer supports Channels, which are encoded in CDF (Channel Definition Format). This is an XML application. Integrating XML support into HTML browsers removes the need for generic XML browsers.

There is another possible strategy, which might act as a fall-back if true integration of XML into HTML browsers isn't forthcoming. XML-aware plug-ins (which could be third-party offerings, written in Java) can take XML, convert it on the fly to HTML, and output the result to the browser's main window. Either way, users get the benefit of XML delivery without needing to acquire a new Web browser.

On the other hand, it is likely that XML-specific browsers and plug-ins will be created to provide specialized client-side support for particular XML applications. For example, if financial transactions are transmitted as XML, plug-ins would be required both to create and to decode them.

More generally, the linking facilities in XML can be used in a number of novel ways, and there is a place for a new generation of hypertext software that supports the creation and use of XML's out-of-line links. (See Chapter 9, "Linking with XML," for the full story.)

XML-Lang: SGML Without Tears

In Chapter 1, I gave you a taste of what generalized markup is and how SGML implements those ideas. I've already established that XML is a simple SGML profile.

In this section I review the main features of the XML language specification. This is just a taster; the first few chapters of Part II give a much fuller picture.

Self-Describing Documents

XML documents that satisfy XML's requirements for validity can be said to describe themselves. (The concept of validity is described later in the section "Valid and Well-Formed Documents.") Every valid XML document starts with header information that does the following:

- Describes the structural rules that the markup in the document aims to follow
- Lists external resources (external entities) that might form part of the document
- Declares internal resources (internal entities) that might be required within the document
- Lists types of non-XML resource (notations) that might be found in the document (and for which helper applications might be required)
- Lists actual non-XML resources (binary data entities) that might be found in the document (and for which helper applications might be required)

This header information (known as the *document type definition*, or *DTD*) helps software that is about to process an XML document. It also allows XML documents to be validated: Do they match up to their own rules? The DTD can be complemented by *processing instructions*, which tell software how to deal with the XML document, and by the other types of resources that might be encountered.

Clearer Is Simpler: Non-Minimized Markup

Clarity is the watchword for the XML markup language. Say what you mean and don't miss anything. XML is very simple-minded and very rigorous about markup.

A lesson learned from SGML (and HTML) is that minimization is something you are better off without in XML. As an example, you might routinely exclude the `</p>` end-tag after each paragraph:

```
<p>Clarity is the watchword for the XML markup language. Say
what you mean and don't miss anything. XML is very simple-minded
and very rigorous about markup.
<p>A lesson learned from SGML (and HTML) ...
```

You can do this because SGML-aware software can infer the presence of the `</p>` end-tag from the arrival of the following `<p>` start-tag. (The DTD says that paragraphs can't nest; therefore, it is assuming a piece of markup is present because your rules say it must be there.)

This sort of cleverness can make life harder for all in the long run—users and software alike. In particular, it makes life hard for programmers who want to process the markup.

Minimization techniques were introduced into SGML with the laudable aim of reducing the number of keystrokes needed to mark up text. This is no longer an issue when a wide range of authoring software can add the markup for you.

Because XML insists on having all the markup be explicit, it is easy to see how all the markup in a document is neatly nested. This nesting means that elements can be described in terms of their contextual position, which has two obvious benefits:

- Simpler information modeling
- Greater precision when searching

In this example, the body text is divided into divisions. div1 is a level-1 division, within which div2 is a level-2 subdivision, and so on:

```
<document>
    <body>
        <div1> <!-- level-1 division -->
            <head>Beginnings</head>
            <p>In the beginning ... </p>
            <div2> <!-- level-2 division -->
                <head>Part of the beginning</head>
                <p>As part of our discussion ...</p>
            </div2> <!-- end of level-2 division -->
        </div1> <!-- end of level-1 division -->
    </body>
</document>
```

Being able to describe a heading as "immediately inside a div1 element" means that you don't need to have, as HTML does, six different element types for headings. Instead, the single element type head is provided, and it is used for headings at any level. It is still possible to distinguish the different levels of headings using their context.

Having a full context for every piece of text in an XML document is also a great help when searching. You can look for a given word anywhere in the document, only inside headings, or even only inside level-1 headings. This added precision for retrieval is particularly important for XML applications whose information content is precisely defined and tightly controlled, but it can still be a major bonus within more textual applications.

Create Your Own Applications

A central feature of XML is that it lets you define your own information structures. This doesn't mean that you personally will have to learn how to design your own DTDs. Most users of XML won't even be aware that they are using a DTD.

In practice, the creation of new XML applications will probably be done as a community venture for specific types of information work. There is really no benefit in creating a different DTD for every document. If a community or industry adopts a common DTD for its documents, it is effectively adopting a common information standard, which means that information interchange and cross-document searching become feasible.

The key point about this flexibility is that standard XML-aware software will be able to work with your custom XML application without any special help. At present, if you load a document full of non-HTML tags into a Web browser, it won't complain but it won't do much with the document either. With XML you will be able to control how your document looks and how its links work, even though your tagset is unique in your application.

Valid and Well-Formed Documents

If you declare a DTD at the head of your XML document and then follow all the rules it prescribes, you will have a *valid XML document*. Better than that, you will also have a valid SGML document. This means that your document is future-proof, because it conforms to an International Standard markup convention. It can be used in any environment that understands SGML—not just the Web.

At another level XML introduces the concept of *well-formed documents*, which are structurally sound but need not be valid. All elements are neatly nested, and all entities referenced by the document are properly declared. However, no check is made that the document's logical structure matches the rules given in the DTD. In fact, the DTD can be dispensed with completely in certain circumstances. A *required markup declaration* (*RMD*) can be used to indicate whether the DTD must be read in order to process a well-formed XML document.

I don't think that much information will actually be created and managed as well-formed XML, except in the simplest of applications. When authoring XML documents, it is actually easier to work with a DTD than without one, because the presence of a DTD allows XML editing software to give the author more help. For example, when the author wants to insert a new element, an XML-aware editor presents a drop-down list containing only those element types that are allowed by the DTD in the current context.

However, the concept of a well-formed XML document provides a legal, convenient, self-contained delivery format for XML-encoded information. For many downstream applications, such as display or indexing, a DTD-less well-formed XML document is perfectly adequate. It therefore removes the need to transmit a potentially large DTD in cases where the client application receiving an XML-encoded stream has no use for one.

Entities: Documents in Chunks

XML supports some practical aspects of document management with its concept of *entities*. Entities are sequences of characters or bit patterns, held within an XML document or external to it.

I introduce entities in my brief introduction to SGML in Chapter 1, where I show how they can be used to represent external resources, such as illustrations, with an added notation to indicate their type. XML supports this approach, and it calls such resources *external binary entities*.

In addition, XML offers two types of entities that can be used to help manage your XML documents.

External text entities are simply resources (usually, but not necessarily, files) containing XML markup. External text entities allow you to build your XML documents in chunks. For example, this book is being written one chapter at a time, and each chapter is a separate text entity. When the time comes to make the whole book into a single XML document, all I need to do is declare each chapter as an external text entity and make reference to them all in the correct order.

In addition to allowing documents to be written by a number of different people, external text entities allow information reuse. A standard warning, for example, could be marked up in XML and held in a file, ready to be pasted into all new customer documentation.

The ability to build up a document in chunks can also be useful when parts of it are in a different character set. Each part can be isolated and placed in a separate entity with its own encoding rules.

XML also supports the idea of *internal entities*, which are shorthand for a piece of XML markup that is held within the document. Internal entities can be used for standard phrases, expansions of abbreviations, and even for single characters (such as the trademark symbol, ™).

I describe XML entities in more detail in Chapter 7, "Physical Structures in XML Documents."

Character Sets

XML has adopted the ISO 10646 (Unicode) standard as the approved framework for encoding characters. This offers a variety of methods of encoding characters as a bit pattern. The 8-bit encoding scheme is compatible with standard ASCII, and the 16-bit and 32-bit encoding schemes offer built-in support for most languages. This means that XML can scale up to whatever level of language support is required for a particular application. In fact, each XML document can contain any mixture of characters and languages. You can even use any alphabet within your markup. For example, you can have cyrillic names for your element types. Putting it another way, internationalization is built into XML.

XML also provides a general-purpose character reference, with which you can refer to any character in Unicode by quoting the numerical value of its bit string. This is useful for characters that you cannot enter directly via the keyboard.

XML-Link: Power Linking

XML provides built-in linking facilities that aim to be powerful enough to cope with most Web-based applications.

Influences on the Design of XML-Link

XML-Link is based on the distillation of many years of experience in the design of hyperlinks. Three standards, in particular, have informed its design:

- *HTML* provides a linking mechanism that is already familiar to everyone who has ever encoded a Web page.
- *HyTime* is an International Standard that contains some useful background concepts.
- *Text Encoding Initiative (TEI) Guidelines* provide a concise syntax for specifying complex links.

The general approach has been to start from the linking facilities supported by HTML, and add value to them. It is quite straightforward to use HTML-style links within an XML document if you choose, like this:

```
<A HREF="http://www.w3c.org/XML/Activity">
```

But you can also do a great deal more with XML links. (For compatibility with HTML, XML has adopted HREF as the name of the special attribute that contains the target of the link.)

Additional Information About Links

XML allows you to state which elements in your XML documents are to be interpreted as linking elements. You do this by specifying the special XML-LINK attribute. This both asserts that an element is to be treated as a link and specifies what type of link it is. For example, the following code states that this is a simple link (as discussed in the next section):

```
<A XML-LINK="SIMPLE" HREF="http://www.w3c.org/XML/Activity">
```

Every link can have a machine-processible *role*. The role is the meaning of the link, and it tends to be specific to a particular XML application. It can also have a human-readable label.

Finally, you can specify the default behavior of a link. The SHOW attribute indicates whether the resource pointed to by the link is designed to be embedded in the current context, to replace it, or to start its own new context. The ACTUATE attribute indicates whether the user has to take action before anything is done with the link.

Simple and Extended Links

HTML-style links are one example of what XML calls *simple links*. Simple links are links that sit in an XML document and point to a single target, or *resource*. (A resource is anything that can be addressed by a link.)

Extended links are a lot less obvious. They can point to any number of targets, and they can live anywhere. In fact, extended links don't need to live inside any of the resources they point to. This might not sound helpful, but in fact it gives you the ability to set up bidirectional and even multidirectional links. Also, taking links out of documents should make it easier to manage them (for example, by checking that their target resource continues to exist).

XML lets you declare one or more XML documents as a *link group*, which makes it easier to manage a set of documents that contain a network of links.

Locators

As I have noted, the value of the HREF attribute identifies the target resource of an XML link, which has a syntax that is upward-compatible with the URL syntax currently used on the Web. This means that all XML links that point to non-XML targets can be interpreted in exactly the same way as similar links found in HTML pages.

The XML syntax, which is based on that of URL, includes the use of # to separate the name of a resource from a part identifier. In the particular case where the target resource is an XML document, the part of the URL after the # must follow a special syntax that identifies which elements within that document form the target of the link. For example, the easiest and best use of this syntax is to specify that the unique ID of the target element is a link to the element with ID equal to CHAP1 within the document MYDOC.XML:

```
<A XML-LINK="SIMPLE" HREF="MYDOC.XML#CHAP1">
```

XML also supports the connector |, which offers the option that only the relevant element, and not the whole XML document, should be returned. This will save loading time when linking to small sections that are near the end of large documents.

The detailed syntax for locating elements within XML documents is described in Chapter 9.

XML-Style: Separate Style from Content

In principle, the existing CSS1 (Cascading Style Sheets, level 1) standard could be applied to give simple control over the on-screen display of XML documents. CSS1 states its rules in terms of element names, IDs, and so on, which are clearly features of XML documents as well as HTML documents.

CSS1 was specifically designed around HTML, and some of its features rely on HTML-specific encoding practices. For example, the a linking element is treated specially so that visited links can look different from unvisited ones. Similarly, the class attribute is treated specially by CSS1: You would have to add that attribute to every element in your XML DTDs to take advantage of that feature of CSS1. However, this is likely to change. The CSS1 specification states an expectation that it will become more generic: "CSS1 has some HTML-specific parts (e.g., the special status of the CLASS and ID attributes) but should easily be extended to apply to other DTDs as well." Such changes will clearly make CSS a more attractive style sheet mechanism for XML documents.

XML provides its own means of specifying style sheets (termed *XS*). Apart from having the advantage of being designed to work with any XML document structure, XS is massively more powerful than CSS1.

Influences on the Design of XS

XS is still at an early stage of development. As of this writing, there is not an initial W3C working draft for it. However, it is clear that XS will be based on the DSSSL (Document Style and Semantics Specification Language) Standard, ISO/IEC 10179:1996.

DSSSL is a standard that supports the transformation and display of SGML documents. The transformation aspect of DSSSL isn't supported in XS, and the style sheet part has been pruned down to the bare essentials.

How XS Works

XS is designed to control the output of an XML document to the screen, the printed page, or any other two-dimensional display device.

It is essentially a data-driven style mechanism. When an XML document is to be displayed, one or more XS style sheets will be called into action. These might be specified in the XML document or selected by the user.

The processing of the XML document is determined by scanning the XML document's structure and merging it with the *formatting specification* derived from the active style sheets. These instructions are then used to create the *flow objects*, such as paragraphs and tables, which determine the layout of the document. This merging process produces a tree structure of flow objects: the *flow object tree*.

Each flow object has *characteristics*, such as font-name, font-size, and font-posture, that can be specified explicitly or inherited from flow objects further up the flow object tree.

What's in an XS Style Sheet?

XS has an extremely flexible *core expression language*, based on Scheme. This is a complete programming language, with facilities for doing calculations, testing conditions, and so on. It can be used to build up complex instructions for the processing of individual elements or even characters within an XML document.

At a higher level, XS supports *construction rules* that declare, in effect, what to do with an element. More precisely, they state what flow objects are to be created, and what characteristics each flow object is to have. For example, an element construction rule for the p element might specify that a paragraph flow object is to be added to the flow object tree, with these characteristics:

```
font-size: 12pt
first-line-start-indent: 20pt
quadding: left
```

This will cause the characters in the paragraph to be 12-point font size, with a 20-point indent at the start of the first line. The paragraph will be left-justified.

Typically, the low-level formatting instructions will be declared as functions. This means that the top-level instructions can be made much clearer to a reader, as in this example:

```
(element NOTE (STANDARD-NOTE))
(element EG (MONOSPACED-TEXT))
(element CODE (UNDERLINED-PHRASE))
```

What XS Offers

Because the core expression language is so powerful, it is possible to use nearly any aspect of an XML document's structure to control how it appears. Most construction rules are pitched at the element level, but you can easily refine their behavior by testing properties of the element, such as its attributes and their values or its ancestor elements.

Although by default the whole document will be displayed in its original order, the core expression language actually gives you access to the full document structure at any point. Therefore, you can rush off and grab a related piece of text from elsewhere in the document. For example, you can create a virtual table of contents from the chapter headings, and place it at the start of your displayed document. It is also easy to suppress parts of the document that you do not want to display at a certain time.

The mathematical functions in the core expression language make it easy to express font sizes, spacing, and so on in relative rather than absolute terms. This means that you can write style sheets in which the user can blow up the whole display in a consistent manner by overriding the base font size.

The XS specification is covered in more detail in Chapter 10, "The XML Style Mechanism."

The XML Processor

The XML Language Specification includes a description of how a beast called the *XML processor* is expected to behave. This is a program that reads XML documents and checks whether they are valid and well-formed.

The general idea is that the XML processor will have no ambitions of its own; it will simply pass information about the XML document to an application that is doing something interesting with it on behalf of an end-user. This could take the form of a one-way brain-dump from the XML processor to the application, but it is more likely that there will be a conversation between the two. As of this writing, the active XML developers are working on a standard API for XML processors.

XML processors will be relatively simple pieces of software, which means that it will be quite feasible to add XML-awareness to existing software. This opens up a whole range of interesting possibilities. The obvious job to do first is to add XML support to existing Web browsers (and both of the major players have indicated that they are looking into this). Beyond that, there are in my opinion potential major benefits (both to users and to the software vendors themselves) of word processing software using XML to structure documents. Then you could have object-oriented databases with built-in XML support, and more. I'll discuss this in more detail in the next chapter.

I discuss the XML processor in more detail in Chapter 11, "The XML Processor."

Summary

In this chapter, you have taken a first, very broad look at XML. I discussed where it came from, and considered the extent to which it is a competitor to HTML. Next, I summarized the three main aspects of XML: the language itself, the linking mechanism, and XML style sheets. Finally, I described the XML processor and discussed the role it might play in a coming generation of XML-aware software.

CHAPTER 3

The XML Advantage

by Richard Light

So far, you've had a brief introduction to the theory and practice of generalized markup, and you've learned where XML came from. You have seen a broad overview of XML's main features. Now it's time to think—again in very broad terms—about the impact that XML might have on the world of the Web.

Let's kick off with a metaphor. Structured information resources might see XML as the Model T Ford of the Web. How's that? Well, think of the car as representing personal transport—being able to get out and about on your own terms. HTML doesn't offer this: Information has to dress up in overalls (adopt HTML tagging) to climb aboard the HTML bus. Up to now, if information wanted personal transport on the Web, it had to buy into a Rolls Royce technology such as SGML. At last, with XML, it can find transportation for a reasonable cost. XML provides a standard packaging/transport mechanism for any type of information—small or gigantic, simple or mind-bendingly complex. XML transports any number of different types of travelers, all heading somewhere they'll be welcome.

Now let's see how far that metaphor will travel!

Documents that Know Themselves

When an XML document arrives, it brings with it a knowledge of its own structure and semantics that make it much more useful in its own right. This occurs before you even start to think about potential applications for XML. In this section, you look at the general advantages of the XML approach to documents.

Header Information: The Owner's Handbook

A key feature of valid XML documents is that they all start with a definition of their own rules and resource requirements. Even when the document type declaration is just a single line, like the following declaration, it is specifying a URL that can, and routinely will, be resolved as the file is read:

```
<!DOCTYPE TEI.2 SYSTEM "http://www-tei.uic.edu/orgs/tei/p3/dtd/
teilite-xml.dtd>
```

Therefore, the complete document type definition (DTD)—in this case, the TEI Lite XML DTD—will always be available to the processor that is trying to interpret the XML document. (See Chapter 8, "Keeping It Tidy: The XML Rule Book," for a full description of the information that can be found in the DTD.)

The DTD states the overall document type, and it goes on to specify which element types are allowed and the properties of each type.

This header information allows XML applications to give a much better service to users. Generic XML tools, such as editors, can use the rules in the DTD to offer context-sensitive lists of allowed elements and to fill out new elements with a template for any mandatory attributes or subelements. Application-specific software can use the document type to recognize the XML documents it is able to process.

Compare this with the HTML case. Even where an external DTD subset is specified at the start of an HTML page, most HTML software will make no attempt to resolve it, and even less attempt to act on the information the DTD contains. Here is an example:

```
<!DOCTYPE HTML PUBLIC "-//IETF//DTD HTML//EN">
```

Yet, useful distinctions can be made between the structure of HTML 2.0 and 3.2 documents and documents using vendor-specific extensions to the HTML tagset. Also, the DTD must be read if software is to correctly infer the implied structure of the HTML document when markup (such as end-tags) has been omitted. As you have already seen, the HTML browser philosophy is to ignore the DTD, and also to ignore any markup that the particular processor doesn't understand. This makes for robustness, but at a considerable price of lost information.

If instead HTML browsers were to insist on having a DTD, and were to actually read it, then a generic HTML browser would be able to deal easily with updates to the HTML spec and variants on standard HTML without itself requiring an upgrade.

Another aspect of the DTD is that it declares up front the full set of resources that constitute the document (or at least that might form part of it). This allows XML processors to spot any potential problems—such as the unavailability of a URL, or a file type that the XML application cannot handle—before the full file is processed. The DTD might also contain processing instructions that link in XS style sheets, which state how the document expects itself to be displayed.

Browseable Document Structure

Thanks to XML's refusal to let you exclude any tags, the internal logical structure of all XML documents is clear for all to see. This is true of well-formed XML documents as well as valid ones. Every XML document can be thought of and processed as a neatly organized tree structure of elements with associated data content. Again, this brings benefits at both generic and application-specific levels.

At the generic level, having all the markup given explicitly means that XML-aware browsers and editors can present the structure of any XML document as a nested set of *folders*. These can work just like the Windows File Manager (or the Windows Explorer in Windows 95). The left pane allows you to open up or collapse the child elements of any element. The right pane shows the content of the currently selected element. Figure 3.1 shows the general idea. This section is being browsed by the SGML Panorama Pro package. The element structure appears on the left, with the current element highlighted.

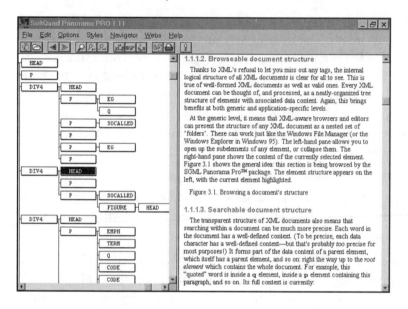

Figure 3.1.
Browsing a document's structure.

Searchable Document Structure

The transparent structure of XML documents also means that searching within a document can be much more precise. Each word in the document has a well-defined context. (To be precise, each data character has a well-defined context—but that's probably *too* precise for most purposes!) Each data character forms part of the data content of a parent element, which itself has a parent element, and so on—all the way up to the *root element*, which contains the whole document. For example, this "quoted" word is inside a q element, inside a p element containing this paragraph, and so on. Its full context is currently as follows:

```
div1 - div2 - div3 - div4 - p - q
```

Therefore, it could be found by any of the following queries:

```
the word "quoted" within a <q> element
the content of all <q> elements
the word "quoted" within a <p> within a <div4>
```

In other words, its data content and its context can both be used, alone or in combination, as search criteria. And, of course, attribute values also can be used to refine the query.

This opens up the possibility of vastly improved searching of *free-text* documents. You have already seen that the current generation of Web search engines are great on recall ("Yes! 15,000 hits!") but pretty poor on precision ("Why should I be interested in *this?*"). XML offers built-in context sensitivity for text retrieval.

Document Classes

All HTML pages share a common core set of tags that will be the same no matter what type of HTML is in use—for example, head, title, and p. In the same way, XML documents that conform to a particular application will form *classes*. These will be either tightly controlled groupings with every document instance conforming to a single DTD, or looser groupings around a family of related DTDs. In both cases, document classes will bring advantages.

When a document class is tightly controlled by a single DTD, application software can treat the rules expressed by that DTD rather like a database schema. This means that all documents in the class can be subjected to very specific processing, as long as they are all valid XML documents, and it is true even when the DTD covers a wide range of possible uses. For example, the XML metadata initiatives that are currently on the table (Meta Content Framework and XML-Data) would both provide information about Web sites and other information resources in a form that search engines and other automated agents could use directly. To quote the MCF proposal, "For interoperability and efficiency, schemata designed to serve different applications should share as much as possible in the way of data structures, syntax, and vocabulary."

If you have a class of documents conforming to a single DTD, you have to do the job of setting up the complete XML application only once—when you develop style sheets, link protocols, and possibly write custom software. Every document that conforms to that DTD can then benefit from its associated application.

Even where there is a looser affiliation of document types, there are benefits in belonging to a class. A good example is the Text Encoding Initiative, a well-established SGML framework for Humanities documents that will shortly be available in XML form. Here, there isn't a single TEI DTD. Instead, there is a framework for designing your own DTD, using the Chicago Pizza Model:

- Choose your pizza base (the basic type of document you are dealing with—prose, poetry, or drama).
- Spread on the cheese and tomato (a set of elements common to all bases).
- Pick toppings to suit your taste (specialized elements for linking, textual analysis, and so on).

The key point here is the "cheese and tomato" layer. Every TEI-based pizza—make that DTD—will use the same element types for common features such as paragraphs, lists, and bibliographic references.

Therefore, it is possible to design a generic XS style sheet for the common TEI elements, which will be useful no matter how you choose to design your TEI application. The modular design of XS allows you to plug in a base style sheet and then add styles for the elements that are unique to your particular use of TEI. Interestingly, XS is also relaxed about which element types you specify in your style sheets. It is quite possible to have a too-broad style sheet that includes elements you are *not* using in your DTD.

In a similar spirit, all TEI applications that use fancy linking will use the same Links "topping," so it will be possible to write support for this into browser software.

> Note: This has already happened in the SGML world, where Synex's Viewport engine—which is used in the well-known Panorama browser from SoftQuad—offers native support for TEI extended pointers. These are the precursors of XML XPointers. See Chapter 9, "Linking with XML," for details.

Finally, it is still possible to gain the benefits of structural precision when running cross-document searches within a loosely grouped class of documents.

Chunk Delivery

One of the problems with using HTML for all your Web content is that sometimes you want to write long documents. There are two ways to deal with this. You could produce a 500KB page, which takes your users forever to download. Or you could put in a few happy hours designing a set of pages into which the document can be broken down, with appropriate buttons so that users can navigate the pages and (hopefully) never get lost. Frames help a bit, but not all of your users will have frames support.

XML doesn't provide any magic to download documents quicker than HTML can download, but it does have a few tricks up its sleeve that help in this area.

For a start, XML's entity mechanism lets you create big documents in bite-sized chunks. You can write your magnum opus in separate sections and have a *master document* that dynamically pulls the sections together. However, this is mainly a convenience at the authoring stage, because the user is still looking at (and downloading) one big document.

A second approach is to use XML-Link's XPointers to link in the sections of the document. This is better because the linked sections are not treated by the XML processor as part of the core document. The XML processor can simply read the core document, indicate that the links exist, and let the user decide which ones to follow. This is rather like the set of linked pages you might design in HTML, except that the navigation between the linked sections will be supported natively by the XML browser without any extra effort on your part.

Finally, it is possible to deliver arbitrary chunks from a large XML document even when it is stored as one big file. Like HTML, XML supports the # separator for parts within the current page, and it works the same way:

```
<a href="http://www.mysite.com/home.htm#pets">
```

First, you download the whole file referenced by the URL: `http://www.mysite.com/home.htm`. Then, when the element marked with `name="pets"` is read, you display the document, starting at that point. The only trouble is that with long documents, you can stare at an empty screen for a long time before that section turns up.

XML has an additional part separator that avoids most of this problem. The part separator `?XML-XPTR=` can be used in place of #. It says, "I only want you to return the part of the document that matches this part code." The server still has the job of reading the whole document, but when it has located the relevant section, it only has to deliver the required chunk to the client. Because much less data is transferred, the operation appears to be much quicker to the client.

> **Warning:** You need to resolve some issues concerning the relationship between the *chunk* and the rest of the document. Obviously, users might want to navigate from that chunk to other parts of the document, but without some additional information their browsers won't be able to do that. The SGML Open industry group is working on a framework for specifying a chunk's context, which could be delivered along with the chunk and would allow you to request items such as the next section in the document.

XML-Based Authoring

Before looking at the advantages that XML will bring to its intended area of application—the World Wide Web—I would like to make a pitch for the more general use of XML. The example I give covers the areas of document authoring and desktop publishing. This might appear to be a digression from the chapter's main purpose, but think about this: If standard word processors knew about XML, we wouldn't need any specialized Web authoring tools!

XML lends itself to well-structured authoring. Word-processor vendors would do well to consider re-engineering their offerings with XML at the center (rather than, say, having XML as an add-on or yet another "save as" format).

The format in which the word processor file is saved would be very simple. It would be a valid XML document with a processing instruction to specify the *editing* style sheet that should be associated with it by default. The beauty of this approach is that the user would no longer have to worry about converting documents from one proprietary format to another, with the seemingly inevitable errors and loss of information.

Elements and Styles

You can treat each XML element as equivalent to one of the *styles* found in traditional word-processing applications. (It isn't an exact equivalence, because the element has a more precise semantic significance and normally won't contain any style-specific information in its own right. However, from the author's point of view, it does basically the same job.)

The presence of a DTD allows you to control the addition of new elements to the document structure. This means that the user always gets a context-sensitive pick list of just those elements that are allowed at the current insertion point. When an element is selected, the program inserts both a start-tag and an end-tag, and places the cursor between the two. By using the DTD, the program also can ensure that mandatory subelements and attribute specifications always are provided, so that documents are automatically valid XML.

A style mechanism such as Cascading Style Sheets (CSS) or XML's built-in XS mechanism can be used to associate a style (in the usual sense) with each element type, which makes it very straightforward to offer WYSIWYG editing with user-defined styles using native XML functionality. (You certainly don't need to have the XML start-tags and end-tags visible, except perhaps as a user option.)

Note: Cascading Style Sheets offer a practicable method of styling XML documents today.

For the future, the power of XS means that you have considerable scope for ingenuity and competition in the design of style support. It is clearly not a good idea to try to offer the full XS language to end-users. Some method of packaging sets of primitive XS commands into useful procedures will be needed.

By default, all instances of a given element will display identically. In most circumstances, this is an advantage. If you want to alter the style of your figure captions, it is helpful to be able to do the job once and know that every figure caption automatically will be updated.

However, sometimes you want to be able to control the style of elements on a case-by-case basis. This can be achieved by specifying attributes that will be picked up by the style specification. For example, this book has different types of note elements, which are controlled by the type attribute. If this attribute is absent, the style sheet generates a boxed note with the heading "note:". If this attribute has the value "hidden", the note element is suppressed. If it has any other value, a boxed note is output with the value of the type attribute, followed by :, as its heading.

In extreme situations, you even can assign a unique ID to an element, and use that identifier to assign it a totally individual style.

Rules and Local Declarations

The XML DTD has a two-part design, which lends itself to a simple strategy for managing standard rules and local declarations. The standard rules for a set of documents (which the user cannot alter) can be declared as the external DTD subset. As you have seen, any non-XML resources that are to be linked into this particular document (such as illustrations) have to be declared in the document header. Suitable declarations can be created by the program and added to the document's internal DTD subset:

```
<!DOCTYPE BOOK SYSTEM "http://www.myorg.org/book.dtd" [
<!-- local declarations added here: -->
<!ENTITY figure1 SYSTEM "fig1.bmp" NDATA BMP>
<!ENTITY figure2 SYSTEM "fig2.bmp" NDATA BMP>
]>
```

This keeps the standard rules and local declarations cleanly separated.

Note: In general, you can expect that XML-aware programs will take on the job of including all the declarations that are required for XML conformance. In this case, for example, all the user has to do is select an image file. As another example, the program can ensure that every element has a unique ID, so that it is a suitable target for XML links.

The Revision Cycle

In more ambitious implementations, XML's linking facilities could be used to support commentary on, and editor review of, a source document. The comments could be held in a completely separate document, with XML links pointing to the relevant passages of the original. This technique keeps the source document "clean." It also allows multiple comments on each document, comments on comments, and even comments that compare and contrast two or more documents.

Link to Desktop Publishing

Using XML as a document storage format also offers a clean interface between word processing and DTP systems. XML-enabled DTP software can read an XML document and decide whether to use its associated style sheet (perhaps as a starting point), or throw it away and use a style mechanism of its own. You don't need to go through the document rooting out or replacing specific word-processing information.

Best of all, this approach solves the "which version do I edit?" problem that normally arises as soon as a document gets to the DTP stage and is converted from a word processor file to a DTP file. This dilemma is caused by the fact that last-minute changes to the document will be made only to the DTP version, rendering the word processor file out-of-date. The DTP file becomes the only one that reflects the printed document, but it is not in a form that allows for easy updating if a revised version is called for in the future. With XML, the *same* document is used as the source for both word processing and DTP. Any changes made to the text within the DTP environment are saved into that single XML document. Therefore, you have no problem when reusing the document in the future.

XML and the Web

What advantages does XML offer in the real world of the Web? You have seen some general XML features that look as though they could be useful. Now let's put them more specifically into a Web context.

> Note: This is just an overview. Chapter 15, "Automating the Web: Rapid Integration with XML," goes into fuller detail.

The Empowered Publisher

For the purposes of this discussion, I consider a *publisher* to be any individual or organization that delivers content on the Web.

The most obvious benefit of XML is that it enables the reliable delivery of any kind of structured information across the Web. As you learned when reading about document classes, the best way to use this flexibility (perhaps ironically) is to limit the number of different applications. This is already happening. Industry-wide collaborative groups are proposing standard XML applications for push data, metadata, and so on. Standard XML applications will mean greater interoperability, and publishers will benefit from adopting them where they exist.

From a publisher's point of view, the information she holds is her stock-in-trade. XML allows this asset to be managed in a coherent manner and deployed efficiently. Large information resources can be broken into *microdocuments*, which can be stored and managed using database techniques. Deliverable results can be retrieved and assembled on the fly via XML's entity management and linking facilities.

This core information asset also can be customized and repurposed easily. By attaching an appropriate style sheet to it, XML-encoded information can be delivered in whatever format the customer requires—on-screen, print, large type, Braille, and so on.

XML's linking facilities can be used to create a *knowledge web* (or indeed several overlapping webs) from what would otherwise be a mass of unconnected documents. These linkages can be held and maintained separately from the documents themselves, simplifying the task of link maintenance.

XML can be used to support resource discovery. When the scale or format of an information provider's existing resources means that they can't feasibly be encoded in XML, they instead can be described by XML-encoded metadata. This is a very cost-effective method of making relevant information findable.

The Empowered Client

From the client's point of view, receiving XML rather than HTML makes it possible to be much more self-contained. Even if clients are receiving only general-purpose information, their generic XML processor will allow them to browse it, using a virtual table of contents generated from the document itself. Clients won't need to go back to the server simply to see a different view of the information. If they want a different view of the information, they only have to load a different style sheet.

However, when the XML-encoded information that is delivered relates to a specific application of interest to the client, its value increases dramatically.

When information is stored in application-specific XML, its markup can reflect very precisely that information's semantics. For a start, this means that Web searching can become a much more precise exercise than it is currently. Also, software on the client's local machine will "understand" the information and be able to process it.

For example, a museum curator might run a Web search and retrieve a set of catalog records describing objects in other museums that are possibilities for an exhibit she is planning. If the records are encoded in XML, she will be able to drop them directly into a "proposed exhibit" entry within her collections management software.

This can be a two-way process. There is no reason why the same curator shouldn't use the Web to send out a set of loan requests, as XML documents, to the museums that hold the objects she wants for her exhibit. Suddenly the Web is supporting peer-to-peer information flow, as well as the traditional publisher-to-client relationship.

Intranets Get Serious

Many companies have developed intranets, as they have realized the advantages of delivering information company-wide. So far, Web technology has typically been adopted directly for intranets, including the use of HTML as the information delivery format. Now, with XML, the whole situation can change for the better.

XML is capable of acting as an interchange format for both documents and database information. In the case of documents, sources with a well-defined structure (such as legal documents and technical manuals) can now be delivered in a form that respects that structure. This, in turn, means that client software can make better use of these documents. For example, a technical manual might arrive with different views built into it—such as one for assembly, and another for troubleshooting and repair.

Database information easily can be *packed* into XML format for delivery, and *unpacked* on arrival. The unpacked information can be loaded into a client's database and worked on directly. This will allow distributed database operations within the intranet.

Chapter 15 takes up the theme of XML-based commerce in more detail.

Summary

This chapter closed the overview of XML by looking at the advantages that it is likely to bring. This started with a discussion of the merits of self-describing documents. You then looked at a specific area where XML might be of general utility—the area of authoring and desktop publishing. I described how XML is likely to make the Web itself a better place for information providers and their clients. I predicted that a democratization will take place, and the flow of information will be more two-way in nature. Finally, you learned about the implications of these developments for the company intranet.

CHAPTER 4

Implementing XML

by Richard Light

At this point, you have learned the definition of XML and examined its advantages. To finish off this introductory part of the book, let's think in very general terms about the realities of implementing XML. Much of the discussion in this chapter is centered on software tools, but you should always remember that the software is just a means of accomplishing a task. This chapter doubles as a checklist of the types of work you might be faced with when you implement XML.

What Software Do You Need?

It is important to remember that XML is just a standard representation for structured information. Without software that can understand that representation, it is not particularly useful.

In this chapter, I review the general types of software that will be required to support XML. In Chapter 16, "XML Software," I review the current state of play in the real world, and describe the software initiatives that are currently taking XML on board.

One general point must be made about software for XML: All valid XML documents are also valid SGML documents. As a result, all existing SGML-capable software should (in principle) work with valid XML documents. Therefore, a pretty good installed base of software exists even before any XML-specific software is developed.

> **Note:** For SGML software to work with XML documents, it needs to be fed—and needs to act on—the XML-specific version of a special header called the *SGML declaration*, which sets things up to support XML's use of the SGML framework. Without this declaration, DTDs designed for XML won't be valid, and things such as the Unicode character set and the special XML syntax for empty elements will cause problems.

> **Warning:** I have used SGML-based software for the figures in this chapter. See Chapter 16 for examples of XML-based offerings.

Authoring

As a writer of Web pages, your first thought will correctly be, "How do I create and update XML documents?" It's a reasonable question, but authoring is actually only one aspect of a more general issue.

Broadly speaking, there are three approaches to creating XML documents:

- "Do it yourself" with a plain text editor.
- Use specialized XML authoring tools.
- Use a standard word processor with plug-in XML support.

The first option doesn't sound very appealing because it implies that you will add all the XML markup by hand. This creates more work and is more error-prone than using software that gives you some help. However, this approach does have the advantage of being free. Suitable software is already included with almost every machine. A surprising number of HTML pages are put together in this way. Some text editors (notably GNU Emacs) have SGML add-ons that can significantly ease the task of adding markup.

Even when an XML document has been authored using some other software, it is useful to know that the document can be read into and edited by a text editor. This gives you a means of making minor edits to an XML document you have received, even if you don't have special XML-aware software yourself.

Warning: You should make sure that the editor you use definitely works in plain ASCII text. Most word processors add lots of hidden stuff to the plainest-looking documents. You might need to use a "save as text" option to get the required result. Also, XML documents created by other software might have few, or even no, newlines. (XML doesn't need them.) This leads to text files with tremendously long lines, which many editors will not be able to process correctly. Finally, if the XML document uses a 16-bit Unicode character encoding scheme, you won't get far with an ASCII-based editor.

The second option is to use a specialized XML-aware authoring tool. These tools are similar in approach to the HTML authoring tools with which you are probably already familiar, such as FrontPage, HoTMetaL, and so on. This option has pluses and minuses. On the plus side, the software is very well designed for the job of adding XML markup. You receive help with adding elements, specifying attribute values, and so on. You won't be able to create a document that isn't valid XML. Figure 4.1 shows this section being written using SoftQuad's Author/Editor SGML authoring software.

The downside is really a matter of personal preference. If you already know a particular word processor (especially if you have spent a long time mastering it), you might not be too eager to learn a different package just to write XML documents. On the other hand, if you pick up new software easily, or if you know that you will be spending a lot of your time with XML, then a specialized package is probably a better bet for you.

The final option is, in principle, the best for the average user. Both Word for Windows and WordPerfect have already introduced versions that offer support for adding SGML markup. When they do the same for XML, you should be able to use your word processor of choice and still get proper help with XML coding.

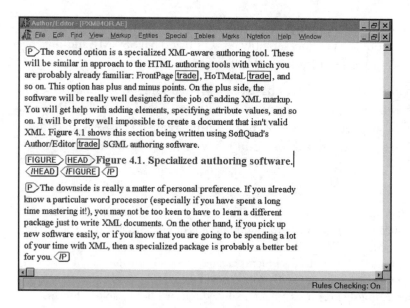

Figure 4.1.
Specialized authoring software.

Note: It will be interesting to see how the marketplace for XML authoring software develops. I have already argued (in Chapter 3, "The XML Advantage") that there is a strong case for word processors being redesigned around XML. The approach adopted for SGML support tends to involve associating SGML element types with styles. This works for simple DTDs, but it tends to break down when a large and complex DTD is in use. In particular, styles usually don't support the idea of nesting, which is central to how XML elements work. It should be the other way around: Store the document as a tree structure of XML elements, and then associate the styles with those elements.

Parsers

What is a parser? It's a piece of software whose job description is to check that an XML document is valid or, failing that, well-formed. Not very interesting to the average user, perhaps, but a vital part of the picture if *validity* and *well-formedness* are to have any real meaning in the XML world.

Any software package that is XML-aware will have a parser built into it in the form of an *XML processor*. (See Chapter 11, "The XML Processor.") As a minimum, the XML processor checks the XML documents you are about to work on, and checks them again when you have finished. Ideally, it is interactive; any errors you introduce are reported and can be sorted out while you work.

You also can get standalone XML parsers, which are important if you take the plain text editor route for your XML authoring. When you have finished working on an XML document in an uncontrolled environment (one that doesn't know about XML tagging conventions), you should always run an XML parser on it to check that it is still valid.

The most widely used parser for SGML and XML is nsgmls, part of the SP suite written by James Clark. This parser does a reliable job of checking the validity of any XML document. However, it isn't the friendliest of programs because it runs from the DOS command line. I have written a Windows front-end for nsgmls called RUNSP, which runs the program for you. If any errors occur in the document or the DTD, it opens up an editing window with the errors highlighted. Figure 4.2 shows RUNSP in action, pointing out an error in this chapter. (I mistyped the HEAD end-tag.) Both the SP suite and RUNSP are freeware.

In addition, there is a rapidly growing number of XML parsers, with many written in Java. Those that are available as of this writing are described in Chapter 16.

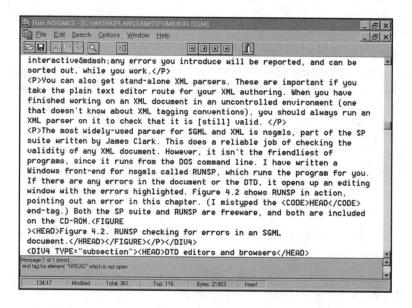

Figure 4.2.
RUNSP checking for errors in an SGML document.

DTD Editors and Browsers

One part of the XML system that must be included, to keep everything in order, is the DTD. Someone (probably not you) has to write that DTD. You can create a DTD with a plain text editor, but once again software can come to the aid of the DTD designer.

The process of developing a DTD for a new application can be complex and time-consuming. You are really analyzing the information requirements of a particular sphere of activity and writing a set of rules that always must be followed. If you make those rules too tight, they might not allow perfectly valid pieces of information. If the rules are too lax, they might encourage sloppy practices that interfere with the operation of your application.

Therefore, it is important to control the process of developing a DTD and to make sure that the element types in the DTD are well documented. DTD creation tools can help with this process, particularly when a number of people are working together on the design of the DTD.

DTD browsing tools can help users visualize the types of document structures that the DTD will support. They can show all the possible subelements of a particular element type graphically. This is much more fun than reading the DTD itself! Figure 4.3 shows a view of the HTML 2.0 DTD being browsed by Corel's Visual DTD tool. In this figure, the subelements that are allowed within paragraphs (the p element type) are shown. In addition to the 13 element types (a, img, br, and so on), character data is allowed. This is indicated by the icon at the top, above a.

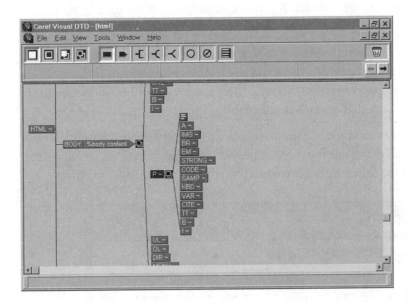

Figure 4.3.
The visual view of the HTML 2.0 DTD.

Style Sheet Editors

The XS style language is based on Scheme, which is a dialect of LISP. In one sense, it is very simple—and it is certainly powerful. However, coding with this language requires high-level skills. It won't be easy to write style sheets of any sophistication without some help. See Chapter 10, "The XML Style Mechanism," for a description of the style language.

An XS style sheet authoring package would know about the primitive components of the XS language and might let you create procedures to carry out common tasks such as outputting a paragraph or one item in a bulleted list. These low-level procedures could then be called up and used to display one or more element types.

Because no one has yet produced commercially available software of this type (even for the DSSSL standard, on which XS is based), it is not so easy to be sure how it would work. Obviously, it would be nice to have an environment in which you design a report format interactively, dragging and dropping components onto a form. However, the way XS works makes it hard to see how you could visualize your report in this way, because the report generation is driven by the content of each XML document, not by the spec.

Probably, you would have an actual document on screen, with the capability to associate styles with elements in that document. If you changed the style of any element, the whole display would be updated, which means that you would need to test your developing XS style sheet against a number of documents in order to be sure that it worked acceptably.

I'll give you an example of a proprietary SGML style sheet mechanism. This is the interactive style editing support provided by Panorama Pro. In Figure 4.4, I changed the font family for paragraphs (the p element type) to Arial.

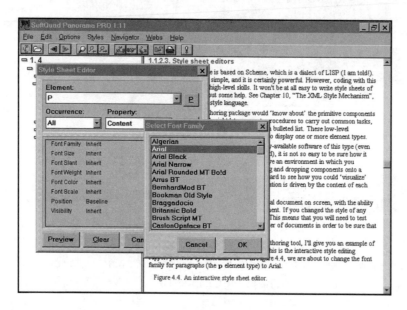

Figure 4.4.
An interactive style sheet editor.

In the immediate future, XML editors will probably support CSS style sheets in a similar way to Panorama Pro.

Link Management Tools

Linking is the third major element in the XML specification. (See Chapter 9, "Linking with XML," for a description of XML-Link.) Linking could also benefit from software support in the following three situations:

- Authoring XML documents
- Specialized link management
- Browsing XML documents

In the first case, I expect standard XML-aware authoring software to support the creation (and traversal) of XML's simple links. These are, after all, firmly based on the HREF links that are supported by HTML authoring packages, so no additional software should be required.

On the other hand, special software probably will be needed to support XML's extended links. Because these need not be physically located at any of the places that they link together, and need not even be in the same document, managing extended links is clearly a different scale of problem.

Extended links offer an exciting range of possibilities for two-way and multi-way linking, for *link farms* containing links within and between a whole set of documents, and so on. It is likely that software to support extended links will take a specific approach, rather than trying to offer a general-purpose solution. Several different approaches could be offered.

It is reasonable to expect that any XML-capable browser will be able to traverse both simple and extended links, although the implementation details for extended links can again be expected to vary. (Browsing of XML documents is covered more fully later in this chapter.)

Conversion

I started by talking about authoring XML documents from scratch, and I covered the software that might be helpful in that task. I said that this is only part of the picture. Then, I discussed software for dealing with DTDs, style sheets, and links. Now let's look at another way to actually create XML documents, which is to convert them from some other format to XML.

Converting to XML

Up-conversion, as it is known, is usually a mixture of software processes and hard work. The software processes are concerned with finding clues in the existing documents that can be mapped automatically to XML markup. This pattern matching can be based on the page layout of the source document, or the conversion software can provide a general-purpose language in which you write scripts to process specific source formats. The hard work can happen on either side of the software process.

A general problem is that current documents typically contain less information than you want in your XML version. For example, italicized words and phrases within paragraphs might be italicized because they are

- Foreign words
- Emphasizing a point
- Technical terms
- Representing irony

You usually should distinguish these cases in your XML markup. So, even if your conversion software is able to pick out these phrases in italics, you still have some manual work to do. You can *seed* the document with clues to help the software before processing it. Or you can edit the document by hand after processing to improve the quality of markup.

Up-conversion is often an iterative process. It makes sense to convert documents to a low-level DTD, which does little more than mirror their original logic in a valid XML form. XML-aware software can then be used to successively enhance the XML markup until it is acceptable.

The scale of an up-conversion project can be very large. If a corporation decides to re-engineer its internal documentation around XML, it might want to convert five years of material to this format. You easily might have to look at tens of thousands of documents in an interesting variety of formats! For this reason, a number of firms earn a living by taking on data-conversion projects. Many of these firms are already proficient in up-conversion to SGML and would find XML no problem.

XML to XML Conversions

When you have your documents in XML format, other types of conversion jobs will crop up. These require a slightly different kind of software because you are now starting from a well-structured source.

One very common need is to convert from one XML-style format to another. For example, you might want to convert documents from an in-house XML DTD to HTML for easier delivery on the Web. Such a process is typically driven by a script that tells you what to do with each element type (convert it to another element type, ignore it, output its data content without surrounding markup, and so on). Like a style sheet, the script is actually driven by the document itself.

XML to Other Formats

Finally comes the process known as *down-conversion*, which entails moving from XML to non-XML form. This is actually the province of the XS style mechanism, although other software also does this job. XS is clearly biased toward a paginated result. It specifies the required result in terms of things that appear on the page, such as paragraphs. Then a *back-end processor* converts this generalized description to the actual format required—RTF, TeX, PostScript, and so on.

This book was authored in SGML and then down-converted to RTF so that it could be fed into Sams Publishing's Word-based production process. I used a freeware package called Jade, by James Clark, which supports the subset of DSSSL on which XS's design was based.

In some cases, you actually want an unpaginated output from your XML. For example, if you are outputting selected elements from an XML document to be loaded into a database, you really want just a comma-delimited file containing only the required elements in the correct order. In this case, a specialized XML-aware down-conversion program is probably required.

Publishing

Publishing from your XML documents can take a variety of forms. In addition to the obvious option of Web-based publishing (enhancing your Web site with XML-based pages), the following possibilities spring to mind:

- Print
- CD-ROM
- On-demand and custom publishing

Let's start with Web delivery of your XML documents. I think it is reasonable to assume that future releases of standard Web browsers such as Netscape and Internet Explorer will offer seamless integration of XML with their current HTML capabilities. Assuming that this happens, you can develop your Web site with whatever mixture of HTML and XML makes sense for your particular circumstances, and you can be confident that your clients will have software that can read all of your pages. On the server side, you simply have to ensure that your XML documents are served with the correct MIME-type—text/xml. In addition, it is quite possible that specialized client-side browsers will be developed for specific XML applications.

The built-in XS style mechanism offers a reasonable quality of printed output directly from your XML documents. Current DSSSL implementations (which support XS) offer a variety of back-end formats that can be fixed (TeX) or revisable (Rich Text Format).

If you require higher-quality print products, your XML documents can be fed to a typesetting/desktop publishing (DTP) program. You have two options here. In the first case, you must convert your XML documents to the input format required by your DTP package. This is an example of a down-conversion (as discussed in the previous section). Alternatively, if you have a DTP program that is XML-aware, all you need to do is load the document as it stands. This is obviously the better route. Apart from avoiding the conversion process, you also avoid the problem of having the same document in two revisable formats. This can (and usually does) lead to inconsistencies between the printed document and its XML source.

Producing a CD-ROM from XML documents leads to a requirement for software that indexes and organizes a set of XML documents into an *electronic book*. This software might be self-contained, holding the documents in a proprietary non-XML format, or it might simply set them up so they can be viewed by a standard XML browser application.

On-demand publishing and current awareness services require some sort of XML-aware search engine that can pick out the relevant material matching a one-off query or a user profile. The selected documents (or parts of documents) can then be delivered using standard Web publishing techniques.

Site Maintenance

Although it is quite feasible to manage a small hybrid XML/HTML Web site by hand, this option becomes untenable at some point as the site grows. If the Web site is actually a company-wide intranet, software support for its maintenance is usually a necessity.

Document management systems allow a whole mass of documents to be managed and served in a coherent manner. This includes operations such as the following:

- Storing all the documents in a single repository
- Enforcing appropriate access rights for each user
- Checking out complete and partial documents for editing
- Locking checked-out documents so that no one else can update them at the same time
- Logging changes to a document when it is checked in after editing
- Creating publications from a set of documents

Ideally, an XML document management system takes account of both the physical organization of your documents (into entities) and their logical organization (into elements). This gives you the best chance to manage your information resources effectively, avoiding redundancy of information. Current experience from the SGML world suggests that a wide range of XML document management systems will be available, offering dramatically diverse solutions to this problem.

Another type of database makes no attempt to support document management, but it simply provides XML-aware retrieval capabilities. I suspect that these capabilities will be added to Web search engines that currently use free-text indexing to track down relevant pages.

Summary

In this chapter I looked at what supporting XML actually means. The main focus has been on the software that will be required, although discussing this has also given an insight into the tasks (and the "people skills") that will be called for.

I reviewed the process of authoring XML documents. In addition to having different possible styles of editing software, I showed that an array of support packages is required to maintain the XML DTD, style sheets, and links.

Moving on to the processing of XML, I discussed the conversion processes that can create XML documents out of other types of information, XML-to-XML transfers, and the creation of "delivery" formats from an XML source. I followed this up with a review of the publishing options currently offered by XML.

Finally, I sketched out the requirements for managing a real-life XML site. These are centered on document management issues, such as version control and security.

Part II, "XML in Detail," is designed to give a fuller picture of what is in the XML specification. If your interest is more in the potential uses of XML, you might find what you are looking for in Part III, "Using XML," and Part IV, "The Future of XML."

XML in Detail

CHAPTER 5

The XML Approach

by Richard Light

Part II, "XML in Detail," takes a detailed look at all aspects of the XML specification. In this chapter, by way of preparation, I outline the general philosophy behind XML. The arguments that determine the design of XML offer you a good insight into XML's overall approach.

After this I describe some general concepts that are necessary to obtain a proper understanding of XML, and some specific conventions that apply throughout the XML standard. The following topics will be covered:

- How XML represents individual characters
- Low-level constructs that are referred to throughout the XML specification
- The distinction between the text in your XML documents (character data) and markup

- A technique for marking sections of an XML document so that markup within them is ignored
- How XML deals with white space (spaces, tabs, and newlines)
- How to insert comments into your XML documents
- What processing instructions are and how they are used
- The distinction between the logical structure and the physical structure of an XML document

XML's Main Objectives

What is XML all about? This is what the XML editors said in the June 30, 1997 draft of XML-Lang: "Extensible Markup Language (XML) is an extremely simple dialect of SGML which is completely described in this document. The goal is to enable generic SGML to be served, received, and processed on the Web in the way that is now possible with HTML. XML has been designed for ease of implementation and for interoperability with both SGML and HTML."

The general intent of this statement is pretty clear, but it might be helpful to expand on a few specific points.

Generic SGML

Generic SGML means any information that follows the SGML syntax. This is the big advantage that XML offers. Unlike HTML, XML gives Web information providers the power to define their own structures for the information they deliver.

In order to let XML offer the same degree of generality as SGML, some compromises had to be made. Many SGML features had to be jettisoned so that XML would be small and light enough to fly. But the ability to define and use your own DTDs is central to XML, and this is what the phrase *generic SGML* denotes.

> Note: In fact, one form of XML—the *well-formed document*—doesn't even require a DTD. This is described in the "Well-Formed and Valid Documents" section, later in this chapter.

Interoperability with SGML

Why should XML be interoperable with SGML? Isn't this a step backward? The answer is that two major types of benefits can be gained from making XML interoperable with SGML.

For a start, what do I mean by *interoperability* in this context? In this case, interoperability means that all valid XML documents can be treated as though they are SGML documents.

> **Warning:** This is definitely a one-way street: It is most certainly *not* possible to treat all SGML documents as though they are XML documents!

Another way of looking at interoperability is to understand that "all valid XML documents are, by definition, valid SGML." This is the first benefit. SGML is an international standard (ISO 8879:1986 to be precise), and all valid XML documents are guaranteed to conform to it, without users having to take any special measures to ensure conformity. Compare this with the HTML experience. Web services that validate HTML documents frequently report errors in pages that work perfectly on the Web. Making sure that all your HTML pages are valid usually involves extra work for little obvious or immediate benefit. If you take the trouble to ensure your XML documents are valid, you get SGML conformance for free.

The second benefit is that a fair amount of powerful software for working with SGML documents already exists: conversion tools, desktop publishing engines, document management systems, search tools, and so on. Interoperability means that this SGML software works, straight out of the box, on your XML documents. No changes to the software means no changes to your documents! This also means that you can set up projects that use SGML software to process a mixture of XML and SGML documents.

> **Note:** As a separate issue, SGML tools vendors might choose to produce lower-cost versions of their products specifically for XML. Although this is clearly to be welcomed, it doesn't remove the benefits to XML of SGML interoperability.

Interoperability with HTML

In what way can XML be interoperable with HTML? The two standards are incompatible in terms of their scope: HTML is a specific application of SGML, and XML is an *SGML profile* that supports many types of documents.

In this case, I think the answer lies in how the two standards are actually used on the Web. XML documents will use the same protocols as HTML: They will be requested and delivered using HTTP. The linking mechanism used by XML is based on the existing URL scheme and is upwardly compatible with it.

Assuming that Web browsers are extended to support XML as well as HTML, it will be possible to set up Web sites that are a glorious mix of XML-encoded and HTML-encoded documents. You will be able to link from HTML pages to XML documents (and vice versa), and your users won't even need to be aware that they jumped between HTML and XML.

HTML interoperability means that XML can be adopted gradually, and your investment in existing HTML pages is safe. If you maintain a Web site, you might choose to write new pages in XML, and leave the rest of your site as it is. Or you might decide to continue using HTML for your core pages, and switch to XML for only a particular set of specialized information that would benefit from a custom DTD and tailored style sheets. Or you might decide not to bother with XML at all. It's your call. HTML won't go away.

Design Goals

XML's designers gave themselves 10 commandments, or design goals. Let's look at each of them to see what they tell us about the XML project.

1: XML Shall Be Straightforwardly Usable Over the Internet

I've already touched on this while talking about interoperability with HTML. XML needs to use the communications protocols, such as HTTP, that are already in place. It shouldn't impose any picky new requirements of its own.

Usable also suggests that you should be able to do something useful with an XML document after it has been delivered to you over the Internet. This is where SGML currently fails, because the structure is too sophisticated to be straightforwardly processed by client-side software. (I foresee a massive growth in new client-side XML software when developers realize the wide range of interesting things they can do with well-structured information packets delivered over the Internet. Much of this software will be application-specific— working with financial transactions, annotated chess games, museum catalog records, and so on.)

I want to stress that this design goal does not *limit* XML to Internet-based applications. Apart from its obvious application within intranets (where the logic for using XML is identical to, or even more compelling than, the Internet case), this design goal might find favor as an information structuring mechanism within stand-alone systems. (For example, I would much prefer my word processing software to be based on XML!)

2: XML Shall Support a Wide Variety of Applications

This design goal requires XML to offer the same level of generality as SGML. This means that the range of applications supported by XML is limited only by users' imaginations.

In practical terms, the rate of adoption of XML will probably depend on the availability of free-standing XML software and XML-aware plugs-ins for existing packages. This is primarily a software issue, not an XML language issue. User-friendly packages for designing XML DTDs and style sheets will also remove a major obstacle to the development of new XML applications.

3: XML Shall Be Compatible with SGML

This is crucial. As you have already seen, making XML documents compatible with SGML yields real benefits to users with XML applications.

In terms of developing the XML specification, this design goal means starting with the full SGML standard and deciding what to leave out. XML can't allow in anything that isn't also valid SGML, so the general approach adopted has been to simplify SGML by removing options and features that are not essential to XML's proper functioning.

You might think that designing XML as "simple SGML" would result in something very similar to HTML. Interestingly, this is not the case: XML and HTML come out looking quite different. As you will see in Chapter 12, "Morphing Existing HTML into XML," HTML actually makes use of some of the sophisticated features of SGML that are outlawed in XML. HTML might look simple, but it isn't!

4: It Shall Be Easy to Write Programs that Process XML Documents

The main barrier to writing software that can claim to be truly SGML-compatible is the sheer size of the SGML standard. The standard reference to SGML (*The SGML Handbook*, by Charles Goldfarb, Oxford, ISBN 0-19-853737-9) is 500 pages long, with another 100 pages of annexes. The equivalent in XML—the language specification—currently totals 26 pages. That just has to be an easier ride. Also, SGML includes programming concepts (such as multiple parsing modes, and inclusion exceptions in content models) that are notoriously difficult to implement.

The developers of XML wanted the language to be simple enough to be implemented as a graduate-student project. (Originally, they talked about a "two-week project," but I haven't heard that phrase used recently on the XML developers' list.)

5: The Number of Optional Features in XML Is to Be Kept to the Absolute Minimum, Ideally Zero

This is another lesson learned the hard way from SGML. The SGML standard includes many optional features, several of which are rarely used. Support for these features (just in case they are needed) is additional baggage that bulks up SGML software and adds to its cost.

Making XML options-free doesn't rule out "beyond XML" software offerings. All three aspects of the XML specification are based on more complete (and more complex) standards: the language is based on SGML; linking is based on HyTime and TEI's Extended Pointer mechanism; and styles are based on

DSSSL. These standards offer a well-defined route for people who want to add extra value to their XML-compliant software products. Meanwhile, producing software that is completely XML-compatible will remain relatively easy.

6: XML Documents Should Be Human-Legible and Reasonably Clear

This is a difficult goal to argue with. I think that this requirement comes in part from a realization that it is very easy to use clever shortcuts that save a bit of typing here and there but lead to markup whose existence can be inferred by machines, but that is not actually present in the document and so is not apparent to a human observer.

Omitting start tags and end tags is a good example of the dangers of shortcuts. In HTML, for instance, you can omit the tags that mark the start and end of the <HTML>, <HEAD>, and <BODY> elements, even though these are a required part of every HTML document. But an SGML system can deduce where these tags should be, and in the system's estimation, the tags will be part of the document's markup, but they will be totally invisible to a human reader!

7: The XML Design Should Be Prepared Quickly

It's a bit of a cliché that speed is of the essence in the world of the Web. The Internet Engineering Task Force's philosophy of "rough consensus and running code" leads to much more rapid development than other methods, such as those adopted by committees working on International Standards. However, in the case of XML, a particular need for urgency was evident. The feeling was that if the SGML community had not offered a way to extend HTML, Web tool vendors would have developed another method, and one that was not compatible with SGML, in the near future.

In order to achieve this speed, the SGML community and W3C formed an ad hoc committee to work on XML. However, guidelines are now being formalized more along standard W3C lines. On July 1, 1997, the group currently known as the *W3C SGML Editorial Review Board* became known as the *W3C XML Working Group*, and it began working under the process rules currently governing the activities of W3C working groups.

8: The Design of XML Shall Be Formal and Concise

The XML language specification uses Extended Backus-Naur Format (EBNF). This is a standard format for declaring programming languages. Wherever possible, EBNF notation is used in preference to a description of an XML feature. Conciseness has also been achieved by including only those parts of SGML that are absolutely necessary, as noted earlier.

9: XML Documents Shall Be Easy to Create

This is perhaps more of a user perspective. Ease of authoring, like ease of DTD design, is most greatly helped by having good authoring software. This software has two main goals. It keeps your documents valid by letting you select only markup that is allowed in the current context. And it saves you keystrokes by putting in the markup for you. Such software lets you select element types (tags) from drop-down lists, add attribute values via dialog boxes, and so on. This is very similar to the aspects of a word processor that have to do with style selection.

Conversely, it is quite feasible to create (and update) XML documents with any simple editor or word processor that can deal with ASCII documents and offers the facility of saving the resulting file as plain ASCII. This might not be an attractive method for creating a major piece of work, but it is very useful to be able to use an editor to tweak XML documents that have been delivered to you requiring minor changes. This compares well with page-oriented delivery methods such as PostScript or PDF, where changes are not possible.

10: Terseness in XML Markup Is of Minimal Importance

This is another lesson from SGML. The SGML standard has options that allow you to omit tags (particularly end tags) and leave an SGML processor to infer their presence. These features were included primarily to save keystrokes and to reduce the disc storage requirements of the resulting documents. However, if software is doing the work of adding the markup, there is little point in your being able to omit it. You don't have to type the tags yourself, and the disc storage overhead is not really an issue these days. (Just look at the size of a typical image file or the large and uncontrollable overhead of "binary stuff" in typical word processor files! The Word file containing this chapter is currently 66,048 bytes, but it contains only 25,197 data characters. Nearly 62% of the file is overhead. So even if markup adds 100% to the size of an XML document, it is still doing better than Word.)

If you minimize markup, the structure of the document is much less clear to the human eye. Also, software finds it more difficult to discern the structure.

Representation of Characters in XML

An XML document consists of a sequence of *characters*, each of which is "an atomic unit of text represented by a bit string." This is a familiar concept to anyone who has probed around inside computer systems. For example, PC-compatible computers use an extension of the long-established ASCII character set. In the original 7-bit ASCII scheme, each letter, number, and punctuation symbol was given a different 7-bit code, similar to the following examples:

- `0110000` stands for the digit 0.
- `0110001` stands for the digit 1.
- `1000001` stands for the letter A.

These bit patterns are commonly represented by a *hexadecimal number,* such as `30` standing for the digit 0. Only 128 different 7-bit patterns exist, so 7-bit ASCII is able to represent only 128 different characters. With the advent of PCs, this proved to be a limitation; therefore, 8-bit character sets have been used most often since the advent of MS-DOS. Going to 8 bits doubles the number of possible patterns to 256, and it allows the PC character set to include accented characters, drawing shapes, a selection of Greek letters, and so on.

XML uses ISO 10646, or *Unicode,* which takes the next logical step and supports the use of 16-bit patterns to represent characters. These allow more than 65,000 different characters to be represented. ISO 10646 provides a standard definition for all the characters found in many European and Asian languages. (16-bit encoding is not mandatory; it's just one of the options supported by ISO 10646. For cases in which a more compact 8-bit character set is sufficient, ISO 10646 offers the UTF-8 encoding scheme.) In addition, ISO 10646 provides *private use areas* for user extensions to the standard character set. Chapter 7, "Physical Structures in XML Documents," discusses character encoding issues in more detail.

XML defines the range of *legal characters* (which are the characters that can appear in an XML document) as those with the following hexadecimal values:

- `09` is the tab.
- `0D` is the carriage return.
- `0A` is the line feed.
- `20`-`FFFD` and `00010000`-`7FFFFFFF` are the legal graphics characters of Unicode and ISO 10646.

Characters are classified for convenience as *letters*, *digits*, and *other characters*. There are detailed rules for dealing with compound and ideographic characters and with layout and format-control characters.

Primitive Constructs

I will introduce here a few low-level concepts that crop up throughout the XML specification. `Name`, `Names`, `NMToken`, and `NmTokens` are used within the definition of many XML constructs, such as start-tags, attributes, and element declarations. They contain `name characters`, so I will define those first. XML defines name characters as

- Letters
- Digits
- Hyphens
- Underscores
- Full stops
- Special characters in classes `CombiningChar`, `Ignorable`, and `Extender`

The four primitive constructs are then defined thus:

- A *Name* consists of a letter or underscore, followed by zero or more name characters.
- *Names* refers to one or more *Name* entries, separated by white space.
- A *Name token* (commonly known as an *Nmtoken*) is any mixture of name characters.
- *Nmtokens* refers to one or more *Nmtoken* entries, separated by white space.

Character Data and Markup

The characters in an XML document represent a mixture of *character data*, which is the actual text of the document, and *markup*, which is information that adds value to that text. The start of some markup in an XML document is signaled by one of two special characters: the ampersand (&) and the left angle bracket (<). XML recognizes the following types of markup:

- Start tags
- End tags
- Empty elements
- Entity references
- Character references
- Comments
- CDATA sections
- Document type declarations
- Processing instructions

In this chapter and the next two chapters, you will learn about these different types of markup.

> Warning: Because & and < are special characters, you can't use them just anywhere. They need to be *escaped* in some way if you want to include them as part of the text of your document. You can use either *character references* (such as & and <) or *entity references* (such as & and <) for & and < respectively. Character references and entity references are described in Chapter 7.

This is an example of mixed text and markup:

```
<p>Once more we consider the wise words of L&eacute;ger:
<q>Get it right first time!</q></p>
```

This example contains the following elements:

- Start tag: `<p>` (a new paragraph)
- Text: `Once more we consider the wise words of L`
- Entity reference: `&eacute;` (the letter é)

- Text: `ger:`
- Start tag: `<q>` (a quotation within this paragraph)
- Text: `Get it right first time!`
- End tag: `</q>` (end the quotation)
- End tag: `</p>` (end the paragraph)

The general rule is that if you strip out the markup, you are left with the character data. This also applies within elements: The character data within an element is all the characters between its start tag and end tag that are not markup. Thus, in the preceding example, the `<P>` element contains the following character data:

```
Once more we consider the wise words of L
ger:
Get it right first time!
```

The `<Q>` element contains the following character data:

```
Get it right first time!
```

> Note: The quoted phrase is part of the character data of *both* elements.

> Note: The accented character appears to have vanished. This happens because it is represented by markup—an entity reference—even though it is only a single character. Obviously, this character will appear correctly as é when the XML document is viewed or printed, but within the document it maintains its separate status. The conversion of `&eacute;` to é happens on the client's machine, which enables XML to represent accented characters correctly on a wide range of platforms despite the fact that they use different encodings.

CDATA Sections

Sometimes it is really tedious to have to escape every & and < character that crops up in your text. What if you are trying (as I am now) to write a book that explains XML and gives lots of examples? Each example will be littered with special characters. XML provides CDATA *sections* to get around this problem. As with comments, & and < can be entered freely within CDATA sections.

CDATA sections can occur anywhere that character data might occur. They are used to escape blocks of text that would otherwise be interpreted as markup. CDATA sections begin with the sequence <![CDATA[and end with the sequence]]>, as in the following example:

```
<![CDATA[ <p>Once more we consider the wise words of
L&eacute;ger: ]]>
```

This is how the first line of the previous markup example was encoded for this book.

In the special case of CDATA sections, *character data* is any string of characters, not including the sequence]]>, that terminates the CDATA section.

Note that CDATA sections cannot occur inside other CDATA sections; that is, they cannot *nest*.

White Space Handling

As an aid to greater readability, you can insert *white space* into XML documents. XML defines white space as any combination of the following:

- The space character
- Carriage return
- Line feed
- Tab

For example, you might indent elements to show their hierarchical structure:

```
<p>Things I would like for my birthday:
    <list>
        <item>a watch</item>
        <item>socks</item>
    </list>
</p>
```

Here new lines and tabs have been used to indent the markup and give a clearer visual layout, even though they are not strictly required. Without the extraneous white space this example would look as follows:

```
<p>Things I would like for my birthday:<list><item>a watch</
item><item>
socks</item></list></p>
```

This is much less clear to a human reader.

This extra white space is treated as part of the document and is passed to an application by the XML processor. However, in the following special cases, an XML processor will flag the white space that occurs immediately before or after markup as not significant:

- When the XML processor is reading the DTD (as discussed in Chapter 8, "Keeping It Tidy: The XML Rule Book")
- When the current element has element content rather than mixed content (as discussed in the "Element Declaration" section of Chapter 8)

In the previous example, you can reasonably assume that the content model for <P> elements allows mixed content, that the content model for <list> allows only <item>, and that the content model for <item> allows mixed content (or just text, which amounts to the same thing). Then an XML processor would mark as non-significant the extra white space within the <list> element, which is the only element type in this example that has element content. An application might then choose to treat this piece of markup as though the white space within <list> did not exist:

```
<p>Things I would like for my birthday:
    <list><item>a watch</item><item>socks</item></list>
</p>
```

In cases when these rules might lead to important spaces being ignored by an application (for example, those in poetry or source code), XML provides a mechanism for signaling to an application that this white space should be treated as significant. The XML-SPACE attribute can be added to any element's attribute list. Its declaration takes the following form:

```
XML-SPACE (DEFAULT ¦ PRESERVE) #IMPLIED
```

Specifying this attribute with the value "PRESERVE" indicates that white space is to be treated as significant within this element:

```
<POEM>
<L XML-SPACE="PRESERVE">One</L>
<L XML-SPACE="PRESERVE"> Two</L>
<L XML-SPACE="PRESERVE"> Three</L>
</POEM>
```

Comments

Comments can be used to annotate your XML documents. They take the form
`<!--`, followed by the text of the comment. They are terminated by the sequence `-->`. Here is an example:

```
<!-- This is a comment. -->
```

Comments can be of any length. The only restriction on their content is that
they cannot contain any pair of hyphens, except for the ones at the start and
end of the comment. Like `CDATA` sections, comments can contain the `&` and `<`
characters with impunity: Markup is not interpreted within comments.

In addition to appearing in your XML documents, comments can be used to
document the Document Type Definitions that control their structure. In these
cases, it is particularly useful to be able to include markup freely:

```
<!-- Declarations for <head> & <body>: -->
```

Comments should be used with a certain amount of caution. They do not form
part of the document's character data, and an XML processor is not required
to let an application access the text of comments. Thus, comments are guaranteed to be good only as a guide for a human reader who is looking at the
source of an XML document or DTD. Information that might be required
when processing XML documents (for example, who last revised the document
and when they revised it) is much better held as markup.

Processing Instructions

Processing instructions (jocularly known as *PIs*) contain instructions for applications that will process an XML document. PIs start with the sequence `<?`
plus a Name, and they are terminated by `?>`. Here is an example:

```
<?XML version="1.0"?>
```

The Name (in this case, `XML`) is called the *PI target*. The PI target indicates
which application is meant to take notice of the processing instruction. XML
itself uses PIs for a variety of purposes. For this reason, it reserves for its own

use all Names beginning with the letters *XML*. However, apart from this minor restriction, the PI mechanism can be used to feed processing information to *any* application that is working with the XML document. Here is an example:

```
<?TAGLINK xref "TEI-P3"?>
```

PIs are not part of the document's character data, but (unlike comments) they must be passed through to the application.

If required, the Name at the start of a PI can be formally declared as a NOTATION. See Chapter 8 for details of how to declare notations.

Logical and Physical Structure

You're getting close to finding out what an XML document is, but first you have to understand some key XML concepts: logical and physical structures, and the relationship between them.

The *logical structure* of an XML document is indicated by the markup that it contains. This markup indicates the declarations, processing instructions, elements, comments and so on that the document contains. The idea of logical markup should be familiar to you from looking at the source of HTML pages. Chapter 6, "Logical Structures in XML Documents," goes into the full detail of the logical structure within XML documents, and Chapter 8 looks at the logical structure of the XML DTD.

Physical structure is a new concept, and a very powerful one. The idea is that you can break an XML document into any number of bits, or *entities*. In the XML world, an *entity* means a physical storage unit. Most of the time, this physical storage unit is just a file on disc, but XML takes care not to limit entities to being files. For example, you might choose to store chunks of XML in a database. The idea is that your XML-aware system will have an *entity manager* that knows how to deliver the required piece of XML on request. This might involve going online to the Internet, querying a database, or just picking up a file from the local system.

The entity in which an XML document starts (and ends) is called the *root* or *document entity*. Chapter 7 looks at the issue of physical XML structures in more detail.

The logical and physical structure of an XML document must be *synchronous.* Broadly speaking, this means that they must nest. Elements must begin and end in the same entity, but they can refer to other entities within their content. Each entity must contain complete, not partial, logical structures. Therefore, you have some additional *containers* representing physical structure, as shown in Figure 5.1.

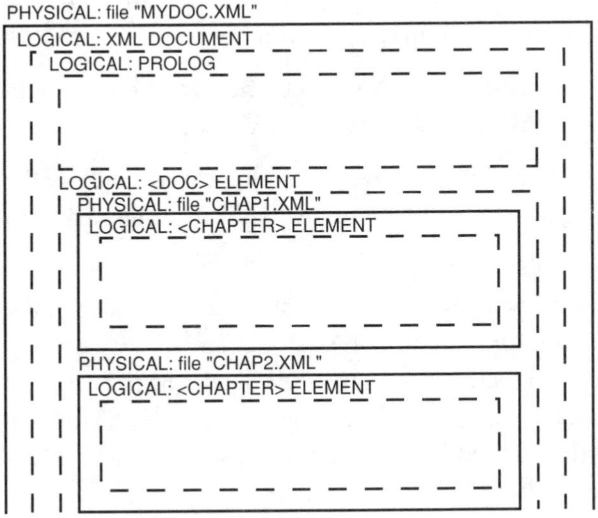

Figure 5.1.
Synchronous logical and physical structures.

You will learn more about the relationship between logical and physical structures in XML in Chapter 7.

Summary

In this chapter, you learned the underlying basics of XML. First, I reviewed and explained the mission statement and design goals that underlie XML. These show you very clearly that the designers of XML are working hard to produce a standard that is as simple and valuable as possible. You saw how some lessons learned the hard way with SGML are being applied to make XML more useful and accessible.

I then reviewed some very basic aspects of XML, which will underpin the rest of Part II, "XML in Detail."

First, you saw how characters are represented in XML, and you learned the distinction between character data and markup. Understanding this distinction is central to a proper appreciation of how XML works. You learned about CDATA sections, which are a handy way of entering text that contains many special markup characters, and you learned about XML's rules for dealing with any white space that is placed around markup to make it more readable.

Next, you learned how to add comments to XML documents and how to send instructions to your applications via processing instructions.

Finally, you found that XML documents have both a logical structure and a physical structure, and that these two structures have to fit together in a well-organized manner.

This chapter has simply set the scene. Chapter 6, "Logical Structures in XML Documents," discusses the logical structure of XML documents. Chapter 7, "Physical Structures in XML Documents," gives full details of the physical structure of documents. Finally, Chapter 8, "Keeping It Tidy: The XML Rule Book," describes how XML provides its own rule book, so that XML documents are genuinely self-describing.

Logical Structures in XML Documents

by Richard Light

In Chapter 5, "The XML Approach," I reviewed the basics of the XML language and discussed types of markup (such as comments, processing instructions, and CDATA sections) that are generally useful but rather incidental to the real job that XML is trying to do. In this chapter, you will see the logical structure of XML documents and what makes them into useful pieces of structured information.

XML Documents

Now that you've learned the basics, you can finally find out what an *XML document* is! This process will be rather like peeling an onion. Each time I define a new XML concept, you will see that some more specific concepts are hidden inside it.

Starting with the whole onion, let's look at the top-level logical structure of XML documents. XML documents have an optional *prolog*, followed by a required element known as the *document element*, and then optional miscellaneous stuff (such as comments, processing instructions, and white space) at the end.

Here is a simple example. Believe it or not, this is a genuine, complete, and *well-formed* XML document:

```
<greeting>Hello, world!</greeting>
```

This example is a document element, without any prolog. You'll take this example and build on it as you go along.

The prolog consists of two main components, both of which are optional.

XML Declaration

The *XML declaration* is a special processing instruction declaring that this is an XML document and quoting the version of XML to which it conforms (currently 1.0):

```
<?XML version="1.0"?>
```

In practice, it is a very good idea to include an XML declaration in even the simplest XML documents. Here is how to add one to your example:

```
<?XML version="1.0"?>
<greeting>Hello, world!</greeting>
```

By including an XML declaration, you are making it crystal clear both to human readers and to software that this is intended to be an XML document. The XML declaration, if present, is always the first piece of markup in an XML document.

The XML declaration can also contain information about the character encoding scheme used in the document:

```
<?XML version="1.0" encoding="UTF-8"?>
```

This is associated more with the physical than the logical structure of the XML document, because it helps software to read the characters in the document correctly. This aspect of the XML declaration is discussed in Chapter 7, "Physical Structures in XML Documents," in the section "Character Encoding in XML Text Entities."

The XML declaration can contain guidelines on whether it is necessary to process all or part of the DTD. These guidelines are the *required markup declaration* (*RMD*) and look like the following:

```
<?XML version="1.0" RMD="INTERNAL"?>
```

This is discussed in Chapter 8, "Keeping It Tidy: The XML Rule Book."

Document Type Declaration

The second main part of the prolog is the *document type declaration*. It must appear between the XML declaration and the start of the document element. The document type declaration indicates the rules that the XML document is following (or at least trying to follow). These rules are collectively known as the *document type definition* (*DTD*).

These rules can be held in another entity (that is, another file), as in the following example:

```
<?XML version="1.0"?>
<!DOCTYPE greeting SYSTEM "hello.dtd">
<greeting>Hello, world!</greeting>
```

Here, the rules for this document can be found in the file referenced by the URL `hello.dtd`. This entity is called the *external subset* of the DTD.

The document type declaration can also include some or all of these rules within itself:

```
<?XML version="1.0"?>
<!DOCTYPE greeting [
<!ELEMENT greeting (#PCDATA)>
]>
<greeting>Hello, world!</greeting>
```

In this case, the single rule for this document (an element declaration for greeting) is actually inside the document type declaration before the start of the document proper. This is called the *internal subset* of the DTD.

In general, you will have both an external and an internal DTD subset in your document type declarations. The general idea behind this two-part approach is that you can use the external subset to refer to a standard DTD. Then you declare any features that are specific to this particular document in the internal DTD subset. (The rule to support this approach states that declarations in the internal DTD subset are read first and take precedence over declarations in the external DTD subset.)

Normally, you should not use your internal DTD subset to change the structural rules defined by the external DTD, although it is quite possible to do that with XML. However, you still need this opportunity to declare, for example, all of the entities that your document uses, such as image files.

The Document Element

So the "meat" of an XML document consists of exactly one element: the *document element*. This doesn't sound like much, until you consider that inside this element any number of subelements can be nested to any depth, and any amount of text can be included.

The key points are that an XML document cannot consist of more than one element, and it cannot be part of an element.

The following is *not* an XML document, because it contains two elements:

```
<?XML version="1.0"?>
<greeting>Hello, world!</greeting>
<response>Hello, XML!</response>
```

On the other hand, the following is a well-formed XML document, because it has a single conversation element containing the greeting and the response:

```
<?XML version="1.0"?>
<conversation>
<greeting>Hello, world!</greeting>
<response>Hello, XML!</response>
</conversation>
```

Well-Formed and Valid Documents

I've casually used the adjectives *well-formed* and *valid* to describe XML documents. What do these words mean, exactly?

Well-Formed Documents

A *well-formed XML document* is one that "looks right," but whose logical structure is not validated against the DTD (if any) associated with the document. In other words, it needs to have a single outermost element (the *root* or *document element*) within which all the other elements and character data are neatly nested. But it isn't necessary for the document's elements and their attributes to be declared in the DTD, and no check is made that each element contains the subelements that the DTD says it should contain.

The fact that an XML document is well-formed does not necessarily mean that no DTD exists for that document. It might be that there is no DTD, but equally the document might have been deliberately delivered without a DTD because the current application doesn't need one. Even if the document has a DTD and that DTD is available, there is nothing to force XML applications to use a DTD if it doesn't suit their purposes.

A well-formed XML document must have a properly declared physical structure. Any entity references it contains must relate to entities that have been declared in the DTD (apart from the predefined entities amp, lt, gt, apos, and quot).

> Note: For an XML document to be valid, as opposed to well-formed, all the entities it uses, including these predefined entities, must be declared in the DTD.

The concept of being well-formed sounds like an invitation to anarchy, but that is not its purpose. The concept is provided in XML because, for many purposes, it is not necessary to provide a DTD or to formally check a document against that DTD. Reading a DTD takes time and bandwidth; checking an XML document against its DTD takes even more time. If a server of XML documents has already ensured that they are all valid and clean, it is a waste of time for each client to have to do the same.

Because an XML document defines its own hierarchical element structure, applications that simply want to display the document might work perfectly well without the DTD. See Chapter 11, "The XML Processor," for a more detailed discussion of how an XML processor deals with well-formed documents.

Valid Documents

In contrast to well-formed XML documents, valid XML documents have to obey all the rules. Not only must they have a DTD, but each element must conform to the rules that the DTD lays down for it. This is the mode in which XML documents will typically be created and updated. Chapter 8 contains further details of the rules that the DTD imposes.

XML's validity rules are an additional layer on top of the rules for being well-formed. Every valid XML document must be well-formed as well.

Whether an application checks that an XML document is valid as well as being well-formed is determined by the XML processor it uses. If a non-validating XML processor is used, it will just check that the XML document is well-formed. If a validating XML processor is used, it will report any validity errors in addition to checking that the XML document is well-formed. Chapter 11 discusses the operation of both types of XML processor in detail.

Elements

Now let's look at *elements* in more detail. First of all, what is an element? It is more than just a tag, or even a pair of tags. Let's start by reviewing what an element appears to be in HTML and then move on to the XML case.

Elements in HTML

In HTML, the concept of an element isn't particularly relevant. HTML tags tend to be used as style indicators, markers, and switches. It's not clear where a thing called *element* would fit into the picture.

For example, paragraphs tend to have only start tags, effectively saying "start a new paragraph here" or "make the following text paragraph style," as in the following example:

```
<p>The boy stood on the burning deck ...
```

Although p elements can have end tags, these end tags are frequently omitted. This means that you know where each paragraph starts, but you have to guess where it ends, and so does any software that is processing the HTML document.

Some tags are included simply to mark where visual elements should be placed. For example, <hr> marks the placement of a horizontal line in the HTML page.

Other tags switch on and off typesetting features such as bold and italic. For example, the following line marks a phrase that is to appear as both bold and italic:

```
<b><i>This is really important</b></i>
```

Each start tag switches the relevant feature on, and each end tag switches it off.

XML Elements: The Suitcase Model

To understand XML elements, you need to put the HTML view of markup out of your mind and dream up a new metaphor. Think of an XML element as a particular type of suitcase, with an optional luggage label on the side giving extra useful information. This suitcase might contain baggage (character data) or smaller suitcases. These smaller suitcases might also have a luggage label and contents. Some suitcases will be empty, but they will be there because their luggage labels hold useful information.

Figure 6.1 illustrates this idea by showing a p element that contains a mixture of character data and subelements (rs and emph). Each of these three elements is represented by a suitcase that has a luggage label containing a single piece of information. Inside the rs and emph suitcases (elements) will be more baggage (character data).

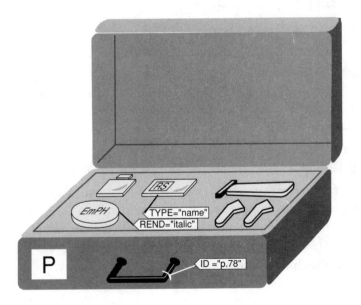

Figure 6.1.
Elements as suitcases.

You learned in Chapter 5 that an XML document consists of a single element. To put that in terms of the suitcase model, if you want to fly XML Air, you must check in with a single item of baggage. Everything else must be packed inside it. (Fortunately, XML Air doesn't impose any size or weight restrictions!)

Start Tags and End Tags

In order to be able to contain things, elements need to have a finite size. Moving from the three-dimensional world of suitcases to the two-dimensional world of structured documents, the finite size of a document is achieved by having a *start tag* and an *end tag*, which mark the boundaries of an element (its beginning and its end). Each of these tags includes a name that indicates the element's *type*. Start tags take the following form:

```
<Name>
```

End tags look like this:

```
</Name>
```

Here is a complete example:

```
<mytag> [content goes here] </mytag>
```

> Warning: In XML, you are not allowed to omit end tags for elements that are not empty. This is in contrast to both HTML and generic SGML, where both start tags and end tags can be omitted in certain circumstances.

Empty Elements

Empty elements have a special format. Because they have no contents, they don't need to have a start tag and an end tag to hold those contents. Instead, they use a format for their start tag that indicates quite clearly (both to human readers and to XML-aware software) that they are empty. This format includes a / just before the end of the empty element's start tag:

```
<Name/>
```

Here is an example:

```
<emptytag/>
```

Empty elements do not have an end tag.

Element Types

The *type* of an element indicates the type of information that the element contains. As you learned in Chapter 1, "Markup in Theory and Practice," the element type should not imply any particular formatting. For example, `heading` is preferable to `bold-centered`. However, in practice this is not always possible. It is very hard to mark up a table without elements to represent rows and columns!

Attributes: The Luggage Label

Now that you understand the suitcase, what about the luggage label? This section looks at the attributes of XML elements.

Attribute Specifications

The luggage label, or additional information that is added to an element, is called its *attribute specifications*. These take the following form:

```
Name Eq AttValue
```

Here is an example:

```
HREF="http://www.w3.org/XML/Activity"
```

In this case, HREF is the *attribute name*, and `http://www.w3c.org/XML/Activity` is the *attribute value*.

Warning: In XML, all attribute values must be quoted. This is different from HTML (and SGML), in which the quotation marks are optional. Matched pairs of either single or double quotation marks can be used for this purpose. Also, note that no spaces are allowed on either side of the = within the attribute specification.

If you need to include quotation marks in your attribute values, the entity references ' and " can be used within attribute values as escapes for single and double quotation marks, respectively.

The attribute specifications appear in an element's start tag. You must have a space between the element type and the first attribute specification, and between each attribute specification if there is more than one. Here is an example:

```
<person KEY="A14768" ROLE="designer">
```

The following example is for an empty element:

```
<IMG ALIGN="left" SRC="http://www.w3.org/pub/icons/w3c_48X48.gif"/>
```

One thing you are not allowed to put into an attribute value is an entity reference to an *external entity*. (See Chapter 7 for details of what these are.) If you refer to an external entity, the XML document isn't even well-formed and is certainly not valid. You can refer to external entities in XML attributes, but you need to use the ENTITY or ENTITIES attribute type and quote them by name. (Attribute types are discussed in the next section.)

Attribute-List Declarations

If you want your XML document to be valid, you don't have the freedom to write just anything on these luggage labels.

Each element type has a list of allowed attributes, which is declared in the DTD as an *attribute-list declaration*. For example, the declaration

```
<!ATTLIST PERSON
ID ID #REQUIRED
ROLE CDATA #IMPLIED
KEY CDATA #IMPLIED
TEIFORM CDATA "PERSON" >
```

states that the person element type has four allowed attributes, called ID, ROLE, KEY, and TEIFORM.

You can add any or all of the attributes declared in its attribute-list declaration to each element in your XML documents, in any order. If you choose not to provide an attribute specification, its value is said to be *implied*.

> Note: A non-validating XML processor will not check the attributes against the DTD, so you can enter any attribute specifications you like and still have a well-formed XML document.

Only one attribute specification is allowed for each attribute definition in the DTD. To put that in simpler terms, attribute specifications cannot repeat within an element's start tag. Therefore, the following is not a well-formed start tag:

```
<person role="author" role="designer">
```

Chapter 8 includes a section on attribute-list declarations, which gives a full description of their syntax.

Attribute Types

Each attribute is declared to have an *attribute type*. For validity, each attribute specification you provide must have a value that is of the correct type for that attribute. In the previous declaration example, ID is an ID-type attribute, which provides a unique identifier for each person element. ROLE and KEY both contain *character data*, which means any text.

XML divides attribute types into three groups: *string types, tokenized types,* and *enumerated types.*

String type attributes are indicated by CDATA in the attribute-list declaration. (ROLE and KEY are string type attributes in this example.) They can take any literal string as their value.

The following are the seven *tokenized attribute types*:

- ID is an identifier for the element, which must be unique within the XML document. Attribute values of type ID must consist of a Name symbol.

- IDREF is a pointer to an ID attribute value. An element with an ID with the specified value must be included somewhere in the XML document.

- IDREFS is the same as the IDREF type, except that the value can contain any number of ID references separated by spaces.

- ENTITY is a pointer to an external entity. The value must consist of a Name symbol, and it must be a case-sensitive match for the name of an external binary general entity declared in the DTD.

- ENTITIES is the same as the ENTITY type, except that the value can contain any number of entity names separated by spaces.

- NMTOKEN contains a value that is a Nmtoken.
- NMTOKENS contains a value that conforms to the Nmtokens production.

Nmtoken and Nmtokens are defined in the "Primitive Constructs" section of Chapter 5.

An *enumerated attribute type* is one that offers a fixed set of options. It is either a *notation type* or a general-purpose *enumeration*.

Notation type attributes offer a set of possible *notations* (as covered in Chapter 7). They take the form

```
NOTATION ( A ¦ B ¦ ... )
```

in which A, B, and so on must be the names of notations declared in the DTD. The following example could be used to specify a range of possible image formats:

```
NOTATION ( BMP ¦ WMF ¦ GIF ¦ TIFF ¦ JPEG )
```

Values must match one of these notation names.

Enumeration attributes consist of a set of Nmtoken tokens, as in the following example:

```
( HAM ¦ BEEF ¦ MUSHROOM ¦ EXTRA_CHEESE )
```

Values must match one of these Nmtoken tokens.

Because an XML processor folds all ID, IDREF, IDREFS, NMTOKEN, and NMTOKENS values to uppercase, it will check these types of attribute values against the values allowed by the DTD in a case-insensitive manner. CDATA, ENTITY, and ENTITIES values, on the other hand, are case sensitive and so must match the declared values exactly.

Mandatory Attributes

Sometimes the DTD declares that it is mandatory to provide a certain attribute. In this example, you are required to specify an ID for each person element.

Default and Fixed Values

Sometimes an attribute is given a default value in the DTD, so you don't have to type it in each time. The TEIFORM attribute has the default value person. Attributes can even be given a fixed value, which you can't change even if you want to.

Content: What's In the Suitcase

If a suitcase isn't empty, obviously it has some contents. In XML, elements can have three main types of content. These can be other elements, data content, or a mixture of the two.

Data Content

The case in which an element has only data content is simplest:

```
<person KEY="A14768" ROLE="designer">Fred Flintstone</person>
```

Here, the person element has no *child elements*, or subelements.

Note the clear distinction in XML between an *empty element*, which has a special syntax as described earlier, and an element whose content is the empty string. The following is not an empty element:

```
<person></person>
```

Element Content

The next simplest case is one in which an element contains only other elements. There is a special name for this: *element content*. It is obvious from the suitcase metaphor that elements have to *nest* neatly: You can't have a suitcase that is partially inside another one. (If you do, you certainly can't close either one!) This means that constructions like the following innocent little piece of HTML are not even well-formed in XML:

```
<b><i>This is really important</b></i>
```

In this example, you start a b element and then you start an i element. Therefore, the i element is part of the content of the b element. This means that the i element has to be closed (by an end tag) before you can close the b element in which it is contained. In fact, it's the other way around: You close the b first and then try to close i. Swapping the end tags fixes the problem:

```
<b><i>This is really important</i></b>
```

Mixed Content

The most complex case is one in which an element contains a mixture of data content and markup:

```
<p>We are going to see <person>Joe Brown</person>
and <person>Elaine</person> on <date>October 15th</date>.</p>
```

Unsurprisingly, this is called *mixed content*.

However, just to confuse you, the term mixed content is also applied to our first case, where an element contains only character data. This is because the key distinction here is between element content and mixed content. Because an element has mixed content if it can contain any data characters, this has to include the case where it contains only data characters and no markup.

Content Models

You can't pack just anything into an XML suitcase. In a valid XML document, each element type has a "packing list" that says what that type of suitcase is allowed to contain. These packing lists are part of the *element declaration* for each element type. These are found in the document's DTD. See the section on element declarations in Chapter 8 for details.

For elements that have element content, the packing list takes the form of a *content model*, which specifies the allowed sequence and number of occurrences of subelements. Content models use a simple grammar, which is described in Chapter 8. Here is an example of a content model:

```
(front, body, back?)
```

This model requires a front element, followed by a body element, and optionally followed by a back element.

For an XML document to be valid, each element in the document must have content that matches the designated packing list for that element's type. If an element has the preceding content model, the following content is acceptable:

```
<front><title>Growing Up</title></front>
<body><div1> ... </div1></body>
```

Note that the title and div1 elements do not affect the situation. When assessing validity, you don't look inside the suitcases you are trying to pack into the currently open suitcase. Or, to put it slightly more formally, an element's content model is checked against only its level-one subelements.

An element with the following content would not be valid, because the mandatory front element is missing:

```
<body><div1> ... </div1></body>
<back><index> ... </index></back>
```

Here is a slightly more complex content model:

```
(head, (p ¦ list ¦ note)*, div2*)
```

This model requires a head element; followed by zero or more p, list, or note elements; and followed by zero or more div2 elements.

Mixed-Content Declarations

Elements with mixed content have a special type of content model called a *mixed-content declaration*, which states that character data (#PCDATA) is allowed and lists the elements that are additionally allowed within this element. The mixed-content declaration is phrased in such a way that no restrictions are placed on the order or number of occurrences of these subelements:

```
(#PCDATA ¦ A ¦ B ¦ ...)*
```

This declaration means "zero or more occurrences of character data or elements A, B, and so on, in any order."

The following form also counts as a mixed-content declaration, even though it allows character data only within the element in question:

```
(#PCDATA)
```

> Note: The presence of child elements within a mixed-content model is always optional, which means that an element containing only character data will always be valid against any mixed-content declaration.

Here are two examples of mixed-content declarations:

```
(#PCDATA ¦ person ¦ date ¦ place)*
(#PCDATA)
```

The first example states that the element can have data content, plus any number of person, date, and place subelements. The following would be valid content for such an element:

```
We are going to see <person>Joe Brown</person>
and <person>Elaine</person> on <date>October 15th</date>.
```

But the following would not be valid content, because the element club does not appear in the list of allowed subelements:

```
We are going to see <person>Joe Brown</person>
at <club>Smokey's</club> on <date>October 15th</date>.
```

> Warning: XML makes itself more restrictive than SGML by defining mixed-content declarations in this way. Content models that combine #PCDATA and other elements in any way other than the preceding form are illegal in XML. Therefore, many content models in existing SGML DTDs need to be rewritten to be valid in an XML context.

Cross-References and Links

The basic XML language provides a considerable amount of power to express cross-references within an XML document and links to resources outside it. This is in addition to the *power linking* facilities that come with XML-Link (which is described in Chapter 9, "Linking with XML"). This section summarizes what you can already do by just using the standard attribute types that XML supports.

Internal Cross-References

The ID and IDREF attribute types are tailor-made for the task of making reference from one part of an XML document to another. This technique can be useful for a whole variety of reasons:

■ Citing a bibliographic reference that is held elsewhere—for example, in a bibliography

■ Pointing to a footnote

■ Putting in "see also" references

It is likely that XML-aware software will provide built-in support for ID to IDREF hyperlinks. This will include the capability to indicate the presence of a cross-reference and, where appropriate, to traverse to the target of the cross-reference.

ID attributes give elements an identifier that is guaranteed to be unique within the XML document. (If an ID isn't unique, the document isn't valid.) This uniqueness makes ID attribute specifications a ready-made target for cross-references. (As you will see in Chapter 9, they are also a handy target for XML XPointers.)

By convention, attributes with type ID are given the name ID, although nothing in the XML specification enforces this approach. It just makes life easier for everyone. Here is an example:

```
<ATTLIST PERSON
ID ID #IMPLIED >
```

Again, there is no reason why XML-aware editing software shouldn't be able to assign unique values to each ID type attribute, saving you the effort of inventing your own names or codes and ensuring that they are unique.

IDREF and IDREFS attribute types have one purpose in life: to point to ID attribute types. If an IDREF or IDREFS attribute value contains an entry that doesn't match an ID, the XML document is invalid.

Setting up a cross-reference is very simple. First you ensure that the target element has a unique ID, like this:

```
<bibl ID="bib.5"><auth>Goldfarb, Charles</auth><date>1990</date>
<title>The SGML Handbook</title></bibl>
```

Then you quote that ID in your cross-reference, like this:

```
<p>As we can see from <ref TARGET="bib.5">The SGML Handbook</ref>,
...
```

Job done! When browsing your completed XML document, you can now expect the phrase The SGML Handbook to be underlined and "hot," just like A elements in HTML. Click on it, and you jump to the full citation.

Note: These internal links can be put to a wide variety of uses; hyperlinks are a very simple application. The fact that the target of the link is an *element*, rather than just a point (as in an HTML internal link), means that XML applications can do a whole range of useful things by traversing these internal links. In effect, they add the possibility of processing XML documents in a nonlinear manner.

External Linking

XML documents can make reference to non-XML resources that are outside the document. Here are some obvious examples:

- Image files
- Video clips

- Audio clips
- Word processor files
- Java applets

The built-in mechanism for linking these external resources is more formal and less direct than the HTML equivalent. In HTML, you just use a standard URL and expect the browser and server to work out between them what type of resource is being addressed. The following line implies a link to an image of type GIF:

```
<img src="/Images/bump.gif">
```

XML makes the type of the target explicit through its use of *notations*.

Before you can link to an external entity from an XML document, you must declare it in the document's DTD. An external entity declaration looks like this:

```
<!ENTITY fig.bump SYSTEM "/Images/bump.gif" NDATA GIF>
```

This declaration specifies the GIF notation through the value given to the NDataDecl, which is the Nmtoken following NDATA. This notation, in turn, must be declared:

```
<!NOTATION GIF SYSTEM "http://www.mainsite.com/support/
gviewer.exe">
```

Now you are free to use the name fig.bump to link the image file to your XML document. If the XML version of your HTML DTD defines the SRC attribute of img as having type ENTITY or ENTITIES, as in

```
<!ATTLIST IMG SRC ENTITY #REQUIRED
```

you can link to the image file in a manner similar to the earlier HTML case, as follows:

```
<img src="fig.bump">
```

But in this case, the entity name is the value of the SRC attribute, rather than its actual filename or URL.

Groves

Groves do not appear on the scene until Chapter 10, "The XML Style Mechanism." However, they are a *logical structure* that is fundamental to how XML works (or at least to how XML documents will be exploited effectively), and as such I will cover them here.

A *grove* is a new way to look at an XML document that makes its content much more tractable to object-oriented programming techniques. Groves provide a method of delivering only those aspects of a document (or parts thereof) that are required for a particular purpose.

This section is provided mainly for the technically minded reader who is eager to understand the potential use of groves when developing XML applications. It can quite safely be skipped if it ceases to make sense to you at any point.

Warning: In the following discussion, I have made every effort to explain the logic of groves as I understand it. I have not made a major effort to use the exact terminology used by the DSSSL standard from which the explanation is derived. If you understand my explanations and want to take things further, be sure to check out the DSSSL standard for an authoritative use of terminology.

Classes and Properties

Your goal is to present an XML document as a well-organized stream of *objects* that can be treated, at some basic level, in a consistent manner. Each object will be a member of a *class*, which might be derived from some base class. Each class will have its own set of *properties*. Some of these properties will be inherited from its base class, and others will be unique to that particular class. Each actual object will *exhibit a value* for some or all of the properties of its class.

If that sounds like a reasonable basis for an object-oriented approach, consider what you have with XML. In order to process the wide range of different structures that make up an XML document, I will generalize things a little bit.

First of all, the different logical structures you have encountered while exploring XML (such as elements, comments, and processing instructions) can be considered your classes. Next, if you say that each class has a property called `class name`, all of your XML logical structures will have this property:

```
Class: class name="element"
Class: class name="comment declaration"
Class: class name="processing instruction"
```

Therefore, class name is an *intrinsic property* of all XML classes. In addition, XMl classes have another 10 or so intrinsic base properties, such as a property that lists the names of all properties exhibited by a particular instance of the class.

Also, certain properties are unique to each class. For example, the element class has the following properties:

■ generic identifier is the GI (element type name) of the element.

■ unique identifier is a unique ID that has been assigned to the element.

■ attributes is a list of attribute assignments—one for each declared attribute of the element.

■ content is the actual content of the element: character data, child elements, and markup such as comment declarations and processing instructions that happen to occur within the element.

Comment declarations have the single property markup, containing the actual comment. Processing instructions have the single property system data.

Each property has a *data type*, such as string, integer, strlist (a list of strings), enum (an enumerated set of possible values), node, or nodelist. The last two (node and nodelist) provide the glue that keeps everything together.

Nodes and Nodelists

To make your object-oriented view of an XML document into a coherent single *object*, you need to be able to connect your objects together. The best way to do this is to consider each object instance to be a *node* in a tree structure that you are building.

For example, consider the following person element with some text and a comment declaration inside it:

```
<person>Fred Flintstone<!-- not! --></person>
```

This person element is a node that exhibits the following properties:

■ class name: element

■ generic identifier: The string person

■ content: The string Fred Flintstone followed by a comment declaration

The key question is, how do you represent the content? It is obviously a sequence of data characters followed by a comment declaration.

If you check out the data type for an element's content property, you find that it is nodelist—that is, a list of nodes or objects. So you can describe an element's content as a list of the objects found within that element. The comment, which is an object in its own right, appears as the last node on that list. (It is quite a long list. Each of the 15 characters in Fred Flintstone is treated as a separate data character object in its own right.)

In a similar way, any attributes that had been declared would be constructed as attribute assignment objects and attached to the element's attributes property. Each nodelist property has an associated list of the types of object that it can validly contain.

This is how the whole grove is put together. The sgml document object is the *root* of the tree structure, or grove, that you are building. This object has properties relating to the whole XML document, such as prolog (a nodelist that in turn contains the document type declaration), docelem (a node that contains the *document element*, or root element of the XML document), and elements (a list of all the elements in the XML document that have unique identifiers).

Grove Plans

Starting from the root of your grove, you can obtain any of the information in an XML document—right down to the tiniest detail of the document itself or its DTD—in a useful object-oriented form. Often, this is much more than you actually need.

A *grove plan* is a list of the object types (classes) and properties in which you are interested. It is used to "prune" the complete grove so that it contains only the aspects of the document that are of interest to your application. Broadly speaking, you take your shears to the root node of your grove structure, and you prune off any objects that are not in the grove plan. For each object that is left, you prune off the properties that are not mentioned in the grove plan.

Then you move on to the subnodes of the root node and do the same thing to them, to their subnodes, and so on. Eventually, you work your way through the whole tree, pruning out all classes and properties that are not in the grove plan. Finally, to tidy up, you remove all references to bits of the tree that are no longer present as a result of your pruning activities.

Summary

In this chapter, you examined the logical structures that are found in XML documents.

The chapter began by outlining the overall logical structure of an XML document. You found that it has an optional prolog, which contains the highly recommended XML declaration, and a document type declaration, which is essential for any XML document that has ambitions to be valid. After this comes the document element, which contains the actual document.

You learned that XML documents can be well-formed, which means that they contain nicely nested elements and are self-contained. Furthermore, they can be valid, which means that they pass all the XML rules.

You then went on to learn just what an element is, and the suitcase metaphor stressed that elements are containers for information and that the start tags and end tags you see in XML documents are there to mark the boundaries of elements. You found that all elements have an element type, and that some elements are officially empty elements. Talking in terms of suitcases also helped you to learn why elements have to nest neatly inside each other and how an XML document is, in one sense, just a single element.

Next, I covered the attributes that can qualify elements. You saw how they can be used to add value to the text of a document without disturbing its flow, by acting as luggage labels. You saw the different attribute types, each with its own particular job to do.

You also reviewed what elements can contain. They can have element content or mixed content (which includes the simple case, in which only data content is present). The content of elements in valid XML documents is controlled by content models in the document's DTD.

Next, you learned how attributes can be used to support hyperlinking. You used the ID and IDREF attribute types to support internal cross-references within an XML document. Then you saw how the ENTITY and ENTITIES attribute types can be used to link to external resources such as images and video clips.

Finally, for the technically minded reader, I introduced the concept of groves as a means of representing all the information in an XML document, using the object-oriented concepts of classes and properties. You learned how to join these objects together into a tree structure by considering them as nodes, and you learned how to prune that tree for efficiency using a grove plan.

CHAPTER 7

Physical Structures in XML Documents

by Richard Light

In Chapter 5, "The XML Approach," you learned that XML documents have two types of structures: a logical structure and a physical structure. The logical structure, which was covered in Chapter 6, "Logical Structures in XML Documents," relates to the markup that the document contains. This chapter examines in more detail the physical structures associated with XML documents.

An XML document can consist of one or more virtual storage units. These storage units are called *entities*. Each entity has a *name* and a *content*. The general idea is that by quoting the name, you receive the corresponding content, which can be anything from a single character to a large file.

Internal and External Entities

Internal entities have a value that is given directly in the entity declaration:

```
<!ENTITY XML "Extensible Markup Language">
```

This entity declaration maps the name XML to the content "Extensible Markup Language". No separate storage unit is involved.

External entities, by contrast, refer in their declarations to a storage unit by means of a SYSTEM or PUBLIC identifier:

```
<!ENTITY chapter1 SYSTEM "chap1.xml">
```

This associates the name chapter1 with the URL "chap1.xml". An XML processor must read the file referenced by that URL in order to find out the content of that entity.

The format for PUBLIC identifiers includes a PUBLIC name before the SYSTEM name:

```
<!ENTITY image1 PUBLIC "-//RBL//NONSGML
 Illustration 1//EN" "images/illus1.gif" NDATA gif>
```

PUBLIC identifiers provide a mechanism for describing an entity, but do not specify any particular storage location. This can be very useful when a particular entity is already widely available. An XML processor may be able to determine, by matching the PUBLIC identifier against a catalog of resources available locally, that it does not need to fetch a new copy of this entity because it is already available.

Text and Binary Entities

External entities can be either *text* or *binary*.

A *text entity* contains text data, which is considered to form part of the XML document. When you insert a reference to a text entity, it is treated as though its content actually appears in the text of your document at that point. For example, the entity XML declared as

```
<!ENTITY XML "Extensible Markup Language">
```

means that references to the entity XML should be replaced by the phrase "Extensible Markup Language". Then the markup

```
<p>We are going to learn about physical structures in &XML;.</p>
```

is equivalent to the following:

```
<p>We are going to learn about physical structures in
Extensible Markup Language.</p>
```

A *binary entity* is basically anything that isn't meant to be treated as though it is XML-encoded. In that sense, the name is misleading: A binary entity could be a plain text file, for example.

Each binary entity has to have an associated *notation*. A notation describes a type of resource (which is usually just a file type, such as BMP, GIF, or JPG). In fact, having a notation is the one thing that distinguishes a binary entity from a text entity. Notation information forms part of the entity declaration in the DTD, like this:

```
<!ENTITY my.picture SYSTEM "mypic.bmp" NDATA BMP>
```

This line declares that the entity my.picture is in the BMP notation. Put more simply, it is a BMP file.

The notation information tells an XML processor what sort of beast the entity is and, therefore, allows the processor to decide what to do with it. For example, if an entity contains mathematical equations using the TeX notation, an XML browser might call a helper application to format the equations and then display the result inline within the document. On the other hand, an entity with a notation of Word6.0 would probably cause an XML browser to call up Word and hand it the relevant file.

> Note: It is possible, and is not an error, for XML documents to contain references to notations not supported by any application on the system where the XML application is running. This means that you might encounter XML documents containing references to entities that your system cannot process. This is similar to the situation that occurs when an HTML browser encounters a MIME-type for which no helper application has been set up.

Entity References

You insert an entity into your XML documents by using &, followed by the Name of the entity, followed by ;, as in the following example:

```
&pub-status;
Fernand L&eacute;ger
```

Before you can make use of an entity, you have to declare it. Chapter 8, "Keeping It Tidy: The XML Rule Book," describes the form that entity declarations take in XML. You must give the entity name exactly as declared, because it is case-sensitive. If the Name you give doesn't match a declared entity, the resulting XML document will not be well-formed.

XML also prohibits recursion: If an entity contains a recursive reference to itself, directly or indirectly, the resulting XML document is not well-formed. (If this were not so, an XML processor would go on inserting the entity into itself until it fell over!)

If the entity in question is a text entity, the entity reference will refer to the content of that entity.

It is important to note that binary entities should not be inserted into text in this way. Binary entities can be referred to only in the values of attributes of type ENTITY or ENTITIES. If you use an entity reference to refer to a binary entity, your XML document will not be well-formed.

Warning: You can't tell by looking at entity references in your XML document whether they refer to internal or external entities. Nor can you tell whether they refer to text or binary entities. This information is held in the DTD as part of the entity declaration. See Chapter 8 for more details of entity declarations.

Parameter Entity References

A variation on the entity reference is the *parameter entity reference*. This starts with % instead of &, but it is otherwise identical. Here is an example:

```
%ISOLat2;
```

Parameter entity references cannot be used within XML documents. They are reserved for use within the DTD.

Note: To be precise, parameter references *can* be used within the internal subset of the DTD, which is part of the prolog at the start of the XML document, as well as in the external DTD subset. But they *cannot* be used within the document element that follows the internal DTD subset.

In order for an XML document to be well-formed, any parameter entity it contains must be declared before it is referred to.

Uses for Entities

What are entities good for? The following list shows the variety of uses of entities:

- Represent non-standard characters within your XML documents.
- Function as shorthand for frequently used phrases.
- Hold chunks of markup that might appear in more than one XML document.
- Hold sections or chapters from a large XML document.
- Organize your DTD into logical units.
- Represent non-XML resources.

Non-Standard Characters

The following example shows an XML text entity being used to represent an e-acute symbol (é):

```
Fernand L&eacute;ger
```

Using eight characters to represent one might seem inefficient. However, accented characters are particularly vulnerable when documents are moved among different computer platforms, because only the first 128 characters of the ASCII character set are used consistently on PCs, Macs, and UNIX systems. Using a text entity to represent accented characters has the following advantages:

- Only characters that appear in 7-bit ASCII are used in the entity reference.
- The result, while not particularly easy to read, is at least clear to the human reader, because eacute is a reasonable mnemonic for the character it represents.

A useful SGML practice that could be adopted in XML applications is to have entity sets. *Entity sets* give standard entity names to groups of related characters, as in the following examples:

- ISOlat1: Latin alphabetic characters used in Western European languages, apart from uppercase and lowercase letters.

- ISOgrk1: The letters of the Greek alphabet.
- ISOnum: Numeric and special graphic characters.

> **Note:** There are two other ways to deal with characters that fall outside the ASCII character set. Character references (described later in this chapter) can be used to represent any ISO 10646 character directly by its numeric or hexadecimal representation. And if the number of such characters warrants it, the whole text entity can be encoded using an ISO 10646 encoding in which they can be encoded natively.

Frequently Used Phrases

If your documents contain phrases that appear repeatedly, you can benefit from using text entities to represent them. For example, when preparing this book I found that I was making frequent cross-references to other chapters. Sams.net Publishing's house style requires these to appear with the chapter number, followed by its title:

```
<p>In Chapter 5, <q>The XML Approach</q>, ...
```

I encoded the chapter headings as entity references, like this:

```
<p>In Chapter 5, &chap5;, ...
```

And this encoding produced the following advantages:

- Speed: After I declared the chapter heading entities, I was able to select their names from a drop-down list in my editing program, and I had to type the full headings only once (when declaring my entities).
- Consistency: There is no possibility of mistyping an individual cross-reference.
- Flexibility: If I decide to rename a chapter heading at a later date, I have to update only my entity declaration for that chapter to ensure that all the cross-references to it will be correct.

Chunks of Markup

Entities can also be applied to larger chunks of marked-up text. For example, if your company has a standard set of conditions for its contracts, these could be encoded in a separate file and declared as an *external entity*. When these conditions are updated, all documents that refer to them will automatically be updated too.

> Warning: Be sure that the markup within these chunks is balanced. Remember that an entity must contain a whole number of elements, plus optional character data at the start and end. Also, be aware that it is possible to insert an entity declaration into your documents at a point where the markup it contains is not allowed.

Sections of Documents

Large multi-authored XML documents can usefully be managed by breaking them into sections and working on each section separately. For example, this book was written as approximately 20 XML documents—one per chapter and one per appendix. The whole book was then put together quickly by having a series of entity references pull in the individual chapters:

```
<doc><body>
&chapter1;
&chapter2;
&chapter3;
...
&appendixd;
</body></doc>
```

One point to watch in this situation is that the embedded chapters must contain only markup. They cannot have their own <!DOCTYPE declaration:

```
<chapter><head>1. Beginnings</head><p> .... </p></chapter>
```

This makes it rather tricky to treat them as XML documents in their own right. One way around this problem is to have a separate file whose only purpose is to act as the document entity for a single chapter:

```
<?XML version="1.0"?>
<!DOCTYPE chapter SYSTEM "mydoc.dtd" [
<!ENTITY chapter1 SYSTEM "chap1.xml">
]>
&chapter1;
```

Organizing Your DTD

Parameter entities are particularly useful when developing DTDs. They have the following benefits similar to those of ordinary entity references:

- Internal parameter entities can be used to ensure consistency and to improve the readability of the DTD for users.
- External parameter entities can be used to modularize the DTD.

Both types of parameter entities can be used with *conditional sections* to develop DTDs that can be tailored by users for individual documents. Most often, this is achieved by including parameter entity declarations in the document's internal DTD subset to act as *switches*, as in the following code:

```
<?XML version "1.0"?>
<!DOCTYPE doc SYSTEM "strict.dtd" [
<!ENTITY % options "IGNORE">
]>
<doc> ...
```

The preceding entry states that the parameter entity options is to have the value "IGNORE" in this document. Typically, this switches off a set of options within the DTD. DTD design is discussed in more detail in Chapter 8.

Non-XML Resources

Binary external entities are provided to represent any non-XML resource that is to form part of an XML document. The open-ended design of binary entities, linking them to notations, allows a framework that can easily cope with any new type of digital resource that is invented.

Storage Strategies for XML Entities

Note the careful phrase "virtual storage units" that I used to define entities. An entity's content can be, and often is, a complete file, but it can also be a part of a file, a stream held in the computer's memory, an object stored in a database, or even the result of a database query. XML gives you the freedom to store and manage your entities in whatever way is most appropriate.

If you decide to take all your supporting files and put them into an object-oriented database, it isn't always necessary to change all your XML documents. (Even when you do have to make changes because you have reorganized your files, XML's design ensures that you don't have to scratch around within the content of your documents. All entities used by an XML document must be declared up front in the DTD, so that's where you update all your references to storage units when files are moved around.)

XML assumes that your XML application will include an *entity manager*, which takes your entity names and finds the correct piece of content for you. As a minimum, any Web-aware XML application will have an entity manager that is able to find the following:

■ Entities contained within your XML documents

■ Any resource that can be addressed by a URL

Synchronicity of Logical and Physical Structures

I mentioned in Chapter 5 that the logical and physical structures in an XML document need to nest neatly within each other. Now that I have described those logical structures in Chapter 6, I can be more precise about the rules.

The first text entity you encounter when reading an XML document is called the *document entity*. This is the starting point for an XML processor, and it acts as the *root* of the tree of entities specified within the XML document.

What's Allowed in a Logical Structure?

First, look at this question from the point of view of logical structures. All tags and elements must be completely inside a single entity. In particular, the *document element* must start and end in the same file; you can't switch files halfway through a document. However, you can have references to other entities inside an element. (This is another type of nesting—more suitcases.) The following is a document entity that describes a complete (three-chapter) book.

```
<?XML version="1.0"?>
<!DOCTYPE doc SYSTEM "mydoc.dtd" [
<!ENTITY chapter1 SYSTEM "chap1.xml">
<!ENTITY chapter2 SYSTEM "chap2.xml">
<!ENTITY chapter3 SYSTEM "chap3.xml">
]>
<doc><body>&chapter1;&chapter2;&chapter3;</body></doc>
```

Here, the three chapters each can be found within its own entities: the files chap1.xml, chap2.xml, and chap3.xml. Note how the document element <doc> (and its subelement <body>) are both completely declared in the document entity, and the embedded entities nest neatly inside the <body> element.

The other logical structures I have mentioned (comments and processing instructions), together with two I will soon introduce (character references and entity references), must also be contained entirely within a single entity.

What's Allowed in a Physical Structure?

Looking at it from the physical structures' point of view, a text entity must contain a whole number of logical structures, possibly together with stray character data that is not inside any element in the entity. (This includes the very common case in which the whole entity contains nothing but character data.) So the following three examples are valid text entities:

```
<chapter><head>1. Beginnings</head><p> .... </p></chapter>
Museum <emph>Documentation</emph> Association
Museum Documentation Association
```

The following two examples are not valid text entities, because they contain elements that are incomplete:

```
<chapter><head>1. Beginnings</head>
Museum <emph>Documentation Association
```

Predefined Entities

XML provides the following predefined entities:

- amp: Ampersand (&)
- lt: Less than, or opening angle bracket (<)
- gt: Greater than, or closing angle bracket (>)
- apos: Apostrophe, or single quote (')
- quot: Quotation mark (")

An XML document that uses only these entities can still be well-formed. (However, to be valid, it needs to declare these default entities if they are used. Also, it must give them the same single-character values that they would have by default.)

Character References

A *character reference* is a code for a specific character in the ISO 10646/Unicode character set. It is useful to be able to do this when you cannot enter the character from your keyboard. The reference is to the character's character number in ISO 10646/Unicode. It can be expressed either as an ordinary number or in hexadecimal.

The syntax of character references is &# for decimal or &#x for hexadecimal, followed by the character number, and terminated by a semicolon (;). For example, the character reference for the copyright symbol (©) is © or ©.

Character Encoding in XML Text Entities

XML uses the ISO 10646 character encoding scheme (also called *Unicode*). This provides a range of encoding schemes, starting with 8-bit characters and moving on to 16-bit or even 32-bit representations of each character. All XML processors are expected to support the UTF-8 and UCS-2 schemes.

Obviously, there is a trade-off between the size of each character and the number of possible characters you can represent. You won't benefit from using 16-bit character encoding (which gives more than 65,000 possible characters) if you never require anything except standard 8-bit ASCII characters, because your documents all will be twice the size they would be otherwise.

Every XML text entity must declare and then stick to a single encoding scheme. However, each text entity in an XML document can use a different encoding for the characters it contains. This means that you can declare separate entities to hold sections of an XML document that contain, for example, Cyrillic or Arabic characters, and assign the 16-bit UCS-2 encoding to these sections. Meanwhile the rest of the document can use the more efficient 8-bit encoding.

By default, the ISO 10646 UTF-8 encoding is assumed. By default, the first part of this encoding matches standard ASCII, so you do not need to take any special action on character encoding unless you have some unusual characters to encode.

You should also bear in mind that switching to a different encoding is not the only way to represent characters that do not fall into the UTF-8 character set. You can reference any character by quoting its ISO 10646 character number in a character reference, or you can declare and then reference an entity that represents the character in question. These techniques are probably best if you have only a sprinkling of non-UTF-8 characters to mark up.

If an XML text entity is encoded in UCS-2, it must start with an appropriate encoding signature, the Byte Order Mark, which is the character with hexadecimal value FEFF. This is not considered to be part of the markup or character data of the XML document.

XML provides a more generalized method of signaling encoding schemes—the *encoding declaration*. This takes the form of a processing instruction (PI). It is part of the XML declaration for the document entity and is a special encoding PI for any other entity. Every XML text entity that is not in UTF-8 or UCS-2 must begin with the following declaration:

```
<?XML encoding="[encodingDesc]" ?>
```

In the declaration, [encodingDesc] is a Name consisting of only Latin alphabetic characters (A to Z and a to z), digits, full stops, hyphens, and underscores. The following values are recognized:

- UTF-8
- UTF-16
- ISO-10646-UCS-2
- ISO-10646-UCS-4
- ISO-8859-1 to -9
- ISO-2022-JP
- Shift_JIS
- EUC_JP

Here is an example:

```
<?XML ENCODING="UTF-8">
<?XML ENCODING="ISO-10646-UCS-4">
```

The idea behind limiting the encoding description to Latin characters is to make it possible for XML processors to read the encoding description unambiguously.

Having recognized the encoding of an XML text entity, an XML processor might not be able to process that encoding. If this is the case, it has the option of treating the entity as a binary entity instead, or of abandoning the attempt to read the entity.

Summary

This chapter primarily addressed the role that physical structures (entities) play in XML. You have seen that there are two types of XML entities:

- Text entities are effectively part of the XML document.
- Binary entities are any other type of resource.

I briefly discussed the main uses to which entities can be put, and how to refer to both general entities and parameter entities. (The latter are useful only when creating a DTD.)

After this, I pointed out that XML entities are a slightly abstract concept that can be physically implemented in a number of ways. The two most common methods are to hold entities as files and to store them as part of an XML document.

I then covered how logical and physical structures can nest within each other in XML, and I finished this discussion by describing the built-in entities included with XML.

I then showed how to insert references to any individual character in the ISO 10646 character set. The chapter was rounded off with a broader review of the character encoding issues and strategies in XML.

The next chapter looks at what is inside XML DTDs. They are the control center that determines what is allowed in your XML documents.

Keeping It Tidy: The XML Rule Book

by Richard Light

In previous chapters, I characterized XML documents as self-describing. Every valid XML document brings its own rule book along with it. In fact, that is the definition of a *valid XML document*: It obeys its own rules. In this chapter, I open up the rule book and see what it can tell us about an XML document.

The XML Prolog

The *prolog* is everything that occurs in an XML document before the start-tag that begins the document proper. This can include the following items:

- An optional *XML declaration*
- A *document type declaration*

- Comments
- Processing instructions
- White space

Here is an example of an XML prolog for this chapter, containing all of the preceding features:

```
<?XML version="1.0" RMD="internal" ?>
<!-- Chapter 8: the XML rulebook -->
<!-- Last edited by rbl, 7 July 1997 -->

<!-- Processing instructions: -->
<?XML-STYLE *** to add *** ?>
<?PCX compression="standard" type="256 color" ?>
<!-- Document type declaration: -->
<!DOCTYPE DIV1 SYSTEM "TEISAMS.DTD" [
<!-- Figures for this chapter: -->
<!ENTITY ch8.fig1 SYSTEM "08PXM01.PCX">
<!ENTITY ch8.fig2 SYSTEM "08PXM02.PCX">
]>

<!-- The chapter starts here: -->
```

The following five sections break down each component of the prolog.

The XML Declaration

I covered the XML declaration in Chapter 6, "Logical Structures in XML Documents." I cover the last aspect of the XML declaration—the *required markup declaration*—at the end of this chapter. Here is the XML declaration:

```
<?XML version="1.0" RMD="internal" ?>
```

The Document Type Declaration

I discuss the document type declaration throughout most of this chapter. Here is the document type declaration:

```
<!DOCTYPE DIV1 SYSTEM "TEISAMS.DTD" [
<!-- Figures for this chapter: -->
<!ENTITY ch8.fig1 SYSTEM "08PXM01.PCX">
<!ENTITY ch8.fig2 SYSTEM "08PXM02.PCX">
]>
```

Comments

Comments are meant to be included purely for user consumption (although I have seen systems in which comments were used as a place to squirrel away information that will be used by the application). Use comments liberally, so that the purpose of the XML markup can be clearly understood by any human reader who is looking at an XML document. Here are the comments:

```
<!-- Chapter 8: the XML rulebook -->
<!-- Last edited by rbl, 7 July 1997 -->

<!-- Processing instructions: -->

<!-- Figures for this chapter: -->
```

> **Note:** Comments are normally thrown away when an XML document is processed, so they won't ever appear on the screen when the document is displayed by a client's Web browser.

Processing Instructions

I cover processing instructions (PIs) in Chapter 5, "The XML Approach." PIs can be placed anywhere in the content of an XML document, but the prolog is where you can expect most of them to appear. Here are the processing instructions:

```
<?XML-STYLE *** to add *** ?>
<?PCX compression="standard" type="256 color" ?>
```

PIs in the prolog will set up a global processing environment for the whole XML document. They can set up the environment for the XML document itself. For example, they can be used to specify which XS style sheet is associated with the document, as in the following:

```
<?XML-STYLE *** to add *** ?>
```

Alternatively, they can give additional information to the helper applications that will be called on to process the various non-XML objects that are linked to the document. The following specifies options for the treatment of PCX images (standard compression; 256 color 8-bit images):

```
<?PCX compression="standard" type="256 color" ?>
```

White Space

Each declaration is laid out on a separate line. Blank lines appear between groups of declarations that belong together. You can space out the prolog any way you want. Try to ensure that its structure is clear to a reader.

The Document Type Declaration

An XML document's *document type declaration* specifies what type of document it is, and says where to find its rule book. This rule book can be in two
parts that together form the *document type definition* (*DTD*) for the document.
The *external DTD subset* is outside the document. It typically is a standard
DTD that someone else wrote. The *internal DTD subset* forms part of the document. It typically contains declarations that specify your usage of the standard
DTD and declarations for the entities that are referred to within the text.

You can have a reference to an external DTD subset on its own, like this:

```
<!DOCTYPE XXX EXTERNAL-DTD-SUBSET-REFERENCE >
```

An internal DTD subset can also be on its own, like this:

```
<!DOCTYPE XXX [
INTERNAL-DTD-SUBSET
]>
```

The two can also be together, like this:

```
<!DOCTYPE XXX EXTERNAL-DTD-SUBSET-REFERENCE [
INTERNAL-DTD-SUBSET
]>
```

Here, XXX must be the same as the element type of the document element. For
example, this would be an error:

```
<!DOCTYPE TEI.2 SYSTEM "TEISAMS.DTD">
<DIV1> ...
```

> Note: One interesting feature of DTDs is that they do not specify which
> element type has to be the document element. When I wrote this book, I made
> each chapter into a separate document and started with the div1 element type:
>
> ```
> <!DOCTYPE DIV1 ...
> ```
>
> When the whole book is put together as a single document, it has the (in-
> tended) TEI.2 element as its document element type:
>
> ```
> <!DOCTYPE TEI.2 ...
> ```
>
> The chapters all are div1 elements inside it.

When the external DTD subset is a standard DTD, it will often have a PUBLIC identifier as well as a SYSTEM identifier:

```
<!DOCTYPE DIV1 PUBLIC "-//TEI//DTD TEI Lite 1.0 For SAMS//EN"
"TEISAMS.DTD">
```

For simple applications, there is nothing to stop you from putting the whole DTD in the internal DTD subset. This memo is a complete, valid, totally self-contained XML document:

```
<!DOCTYPE memo [
<!ELEMENT memo (from, to, cc, date, content)>
<!ELEMENT from (#PCDATA)>
<!ELEMENT to (#PCDATA)>
<!ELEMENT cc (#PCDATA)>
<!ELEMENT date (#PCDATA)>
<!ELEMENT content (p+)>
<!ELEMENT p (#PCDATA)>
]>
<memo><from>Frank</from>
<to>Joan</to><cc>Joseph</cc><date>July 4 1997</date>
<content><p>Thanks for the meeting minutes.</p>
<p>I'll try to update the background materials in time
for next week's meeting.</p></content></memo>
```

> Note: Remember that the DTD is important even when you are not pitching for validity. In order to be well-formed, XML documents must also have all their external entities declared in the DTD. In a well-designed application, it should be possible to place all of these declarations in the internal DTD subset, thus avoiding the need to read and process the external DTD subset when well-formedness is all you are interested in.

When an XML document has both an internal and an external DTD subset, the internal one is processed first, so it takes precedence. Later in this chapter, you learn how this feature can be used to control a standard DTD via the use of parameter entity declarations.

Element Declarations

The element declarations in the DTD determine the possible structure of your XML documents. They each take an element, state its name, and define its possible content by means of a *content specification*. Here is an example:

```
<!ELEMENT memo (from, to, cc, date, content)>
```

This specifies an element type called memo and states that it can (in fact, it must) contain the elements from, to, cc, date, and content, in that order. Each of these elements will, in its turn, have an element declaration that registers its name and states what it can contain:

```
<!ELEMENT from (#PCDATA)>
<!ELEMENT to (#PCDATA)>
<!ELEMENT cc (#PCDATA)>
<!ELEMENT date (#PCDATA)>
<!ELEMENT content (p+)>
```

The elements from, to, cc, and date all contain character data (#PCDATA). The content element must contain one or more p elements, which in turn contain character data:

```
<!ELEMENT p (#PCDATA)>
```

This is a very simple, rigid model. For an XML document to be a valid memo, the elements must be specified in exactly the right order. None of them can be missed, and none (apart from p) can be repeated. In practice, very few DTDs are this prescriptive, because real-life applications normally require more flexibility than this (even for memos).

As you will see, there are methods for specifying that elements are optional or repeatable, and that they can occur in any order. This makes it much easier to model real-life information. However, the real power of this approach to modeling comes from recursion—the capability of elements to contain themselves. Here is a simple example:

```
<!ELEMENT node (desc, node*)>
<!ELEMENT desc (#PCDATA)>
```

This says a node contains a mandatory desc, followed by zero or more subnodes. This simple two-element model can describe an arbitrarily complex tree of node elements:

```
<node><desc>top node<desc>
<node><desc>level 1, #1</desc></node>
<node><desc>level 1, #2</desc>
<node><desc>level 2, #1</desc>
<node><desc>level 3, #1</desc></node>
<node><desc>level 3, #2</desc></node>
</node></node></node>
```

In this case, the node element can contain itself directly. More frequently, the recursion is less direct, with a child or grandchild of an element itself being able to contain that element.

EMPTY and ANY

Before looking at more complex cases, examine these simple types of content specifications. The following element is declared as being EMPTY:

```
<!ELEMENT image EMPTY>
```

It cannot have any contents, and it must always appear as an empty element in the document: `<image/>`.

Clearly, empty elements are not of much use on their own (although the hr and br element types in HTML would qualify as EMPTY in XML). They usually have attributes that give them useful properties.

If an element has a content specification of ANY, it's open season. There are no restrictions on what that element can contain. As in the following example, it can be a mixture of character data and any element types allowed by the DTD, in any order:

```
<!ELEMENT experimental ANY>
```

Element Content

You can choose to define element types that can contain only other elements as their children. They cannot contain character data. The possible occurrences and sequence of child elements is specified by a simple grammar tool called a content model. You have already seen the content model for the memo element type in the memo DTD:

```
<!ELEMENT memo (from, to, cc, date, content)>
```

> Note: Content models apply only to the immediate children of an element. After a child element is inserted into the document, its own content specification is used to determine what it, in turn, is allowed to contain.

Element content is a useful technique for structuring the higher levels of a DTD cleanly. It comes with a rather cool expression language for specifying the allowed patterns of child elements. This language uses the following:

- Parentheses, ( ), surround a sequence or a set of alternatives.
- The , character precedes each element type, except the first, in a sequence.

- The ¦ character precedes each element type, except the first, in a list of alternatives.
- The ? character follows an element or group of elements and indicates that it occurs zero or one time.
- The * character follows an element or group of elements and indicates that it occurs zero or more times.
- The + character follows an element or group of elements and indicates that it occurs one or more times.

Here are some simple examples.

Here is the memo content model refined by including some qualifiers on the individual elements:

```
<!ELEMENT memo (from, to+, cc*, date?, content)>
```

Obviously, the commas between the elements are significant. They indicate a *sequence*—meaning that the elements have to occur in the order specified. The unadorned from element type mandates that a memo must have precisely one sender. By adding + after the to element type, you are allowing a memo to have any number of recipients (while mandating that there must be at least one). It is not necessary to send copies (cc), but they can be sent to more than one person—this is indicated by the * qualifier. The ? after date indicates that it is an optional element.

You can develop the content element type by allowing a mixture of p (paragraph) and note (note) elements:

```
<!ELEMENT content (p ¦ note)+ >
```

This states that you can have one or more paragraphs, or notes, in any order. There must, however, be at least one p or one note element.

By combining these expressions, you can build a content model for your memos that dispenses with the content element completely:

```
<!ELEMENT memo (from, to+, date?, (p ¦ note)+)>
```

This nesting of bracketed expressions can go on to whatever level is required. So, with this grammar you can build up quite complex content models.

Mixed Content

If you want an element to be able to contain character data, different rules apply. This is called *mixed content* (even when there is just character data, not mixed with any subelements).

To express the rules for mixed content, you use the preceding content model grammar. However, you can use it only in a particular way. The content model has to take the form of a single set of alternatives, starting with #PCDATA and followed by the element types that can occur in the mixed content, each declared only once. Except when #PCDATA is the only option, the * qualifier must follow the closing bracket, as in this example:

```
<!ELEMENT x (#PCDATA ¦ a ¦ b ¦ c)*>
<!ELEMENT x (#PCDATA)>
```

It is worth being clear about the limits of this process. XML's content models relate only to the structure of an XML document. They make no attempt to control its content. In fact, even an element that is totally devoid of data matches a #PCDATA content model:

```
<p></p>
```

This is a valid paragraph. If you require any form of data validation support in your XML applications, you will have to add this support in an application-specific manner.

Note: Typing of XML elements is being actively discussed, and it is likely that a mechanism for specifying allowed data types within XML will be developed.

Warning: It is possible to write content models that are not valid in XML by including #PCDATA in a model that does not follow the allowed pattern for mixed content. A well-behaved XML processor will complain about such errors. Be warned, however, that an SGML parser will not complain, because such constructions are valid (although deprecated) in SGML.

Attribute List Declarations

Having declared an element and learned where it can fit into the structure of documents conforming to your DTD, you can now give that element one or more *attributes*. To do this, you include *attribute list declarations* (called a list because each element can have a number of attributes, which are listed in a single declaration).

In XML documents, attribute specifications occur in start-tags and consist of an attribute name followed by a value:

```
<head level="subhead2">
```

The preceding assigns the value `"subhead2"` to the attribute `level`. In the DTD, your attribute specification list will do the following for each element:

- Declare the names of allowed attributes.
- State the type of each attribute.
- Provide a default value for each attribute.

This example declares the attributes for the `person` element:

```
<!ATTLIST PERSON
ID ID #IMPLIED
ROLE CDATA #IMPLIED
KEY CDATA #IMPLIED
TEIFORM CDATA #FIXED "PERSON">
```

Types of Attributes

In general terms, there are three types of attributes:

- String attributes consist of any character data and always have the declared type CDATA.
- Tokenized attributes consist of one or more *tokens* that are significant to XML.
- Enumerated attributes are one of a specific list of possible values declared in the DTD.

String-type attributes are the most common. The following is the form to use when you don't have a more specific purpose for the attribute:

```
ROLE CDATA #IMPLIED
KEY CDATA #IMPLIED
```

Tokenized attributes have one of the following types:

- ID: An identifier for the element that, if specified, must be unique within the document. Consists of a Namestart character, followed by a sequence of Name characters.
- IDREF: A pointer to an ID. Must match an actual ID declared somewhere in the same document.
- IDREFS: Like IDREF, except that the value can consist of multiple IDREFs separated by space.
- ENTITY: A pointer to an external binary general entity (defined in the section "Text and Binary Entities," later in this chapter) that has been declared in the DTD. Consists of name characters only.
- ENTITIES: Like ENTITY, except that the value can consist of multiple ENTITYs separated by space.
- NMTOKEN: A string that takes the form of a NMTOKEN.
- NMTOKENS: Like NMTOKEN, except that the value can consist of multiple NMTOKENs separated by space.

> Note: NMTOKENS were defined in Chapter 5, "The XML Approach," under the heading "Primitive Constructs."

> Warning: The ID attribute type can be applied in principle to any attribute. However, it is standard practice to restrict its use to an attribute that is also called ID.

Enumerated attributes simply take a list of possible values. The only restriction is that each value has to be a valid NMTOKEN. Here is an example:

```
<!ATTLIST box
SHAPE (ROUND ¦ OVAL ¦ SQUARE) "SQUARE">
```

> Warning: For compatibility with SGML, you should not use the same NMTOKEN more than once in the enumerated attribute types of a single element type. Although this restriction has now been removed from the SGML standard, the

> existing base of SGML-aware software will continue to enforce it. However, if you do use the same `NMTOKEN` within the enumerated attribute types of a single element type, no XML processor will complain.

It is a special situation when the enumerated list gives a set of possible notations. In this case, the notations must all have been declared, and the list is preceded by `NOTATION`. Here is an example:

```
<!ATTLIST IMAGE
FORMAT NOTATION (GIF ¦ JPEG ¦ BMP) "GIF">
```

When matching an attribute value against the allowed values specified in the attribute definition, an XML processor will carry out a case-insensitive match for all attributes, except those of type `CDATA`, `IDREF`, or `IDREFS`.

Default Actions

The last part of the declaration of each attribute states which action the XML processor should take when users choose (as they often will) not to provide that attribute in a particular start-tag.

Here are the three options for the last part of the declaration:

- `#REQUIRED` means the attribute should have been there. Missing it makes the document invalid.

- `#IMPLIED` has the XML processor tell the application that no value was specified.

- The declared default value is passed through to the application as though that value had actually been specified. If the default value is preceded by `#FIXED`, any value that is specified must match the default value, or the document will be invalid.

> Warning: The default value, like all actual attribute values, must be quoted. This even applies to default values of enumerated attributes. For example, the following attribute definition (taken from the HTML 3.2 DTD) would not be valid in XML:
>
> ```
> <!ATTLIST BR
> clear (left¦all¦right¦none) none -- control of text flow --
> >
> ```
>
> The default value should read `"none"`.

Here are examples of attribute declarations with default values:

```
<!ATTLIST termdef
id ID #REQUIRED
name CDATA #IMPLIED>
<!ATTLIST list
type (bullets¦ordered¦glossary) "bullets">
<!ATTLIST form
method CDATA #FIXED "POST">
```

Entity Declarations

In Chapter 7, "Physical Structures in XML Documents," I discussed the different types of entities that XML supports and the things you can make and do with them in your documents. In that discussion, I demonstrated some examples of entity declarations. Here I review those declarations and look at a new type of entity—the *parameter entity*—which can be used only within your XML DTDs.

> Note: Remember that you do not need to provide entity declarations for resources to which you are linking via XML's linking facility. This applies only to entities that are part of the XML document itself.

Internal and External Entities

Internal entities have a value that is actually part of the entity declaration:

```
ENTITY chap8 "Chapter 8, <q>Keeping it Tidy: the XML Rule Book
</q>">
```

This entity declaration is self-contained. It maps the name chap8 to the content Chapter 8, <q>Keeping it Tidy: the XML Rule Book</q>. No separate storage unit is involved.

You see in Chapter 7 that an XML document can be made up of as many physical storage units (usually files) as you like. However, these external objects must always be declared up-front in the DTD.

External entities are declared by associating a name with a storage unit that is physically identified by means of a SYSTEM or PUBLIC identifier:

```
<!ENTITY chapter1 SYSTEM "chap1.xml">
```

This associates the name chapter1 with the file chap1.xml.

> **Warning:** You can choose any name you like for your entities. However, entity names must conform to XML's rules for a name, which strictly limit the non-alphanumeric characters you can use within the entity's name. Also, entity names must be unique within each XML document. If you declare the same entity name more than once, the first declaration is used and all the others will be ignored. You might not be warned that this has happened.

> **Note:** Because external entities tend to be uniquely associated with particular documents, their declarations are usually found in the document itself, as part of its internal DTD subset.

Text and Binary Entities

In Chapter 7, I also discussed the distinction between binary and text external entities. A *text entity* contains text data that is considered to form part of the XML document. A *binary entity* is basically anything that isn't to be treated as though it is XML-encoded.

The difference between the declarations of a text entity and a binary entity is that each binary entity has a notation associated with it. This is a binary entity:

```
<!ENTITY my.picture SYSTEM "mypic.bmp" NDATA BMP>
```

The following is a text entity:

```
<!ENTITY chap4 SYSTEM "chap4.xml">
```

> **Warning:** In order to be valid, the notation name (BMP in this example) must be declared in the DTD. Notation declarations are discussed later in this chapter.

Parameter Entities

Parameter entities have the same job description as general entities. The only difference in their scope is that parameter entities can appear only in the DTD.

The only difference in their declaration and use is an extra % symbol. A parameter entity declaration has % between the initial <!ENTITY and the entity's name:

```
<!ENTITY % HTML.Version
"-//W3C//DTD HTML 3.2//EN">
```

A parameter entity reference uses % in place of the & that precedes general entity references:

```
<!ATTLIST HTML
VERSION CDATA #FIXED "%HTML.Version;">
```

> **Warning:** Note that there is white space on either side of the % in the parameter entity declaration, but no space between % and the entity's name when it actually is used.

Later in this chapter, you find out how to use parameter entities to help in the design of flexible, user-customizable XML DTDs.

Notation Declarations

Notations are declared in the DTD in a similar fashion to entities. They declare a name as signifying a notation, and they associate it with a SYSTEM or PUBLIC identifier:

```
<!NOTATION JPEG SYSTEM "/programs/viewjpg.exe">
```

The general intention here is that the external identifier in the notation declaration will help your XML application to deal with other stuff in this strange non-XML format. In this case, for example, it could be the filename of a program that can view JPEG images. However, the XML-Lang standard leaves it slightly open as to exactly how this information will be used. It does not force applications to treat notations as helper applications.

DTD Design Tips

Although I have reviewed the actual declarations that make up an XML DTD, I haven't talked about how you might actually go about designing your own DTD. In an introductory book like this, I can't go into any sort of detail (although, in the SGML world at least one whole book is devoted to just this single topic), but I can at least outline some useful techniques that are suggested by XML's built-in facilities.

In Chapter 13, "Developing an XML Memo Application," I cover how you might actually design a DTD for a simple XML application. If you want to review a more complex example, the XML version of the HTML 2.0 DTD on the CD-ROM is the basis of many of the examples discussed in this section.

External Versus Internal DTD Subset

When designing a DTD, you are actually designing a file (or several, see the next section) that can act as the *external DTD subset* for a class of similar XML documents.

> Warning: For the rest of this section, the term *class DTD* will be used as a shorthand for "an external DTD subset designed for a class of similar XML documents."

As you design a class DTD, it is worth bearing in mind that the XML document author is at liberty to create an internal DTD subset before the start of the document, and that declarations in the internal DTD subset will override corresponding declarations in your class DTD. This feature of XML can be used to your advantage, but only if authors work to an agreed plan and do not introduce gratuitous changes to the class DTD in their internal subsets.

In general, it makes sense to include a complete logical structure (including all the element and attribute declarations) in your class DTD. You might give users some options to switch on and off, but they shouldn't be expected to design new structural elements. (I discuss how to provide user options in the section "User Switches," later in this chapter.)

Entities and notations can be more of a gray area. Normally these vary from one document to another, so they shouldn't appear in the class DTD. However, if your class DTD has a well-understood sphere of operation, it might be possible to include declarations for entities that are widely used within that application. For example, for an intranet XML application, a company's logo could be declared as a standard entity in the class DTD:

```
<!ENTITY logo SYSTEM "/resources/logo.gif" NDATA GIF>
```

Again, if you know in advance which notations are likely to be used, it saves authors work (and improves consistency) if you include their declarations in the DTD:

```
<!NOTATION GIF SYSTEM "/resources/gifviewer.exe">
```

Putting entity and notation declarations in the DTD does not constrain authors. They are at liberty to add any number of entities and notations to their internal DTD subset.

On the other hand, including a large number of predefined declarations in the class DTD does not impose too big an overhead. Clearly, the XML processor has to read the declarations, but it does not have to do anything about them (such as fetching the files they mention) until a document actually references them.

Conditional Sections

Conditional sections are allowed only within the external DTD subset. They are a piece of markup that can be placed around one or more declarations, comments, and white space. They cause the markup they contain to be included in the DTD or ignored, depending on the value of their initial keyword, which must be either INCLUDE or IGNORE:

```
<![INCLUDE[
... included markup ...
]]>

<![IGNORE[
... excluded markup ...
]]>
```

Conditional sections can nest inside each other:

```
<![INCLUDE[
... included markup ...
<![IGNORE[
... markup is still excluded ...
]]>
]]>
```

Be warned, however, that when inside an IGNORE conditional section, everything—including INCLUDE conditional sections—is ignored:

```
<![IGNORE[
... excluded markup ...
]]>
<![INCLUDE[
... this markup is ignored, despite being marked 'include' ...
]]>
]]>
```

Conditional sections become interesting only when you use them in conjunction with parameter entities. I'll discuss how to do that in the next section.

Parameter Entities

Parameter entities can be used in the external DTD subset as a shorthand for a group of elements that come up repeatedly in the DTD. By giving parameter entities a suitable name, you can make the logical structure of your class DTD much clearer to a reader.

> **Warning:** Parameter entities can also be used in the internal DTD subset, but in a much more restricted way than I describe in this section.

For example, in the HTML DTD, the parameter entity `list` is used to refer to all the elements that contain lists of various types:

```
<!ENTITY % list " UL ¦ OL ¦ DIR ¦ MENU ">
```

This parameter is then used as a shorthand for "…and all the list-type elements" in the declaration of the parameter entity `block`, which in turn means "all block-type elements":

```
<!ENTITY % block "P ¦ %list; ¦ DL ¦ %preformatted; ¦
%block.forms;">
```

In turn, `block` is used within the `body.content` parameter entity:

```
<!ENTITY % body.content "(%heading;¦%block;¦HR¦ADDRESS¦IMG)*">
```

Eventually, the `body` element type's content model becomes a single `body.content` parameter entity:

```
<!ELEMENT BODY %body.content;>
```

Without these parameter entities, the declaration of BODY would be something like this (depending on which options, covered in the next section, are in force):

```
<!ELEMENT BODY
(H1¦H2¦H3¦H4¦H5¦H6¦P ¦ UL ¦ OL ¦ DIR ¦ MENU ¦ DL
¦ PRE ¦ BLOCKQUOTE ¦HR¦ADDRESS¦IMG)*>
```

This is longer, but more importantly it has lost the sense that these element types fulfill certain well-defined types of roles within the class DTD.

Another common use for parameter entities is to act as a shorthand within attribute declarations. For example, the HTML DTD contains the SDAPREF parameter entity, which introduces generated text prefixes for use when displaying HTML pages for the print-impaired:

```
<!ENTITY % SDAPREF "SDAPREF CDATA #FIXED">
```

This handy shorthand is used throughout the DTD, as in the following example:

```
<!ATTLIST XMP
%SDAPREF; "Example:&#RE;">
```

A parameter entity also can be used for a whole group of attribute declarations. The following is a definition of a.global:

```
<!ENTITY % a.global "
id ID #IMPLIED
n CDATA #IMPLIED
lang IDREF #IMPLIED
rend CDATA #IMPLIED">
```

With this, you have a set of global attributes that can be associated with any element:

```
<!ATTLIST PERSON %a.global;>
```

Part of the value of this approach is that if you decide to add another global attribute, you have to update only the definition of a.global to achieve this.

The Modular Approach

You have already seen that XML's general entities can be used to help authors by breaking up large documents into manageable chunks. In a similar spirit, parameter entities can be used to break up a large class DTD.

In general, each module should have a clearly defined purpose. It might contain element and attribute declarations for a part of the document structure. For example, this code declares and then includes a module containing declarations for the components of tables:

```
<!ENTITY % basic.tables SYSTEM "table1.dtd">
%basic.tables;
```

You could also use a module to include declarations for a set of commonly used entities:

```
<!ENTITY % common.files SYSTEM "common.dtd">
%common.files;
```

One advantage of the modular approach to DTD design is that you can easily switch in a whole replacement module. For example, if you decide to adopt a new approach to modeling tables, all you have to do is remove the reference to basic.tables and replace it with a reference to another table module.

User Switches

Now you are ready for the subject of customizing class DTDs.

You can use conditional sections and parameter entities in combination to make your class DTD user-customizable. The general technique is to place a parameter entity reference at the point where the keyword INCLUDE or IGNORE occurs in a conditional section:

```
<![%user_option;[
... conditionally included declarations ...
]]>
```

If the parameter entity user_option has the value INCLUDE, the declarations in the marked section will be part of the DTD. If it is IGNORE, they will simply be ignored.

A common method of using this technique is to place switchable conditional sections in the external DTD subset, and to advise users that they can switch various features of the class DTD on or off as they please, by declaring the parameter entity in their internal DTD subset. The following document type declaration declares the parameter entity HTML.Recommended to have the value INCLUDE, which switches in the set of markup declarations that count as good practice in the HTML DTD:

```
<!DOCTYPE HTML SYSTEM "HTML2_X.DTD" [
<!ENTITY % HTML.Recommended "INCLUDE">
]>
```

This includes all those CDATA sections in the DTD that are introduced by a reference to HTML.Recommended. For example, this CDATA section from the HTML DTD will be included:

```
<![%HTML.Recommended;[
        <!ENTITY % HTML.Deprecated "IGNORE">
]]>
```

Using switches requires a certain amount of care. If the user declares this parameter entity to have any value other than INCLUDE or IGNORE, the user will render the whole DTD, and the document, invalid. It is certainly essential to declare a meaningful value for the parameter entity in the class DTD before using that parameter entity to introduce a conditional section in your DTD:

```
<!ENTITY HTML.Recommended "IGNORE">
```

The parameter entity will then have a sensible value that can be used if the user does not specify a value for it in his or her internal DTD subset.

When a switch has been set, you can use it as often as necessary within your DTD. The HTML DTD uses the HTML.Recommended switch in four different places to enforce recommended practice.

Switches can trigger other switches. For example, HTML has another parameter entity switch called HTML.Deprecated, which guards declaration of markup that is no longer seen as good practice. If a user switches in HTML.Recommended, it suggests that he doesn't want any deprecated features, so, as you have seen, this conditional section automatically switches them out:

```
<![%HTML.Recommended;[
<!ENTITY % HTML.Deprecated "IGNORE">
]]>
```

Each switchable section is normally followed by declarations that will apply if that section is switched out. This example, again taken from the HTML DTD, says that the parameter entity preformatted will apply to only the PRE element unless the HTML.Deprecated switch has been set, in which case it will also include the deprecated elements XMP and LISTING:

```
<![%HTML.Deprecated;[
<!ENTITY % preformatted "PRE ¦ XMP ¦ LISTING">
]]>
<!ENTITY % preformatted "PRE">
```

How does this work? This technique relies heavily on the fact that the first declaration is the one that counts if an entity is declared more than once. All subsequent declarations are ignored. So, if HTML.Deprecated is switched in, the conditional section is part of the markup, and it is processed as follows:

```
<!ENTITY % preformatted "PRE ¦ XMP ¦ LISTING">
<!ENTITY % preformatted "PRE">
```

The parameter entity preformatted is declared twice, so the first declaration counts, and the second one is ignored.

If HTML.Deprecated is switched out, the whole conditional section disappears, and it is as though only the following appeared in the DTD:

```
<!ENTITY % preformatted "PRE">
```

This gives the required default setting.

You can use these switches in many ways. However, you should bear in mind that user switches in the internal DTD subset are meaningful only if you tell your users what switches they have available to them and which aspects of the DTD's behavior will be affected by each switch.

The Required Markup Declaration

In the case where an XML document is to be treated as well-formed rather than valid, it is not always necessary to read and process the whole DTD. Time and bandwidth can be saved by skipping this job. However, there is a problem here. Some information that might be found in the DTD is essential for the correct processing even of well-formed XML documents. This information consists of declarations of the following:

- Attributes with default values, if these default values are required by the document (because the attribute in question isn't always specified)
- Entities (apart from the five predefined entities amp, lt, gt, apos, and quot) that are referenced in the document
- Element types with element content, where the document has white space that needs to be treated differently because it falls inside instances of those element types

The problem is that the XML processor cannot know if any of these situations have arisen without reading the DTD. So how can it decide whether to read the DTD without first reading the DTD? Obviously, a little help is called for, and this is where the required markup declaration comes in.

The *required markup declaration*, or *RMD*, is the last component of the XML declaration. It is provided by the document's author as a guide to the XML processor, as in the following example:

```
<?XML version="1.0" RMD="INTERNAL"?>
```

The RMD can take one of three values:

- NONE means that the document can be parsed correctly without reading any part of the DTD.
- INTERNAL means that the XML processor must read and process the internal DTD subset, if provided, in order to interpret the document correctly.
- ALL means that both the internal and the external DTD subsets must be read in order to interpret the document correctly.

If an RMD isn't provided, the value ALL is assumed by default.

Note: The XML language specification sternly calls it "an error" to get this wrong and to imply in the RMD that the XML processor can skip part or all of the DTD when in fact it shouldn't. However, this isn't the sort of error that the XML processor can pick up (apart from entities that it will know haven't been declared). So misuse of the RMD can lead to your XML documents being incorrectly parsed, without any warning.

Summary

In this chapter, I discussed the aspects of XML that control the form of valid XML documents. I started by finding out what the rules consist of, and where they are to be found.

For much of the chapter, I discussed the four main types of declarations that are found in a document type definition:

- Element declarations
- Attribute list declarations
- Entity declarations
- Notation declarations

I then discussed how to use built-in XML features—specifically conditional sections and parameter entities—to produce clear, modular DTDs.

Finally, I described the role of the required markup declaration in helping XML processors to read well-formed XML documents efficiently and accurately.

CHAPTER 9

Linking with XML

by Richard Light

In Chapter 2, "Enter XML," you learned about XML's linking facilities at an outline level. This chapter explores linking in more detail.

To begin, I review the way Web links currently work, and I contrast that with XML's approach. Then I describe some specifics of XML links, such as the following:

- How XML links are identified
- Information associated with XML links
- XML simple links
- XML extended links
- XML's facilities for addressing portions of target documents
- Extended link groups

Putting XML Links into Context

XML-Link aims to provide a much more powerful range of options for linking than HTML offers. Certainly, the familiar "click and jump" type of link will be supported. However, there will be significant new functionality in a number of areas, including the following:

- Typed links: Links with a specific role or behavior.
- Two-way links: Links that can be traversed with equal ease in either direction.
- Multidirectional links: Links that connect two or more targets.

The XML-Link specification simply allows authors to assert the presence of links in XML documents. It gives each XML application the freedom to decide exactly how links, and the effects of clicking on them, should be represented visually. The specification claims that it will provide "an effective yet compact structure for representing links."

XML-Link is built upon years of research and experience into linking. In particular, it takes its ideas from HTML, an International Standard called HyTime (ISO 10744:1992), and an SGML application called the Text Encoding Initiative (TEI). In this section, I cover HTML links and how they have affected the design of XML-Link.

HTML Links

Let's start by reviewing the linking syntax provided by HTML, basing the discussion on the recently released draft for HTML 4.0. Links can be made from only two element types in the HTML 4.0 DTD: <A> and <LINK>.

<LINK> elements occur in the header information, and they indicate relationships between the HTML document as a whole and other resources. <A> links can point to somewhere else in the current page, to another page on the same site, or to anywhere else on the Web.

<LINK> elements must have either a REL or a REV attribute, and <A> elements can have one of the two. These attributes serve two purposes. They state the intended direction of the link (because REV is a *reverse* link into the current document). They also indicate what type of resource they are connecting this document to, by taking values such as the following:

- ■ Contents: A link to a document that acts as a table of contents.
- ■ Start: A link to the first document in a collection of documents.
- ■ Next: A link to the next document in an ordered sequence.

The key part of the link is the HREF attribute. This contains the target of the link, expressed as a *URL* (Uniform Resource Locator).

URLs take the following general form:

```
<scheme>:<scheme-specific-part>
```

RFC 1738 describes the following *schemes*:

- ■ ftp: File Transfer Protocol
- ■ http: Hypertext Transfer Protocol
- ■ gopher: The Gopher protocol
- ■ mailto: Electronic mail address
- ■ news: USENET news
- ■ nntp: USENET news using NNTP access
- ■ telnet: Reference to interactive sessions
- ■ wais: Wide Area Information Servers
- ■ file: Host-specific filenames
- ■ prospero: Prospero Directory Service

Links to other HTML pages use the HyperText Transfer Protocol (HTTP) scheme. An HTTP URL takes the following form:

```
http://<host>:<port>/<path>?<searchpart>
```

Here are some examples:

```
http://www.anothersite.org/xml/bigintro.html
http://www.anothersite.org/
cgiwin.exe?getrecord:1014:field1=archives
```

The characters that can be entered directly within a URL's *path* or *searchpath* are limited to letters, digits, *safe* characters ($, -, _, ., and +), and *extra* characters (!, *, ', ,, and space). Any other character has to be *escaped*, using % followed by that character's code expressed as a hexadecimal number.

Characters that always need to be escaped within a URL include the following: #, <, >, ", %, and the space character.

Within the HTTP scheme, the characters ?, /, and ; are reserved, which means that they must be encoded if the actual character is required in the URL.

The URL might be followed by the symbol # and a *fragment identifier*:

```
http://www.anothersite.org/xml/bigintro.html#section2
```

The fragment identifier should match the name attribute of an <a> element within the target document:

```
<a name="section2">
```

The fragment identifier is *not* part of the URL itself.

> Note: Starting with HTML 4.0, the fragment identifier can instead match the ID of any element in the target document. This brings HTML practice more into line with the XML approach, discussed in the following section.

Interoperability with HTML Links

The designers of the XML link syntax took care to build on what already works in HTML.

As you know, the XML language is intended to support generalized markup on the Web. This clearly means that XML's linking facilities need to work in that environment as well. In particular, HTML and XML must be interoperable. This means that your Web site can freely "mix and match" HTML pages and XML documents, with links running between them as necessary. To achieve this, the following (new) types of links need to work:

- Links from an XML document to an HTML page
- Links from an XML document to another XML document
- Links from an HTML page to an XML document

XML-Link achieves interoperability with HTML by adopting the familiar HREF attribute and giving its value the same general meaning as in HTML. HREF's value is a URL identifying the *resource* that is the target of the link, optionally qualified by # (or ¦) and a fragment identifier, or by ? and a query. Furthermore, XML-Link conforms to RFC 1738's conventions regarding the characters that can appear within the URL itself.

This compatibility means that XML links have the same look and feel as HTML links. The following links can be as valid within an XML document as they would be within an HTML page:

```
<A HREF="http://www.anothersite.org/pub/doc3.xml">
<A HREF="http://www.anothersite.org/pub/doc3.xml#section2">
<A HREF="http://www.anothersite.org/pub/doc4.html">
```

Because URLs have the same form in both HTML and XML documents, there is equally no problem in including a link to an XML document within an HTML page. The only difference between a link to an XML document and a link to another HTML page is that any fragment identifier or query that follows the URL is interpreted in an XML-specific manner when the target is an XML document:

```
<A HREF="http://www.anothersite.org/pub/doc3.xml#chap.2">
```

Here, the fragment identifier `chap.2` specifies an element within the XML document `doc3.xml`, with an `ID` attribute value equal to `chap.2`.

So XML links fulfill the interoperability requirement very neatly.

Additional Linking Facilities

However, if XML-Link were content to simply mimic HTML's links, it wouldn't add any new functionality. Also, one principle of generalized markup is that users must be free to define tagsets that are meaningful to their own application. This means that XML cannot insist (as HTML does) that a limited number of element types be reserved for links.

The XML-Link specification *extends* HREF links in the following ways:

- Allowing any element type to indicate the existence of a link
- Defining the precise meaning of the *fragment identifier* (the part of the URL that follows the # or ¦) in cases when the target of the link is an XML document
- Providing links with human-readable labels
- Providing links with machine-readable labels
- Specifying policies for the context in which links are displayed and processed
- Specifying policies for when links are traversed
- Supporting extended linking groups
- Supporting multi-ended links

Some Linking Concepts

The XML-Link specification talks about some rather specialized concepts, which are best defined before you get into the details.

- *Resource*: This is any addressable object that is taking part in a link. Examples include documents, parts of (and points within) documents, images, programs, and query results.

- *Linking element*: This is a special element within an XML document that asserts the existence of a link and contains a description of the link's characteristics.

- *Locator*: A character string appearing in a linking element that is the address of a resource and can be used to locate that resource.

- *Title*: This is a caption associated with a resource, suitable for explaining to human users the significance of the part played in the link by that resource.

- *Traversal*: This is the action of using a link to access a resource. Traversal can be initiated by a user action (for example, clicking on a displayed portion of a linking element), or it can occur under program control.

- *Multidirectional link*: This link can be traversed starting at more than one of its resources. Note that being able to go back after following a one-directional link does not make the link multidirectional.

- *Inline link*: This link is indicated by a linking element that serves as one of its own resources. HTML <A> elements are examples of inline links.

- *Out-of-line link*: This link is indicated by a linking element that does not serve as one of its own resources (except perhaps by chance). It need not even occur in the same document as any of the resources it serves to connect.

A Concrete Example

These definitions rightly suggest that I want you to think about links in a more abstract way than usual. To give the discussion a more concrete basis, let's try to describe a standard HTML <a> link using this terminology.

Here's the concrete example. The link

```
<a NAME="link14"
HREF="http://www.othersite.org/pub/doc4.html#chap4">
```

points to an `<a>` element in the document `doc4.html`:

```
<a NAME="chap4">The target</a>
```

Let's start with the target of the link. This is a *resource*, which is an addressable unit of information participating in a link. The `<a>` element is an addressable unit because it has been given a `NAME` attribute value, which is how HTML specifies link targets within documents.

Note: When using HTML, you tend to think of within-document link targets as just the point at which you start reading, but the XML concept of a *resource* has more substance. If the target of this link were within an XML document instead of an HTML one, the resource you are pointing to would be the whole `<a>` element, including the text `The target` that appears before its `<a/>` end-tag. As you will see, resources in XML can be very meaty chunks of information!

Next, consider the `<a>` element itself. This is quite clearly a *linking element*, because its `HREF` attribute value asserts the existence of a link.

The link's `HREF` attribute value `http://www.othersite.org/pub/doc4.html#chap4` is an example of a *locator*.

This link is traversed when you click on the link and move to the target page.

The `<a>` element also is an inline link. The definition says that it serves as one of its own resources. What does that mean? All links must have at least two ends, so think of a link as a piece of string connecting two things. You can pin the far end of the piece of string onto the target of the link (the URL specified in the `HREF` attribute value), but where do you pin the near end? On this `<a>` element, of course!

Another point is that `<a>` (*anchor*) elements can also act as a resource if their `NAME` attribute is specified. For example, the following is a link whose target resource (the far end of the piece of string) is the example `<a>` link element:

```
<a HREF="#link14">Here's a link</a>
```

The following points sum up the world of HTML links using XML-Link terminology:

- Within HTML pages, <a> elements are used as linking elements.

- Any <a> element containing an HREF attribute specification is a linking element, specifying an inline link.

- Any <a> element containing a NAME attribute specification is potentially a resource in one or more links, although it has no means of knowing in what links it is participating.

- HTML links are normally traversed by user action—clicking on the linking element.

- The HTML linking scheme offers no way of expressing multidirectional or out-of-line links.

Identifying XML Links

Before you can do clever things with your links, you first have to find them. As I already noted, XML needs to give users the freedom to say that any element type in their applications is to act as a linking element. So how do you specify in XML which elements are to be treated as links?

This is achieved by specifying the reserved attribute XML-LINK for each element that is to act as a linking element. In addition, the value of the XML-LINK attribute indicates what *type* of link the element expresses. For example, this tells an XML processor that it is dealing with a simple (inline) link:

```
<A XML-LINK="SIMPLE" HREF="http://www.w3.org/">The W3C</A>
```

The full list of link types supported by XML is as follows:

- SIMPLE: A simple inline link
- EXTENDED: An extended or out-of-line link
- LOCATOR: A locator, pointing to an actual target resource
- GROUP: An extended link group
- DOCUMENT: An extended link document

Of these, only SIMPLE and EXTENDED are actual linking elements; the others play supporting roles, which will be described later in this chapter.

Fixed XML-LINK Attributes

To avoid having to declare the special XML-LINK attribute every time you use an element, you can declare it one time as follows, in the DTD, as a fixed value and then forget about it:

```
<!ATTLIST MYLINK
XML-LINK CDATA #FIXED "SIMPLE">
```

> Note: The preceding attribute list specification says "the <MYLINK> element always has an XML-LINK attribute with the value "SIMPLE" whenever it occurs."

With that declaration out of the way, your XML <MYLINK> links start to look just like HTML hyperlinks:

```
<MYLINK HREF="http://www.w3.org/">The W3C</MYLINK>
```

> Warning: A technical issue has arisen over the placing of this default declaration. If it lives in the main DTD (its *external DTD subset*), an XML client has the overhead of downloading the whole DTD in order to find out about linking rules. If it lives in the internal DTD subset, which is transmitted with the document, this breaks SGML interoperability unless the element's other attributes are declared there as well. SGML currently mandates that you can have only one attribute list declaration per element. It is almost certain that this issue will be resolved by a forthcoming change to the SGML standard. If not, a new mechanism for flagging links to XML would have to be defined.

Declaring Your Own XML-LINK Attributes

The XML-LINK specification declares that certain attributes are to be treated specially. This could be a major headache if your own XML application already uses one or more of those attributes for another purpose. This is quite possible, because only one of these attributes (XML-LINK) begins with the reserved prefix XML. Some attribute names, such as ROLE and TITLE, could easily be used for other purposes. For that reason, XML-LINK provides a mechanism that it calls *attribute remapping*, which allows you to change the attributes that are significant for linking within XML.

The XML-ATTRIBUTES attribute is used to accomplish attribute remapping for a given type of linking element. It should take a value consisting of pairs of names, with each pair being the name of an attribute that is significant to XML, followed by the name of the attribute that is to actually fulfill this function. Here is an example:

```
<!ATTLIST person-link
        ROLE CDATA #IMPLIED
        XML-LINK CDATA #FIXED "SIMPLE"
        LINK-ROLE CDATA #IMPLIED
        XML-ATTRIBUTES CDATA #FIXED "ROLE LINK-ROLE">
```

This example maps the XML-LINK concept of *role* to the LINK-ROLE attribute for the person-link element type, which allows a person-link element to take the following form:

```
<person-link role="parent" link-role="footnote">
```

In this example, role="parent" indicates the role that the person is playing, and link-role="footnote" describes the role that the link is to have.

Warning: When remapping attributes, remember that you are not allowed to use any attributes beginning with XML. It would be tempting, but wrong, to remap the ROLE attribute to XML-ROLE.

Information Associated with XML Links

HTML provides some attributes you can use to add value to your links, in addition to the HREF and NAME attributes already covered. These attributes include the following:

- REL: The relationship of this resource to the destination of link
- REV: The relationship of the link destination to this resource
- TITLE: A description of the nature of the link
- CHARSET: The character encoding of the text at the link destination

Like HTML, XML allows you to associate additional information with your links. However, the XML-Link specification carefully defines how key aspects of this additional information are used. This gives you an important additional level of control over the way your links behave.

This section reviews all of the information associated with XML linking elements.

Resources

Every locator within an XML simple link or extended link must identify a resource. This is specified by the value of the HREF attribute. The value of HREF is always a URL, like this one:

```
<A HREF="http://www.w3.org/">The W3C</A>
```

This is just the same as in HTML, except that for locators within XML documents, the HREF attribute value must always be specified, whereas A elements in HTML do not have to specify HREF.

Note: I deal with the case of a target resource that is a fragment of an XML document later in this chapter, in the section called "Addressing."

Link Behavior

XML gives you the chance to control how links behave. The information described in this section can be applied to both simple and extended XML links.

Let's start by describing the behavior of HTML links. When you click on an <A> link in HTML, the browser follows the link and returns its target resource to you. (Note that this isn't always another page; depending on the URL, it might be an ftp download or an invitation to send an e-mail.) This process is called traversing the link. In HTML, you can always see that the link is there, and it is never traversed until you take action by clicking on it.

When you author an XML document, you have a much wider range of options. However, you can only state a policy for your links. It is up to the XML application to decide how to best implement that policy.

First, the SHOW attribute lets you control how the resources that you link to are displayed and processed. It has three possible values:

- INCLUDE: The target resource is embedded into the body of the resource where the traversal started.
- REPLACE: The target resource replaces the resource where the traversal started.
- NEW: The target resource is displayed in a new context, not affecting that of the resource where the traversal started.

The abstract nature of these definitions reflects the fact that XML links can be used for any sort of connection between information resources. To give you a more concrete idea of how the SHOW attribute works, let's review the behavior of a typical HTML browser.

<A> hyperlinks cause the current screen to be cleared and replaced by the one you have just linked to. (This is what REPLACE does.) Conversely, if the link is to an ftp download, that operation is carried out in a separate window. (This is what NEW does.)

There isn't really an equivalent for INCLUDE in HTML. Its action is similar to pasting a picture into your Web page using the IMG tag, except that what you are pasting is all or part of another page.

The second aspect of link behavior that you can control is timing—when the link should be traversed. The ACTUATE attribute has two possible values:

- AUTO: The link is to be traversed as soon as it is found. Reading the link and fetching its target resource are considered part of the process of reading the current resource.

- USER: It is up to the user to ask for the link to be traversed; otherwise, it doesn't happen.

Using these terms in combination, as in

```
<MYLINK HREF="X" SHOW="EMBED" ACTUATE="AUTO" ...>
```

has the same meaning as the following HTML coding:

```
<IMG SRC="X">
```

The meaning is the same because it causes the application to treat the linked resource as though it is part of the current document (even though it isn't).

Similarly, the combination

```
<MYLINK HREF="X" SHOW="REPLACE" ACTUATE="AUTO" ...>
```

has the same effect as the following HTML coding:

```
<A HREF="X">
```

The effect is the same because it causes the current screen to be replaced by the linked resource, but only when the user asks for it to be replaced.

Finally, if the SHOW and ACTUATE attributes don't control the behavior of the link sufficiently closely, you can use the BEHAVIOR attribute to provide your own detailed instructions.

> Note: XML doesn't specify how to use BEHAVIOR; it just recommends that
> XML processors should look there for detailed guidance on how the link
> should behave. This probably means that BEHAVIOR will be used in a variety of
> ways, which are specific to particular XML applications.

Link Roles

Every XML link can have a *role*. This appears in the link's ROLE attribute, and
it states the meaning of the link. Each resource that participates in a link also
can have its own role.

To put this a bit more generally, links are usually included to express relationships between the things they connect. Some links connect to subsections of
the current document, others add support or background, and others have a
very different meaning such as providing access to metadata (author, date of
publication, and so on) about the current document.

> Note: The ROLE attribute is designed to be used by an application program
> and, therefore, is an aid to the machine. The TITLE attribute, described next, is
> provided for human consumption.

In an XML application for thesauri, for example, links might be used to connect a mini-document for a single term to other mini-documents describing
the following items:

- Its broader term
- Each of its narrower terms
- "See also" terms

Each of these types of links should have its own specific role.

The XML standard doesn't predefine any "approved" values for link roles. The
roles assigned, and their semantics, will be specific to the particular XML application within which they are used.

Knowing what type of link you are dealing with is a tremendous advantage.
For a start, it allows better control over display. In the thesaurus example, links
to broad terms and to narrower terms should look different.

> Note: To maintain fine control over how an application's links are displayed, you might require a custom XML browser that "knows about" that particular application and interprets its link roles correctly. Alternatively, it should be possible to simply write an XS style sheet for the application because the link role information is part of the document, so it can be tested within the style sheet. Then you can use a generic XML browser to view the application's documents.

Link roles also offer a whole new dimension for searching. If you can include a search on the link role as part of a query, it becomes possible to search for pages that have a particular relationship, and to find information that is spread among two or more documents linked in a particular way.

> Note: When an out-of-line link involves two or more locators, each can be given its own ROLE. This allows asymmetrical relationships (such as parent-child links) to be expressed clearly.

Labels for Links

Every locator can have a TITLE attribute, which acts as a label:

```
<A TITLE="W3 Consortium Home Page" HREF="http://www.w3.org/
">The W3C</A>
```

XML applications decide whether to use this label and what to use it for. However, TITLE follows the same concept as in HTML, so it probably will be used in a similar way. In general, TITLE is expected to provide a human-readable description of the link, which could be used as a pop-up hint within an XML browser. This contrasts with ROLE, which is intended for machine consumption.

> Warning: The current draft notes that, "The simple labeling mechanism described in this draft is insufficiently flexible to cope with internationalization or the use of multimedia in link labels. A future version will provide a mechanism for the use of structured link titles."

Simple Links

Most of the XML links you add probably will be SIMPLE links, so I'll start with them and then move on to extended links.

XML's simple links are very much like HTML <A> elements. However, you can achieve a greater variety of effects with XML simple links by controlling their behavior and assigning roles to them, as I discussed in the previous section.

An XML simple link points to a single resource. This is specified as the value of its mandatory HREF attribute:

```
<LINK HREF="http://www.w3.org/">The W3C</LINK>
```

In addition to the HREF attribute, simple links can have any of the additional features covered in the last section.

Here is an example of a thesaurus application of XML:

```
<broad-term ROLE="BT" SHOW="EMBED" HREF="mats.xml">
materials
</broad-term>
```

This application associates a specific role "BT" and a SHOW behavior of "EMBED" with a broad-term linking element.

The "BT" role allows an XML thesaurus application to display the link in a different way from a link to a narrower term. The SHOW behavior indicates that the details of the broader term should be embedded in the current screen if the user clicks on the link.

In practice, this additional information is often incorporated into the DTD by using #FIXED attribute values. This removes the need to specify it for each linking element in your XML documents. For example, the attribute list declaration for the broad-term element type might look like this:

```
<!ATTLIST broad-term
    XML-LINK CDATA #FIXED "SIMPLE"
    ROLE CDATA #FIXED "BT"
    HREF CDATA #REQUIRED
    TITLE CDATA #IMPLIED
    SHOW (EMBED|REPLACE|NEW) "EMBED"
    ACTUATE (AUTO|USER) "USER" >
```

This definition automatically gives all broad-term elements the desired attribute values by default. Now all you need to do each time you include a broad-term element is specify the HREF attribute value, like this:

```
<broad-term HREF="mats.xml">
materials
</broad-term>
```

> **Warning:** In fact, it would be an error to specify another value for the ROLE attribute within the broad-term element, because the default value is #FIXED.

When you include the additional information about the behavior of each linking element type as a set of default values in the DTD, you gain the benefits of that information without any extra work at the marking-up stage.

In XML, you don't need to limit yourself to a single linking element, as you often do in HTML. You can declare any number of different element types, representing all the different styles of simple links that your application requires. For the thesaurus example, you might have the following element types:

- broad-term
- narrow-term
- see-also
- use-for

Simple Links and Resources

A simple link is an example of an inline link. As you have seen, this means that it acts as one of its own resources. What exactly is this resource? The answer becomes clearer when you realize that it is an element; the linking element *is* the resource. If that element has any content, the resource includes that content.

XML allows you to state whether or not you want your linking elements to be considered as a resource of the link. All linking elements have the attribute INLINE. This attribute can take the values TRUE, which means that the linking element is a resource of the link, and FALSE, which means that it is not considered to be a resource. By default, INLINE takes the value TRUE.

If the linking element is a resource of the link, you need to be able to provide additional information about this inline resource (TITLE and ROLE). For a simple link, there is nowhere to put this information because these attributes are already used for the title and role of the target resource. As a result, XML defines two additional special attributes, CONTENT-TITLE and CONTENT-ROLE, which describe the linking element's own role within the link.

As an example, you might extend the attribute list for the broad-term element within the thesaurus application. By including a CONTENT-ROLE as well as a ROLE, you can indicate that the current term is a narrow term (NT) of the broad term to which you are linking:

```
<!ATTLIST broad-term
        XML-LINK        CDATA    #FIXED "SIMPLE"
        ROLE            CDATA    #FIXED "BT"
        CONTENT-ROLE    CDATA    #FIXED "NT"
        HREF            CDATA    #REQUIRED
        ...
```

In HTML, you are used to linking elements containing a short phrase that acts as a cue for the link:

```
<A HREF="http://www.w3.org/">The W3C</A>
```

So in XML's terms, this phrase is part of the resource at the near end of the link.

It is quite possible for an XML simple link to contain a resource that is not simply a phrase for the application to underline. At one extreme, nothing stops a simple link from being expressed by an empty element. At the other extreme, a linking element could contain a large amount of subelements and data content.

Why does this matter? For one thing, it will be less convenient to indicate that the link exists if there is nothing to underline (for the empty element), or if you have to underline several pages.

More importantly, the SHOW attribute allows the behavior "EMBED". You need to be aware of the implications of using this strategy, particularly if your simple links have significant contents. If you traverse an "EMBED" link, the target of the link will be displayed at the location where the traversal started. However, the XML-Link specification doesn't make clear exactly where that will be in relation to the content of the element containing your simple link. In general, it's probably a good practice to keep the contents of linking elements small.

Simple Links and Link Rot

A simple link is a one-way street to its destination. Although an XML processor, like an HTML browser, might be able to go back from the target of a link to the link element (the *source* of the link), this is not mandated by the XML standard. And, as with HTML, nothing in the target document tells it that it is being pointed at. Therefore, XML simple links are subject to the same ills that beset HTML hyperlinks—in particular, the "link to nowhere," pointing to a page or document that no longer exists.

Extended Links

The XML extensions for simple links are useful, but XML simple links share the fundamental limitations of all inline links. The real breakthrough comes with *extended links*. Have you ever wanted to be able to make your links two-way, and fudged them by putting in two one-way links? Or have you wanted to link to more than one target, but resorted to putting in several links side by side? XML extended links enable you to do these things cleanly.

How does this work? Surprisingly, the one thing holding back simple links from doing greater things is the most obvious thing you do with them, which is putting them into your text at the place from which you want the link made. As I have said, this makes them inline links. What you need for greater flexibility is an *out-of-line link*.

Out-of-Line Links

I've already defined out-of-line links in the "Some Linking Concepts" section earlier in this chapter. Now let's try to understand the concept. (In Chapter 13, "Developing an XML Memo Application," the section "Advanced linking—Out-of-Line Links" provides a practical example of this concept.)

The basic idea is simple enough. Suppose you have two related paragraphs in your XML document that you want to link together. You could put in a couple of simple inline links, one in each direction, like this:

```
<P ID="para.1"><LINK HREF="#para.3">In general terms ... </LINK>
</P>
<P ID="para.2"> ... </P>
<P ID="para.3"><LINK HREF="#para.1"> Specifically, ...</LINK></P>
```

Or you could step away from the actual paragraphs, and make the connection between them somewhere near the start of the document, like this:

```
<EXTENDED-LINK ROLE="sibling">
<LOCATOR HREF="#para.1" TITLE="overview"/>
<LOCATOR HREF="#para.3" TITLE="detail"/>
</EXTENDED-LINK>
...
<P ID="para.1">In general terms ... </P>
<P ID="para.2"> ... </P>
<P ID="para.3">Specifically, ...</P>
```

This means that the connection between paragraph 1 and paragraph 3 is now made elsewhere. (In fact, it doesn't even have to be in the same document, as you will see!) Now the markup of the text is simpler, because it isn't cluttered with linking information. Because the out-of-line link associates the two paragraphs in a neutral way, it can be traversed with equal ease in either direction—so it becomes a bi-directional link.

Of course, for this magic to happen, the software must work a bit harder. An XML application must search for extended links, and work out where the endpoints of each one fall. In this case, it then marks a link from paragraph 1 pointing at paragraph 3, and it marks a second link pointing back the other way. From the user's point of view, each of these links then behaves in exactly the same way as the equivalent simple link would behave.

To take the thesaurus application as another example, extended links would be a very clean method of grouping related terms together:

```
<related-term-group>
<related-term HREF="pine.xml" TITLE="pine"/>
<related-term HREF="beech.xml" TITLE="beech"/>
<related-term HREF="oak.xml" TITLE="oak"/>
<related-term HREF="willow.xml" TITLE="willow"/>
</related-term-group>
```

In this case, the link contains four locators. It states that when you are positioned at any of the four documents mentioned ("pine.xml", "beech.xml", "oak.xml", or "willow.xml"), you have a potential link to any of the other three documents. This is much more concise than having three simple links out of each of the four documents, and it is much easier to maintain. (Think about what happens when you want to add or remove an entry from the related group!)

The XML processor might have to search for extended links in a number of places. The XML-Link specification tries to make the processor's life easier by specifying exactly where the links are likely to be found. I talk about *link groups* in the "Extended Link Groups" section, later in this chapter.

So, how exactly are extended links specified? Let's go back over the paragraph-to-paragraph link and see what's there. The out-of-line link is constructed from two types of elements, called EXTENDED and LOCATOR.

EXTENDED Elements

You might be surprised to learn that an EXTENDED link element doesn't point or link to anywhere at all. It simply groups together a bunch of LOCATOR elements, and by so doing it indicates that *together* they form an extended link:

```
<EXTENDED>
<LOCATOR .../>
<LOCATOR .../>
</EXTENDED>
```

You can use the attributes of your EXTENDED link element to state how the LOCATOR elements within it will behave by default. You can give it a ROLE and a TITLE, and you can specify behaviors, as in the following case:

```
<EXTENDED-LINK ROLE="sibling" TITLE="see also">
```

> Remember that an EXTENDED link element doesn't have to be an element with an element type of extended. It is *any* element that has an XML-LINK attribute with the value "EXTENDED". So, once again, you can declare as many types of extended link groups as your application requires.

The related-term-group element type for the thesaurus example might have the following element and attribute list declaration:

```
<!ELEMENT related-term-group
    (related-term)+>
<!ATTLIST related-term-group
    XML-LINK CDATA #FIXED "EXTENDED"
    ROLE CDATA #FIXED "RT"
    TITLE CDATA #IMPLIED
    SHOW (EMBED|REPLACE|NEW) "REPLACE"
    ACTUATE (AUTO|USER) "USER"
    BEHAVIOR CDATA #IMPLIED>
```

This declaration enforces the role `"RT"` as a default for all locators within `related-term-group`, and it leaves all other linking attributes with their default behavior.

Note: In the example, the content model for `related-term-group` states that it can contain only `related-term` elements. However, the XML-Link specification doesn't limit the content an `EXTENDED` element type can have, as long as any `LOCATOR` elements are its immediate children. An `EXTENDED` element can contain a mixture of different `LOCATOR` element types or `LOCATOR` elements interspersed with character data and other subelements.

LOCATOR Elements

Each `LOCATOR` element defines one resource that is participating in an extended link.

Just like simple links, each `LOCATOR` element can be qualified by a `ROLE` or `TITLE`, and its behavior can be specified by `SHOW`, `ACTUATE`, and `BEHAVIOR` attributes. If any one of these attributes is not specified, its value will be *inherited* from the value of the corresponding attribute in its parent `EXTENDED` element.

In the extended link example, you have two locator elements:

```
<LOCATOR HREF="#para.1" TITLE="overview"/>
<LOCATOR HREF="#para.3" TITLE="detail"/>
```

However, in principle, any number of `LOCATOR` elements could be in this link.

If you have the following three linked paragraphs, the XML processor marks all three as being resources of a hyperlink, just as before:

```
<LOCATOR HREF="#para.1" TITLE="overview"/>
<LOCATOR HREF="#para.3" TITLE="detail 1"/>
<LOCATOR HREF="#para.9" TITLE="detail 2"/>
```

But when a user clicks on one of these links—for instance, the one anchored at paragraph 3—things will be rather different. Now you have two potential targets: paragraph 1 and paragraph 9. How the processor deals with this situation depends on the information available. In the absence of any specific guidance, it might just offer the user a menu, giving the `TITLE` of each target to help the user choose. However, the `BEHAVIOR` attribute of the `EXTENDED` link element or of its `LOCATOR` subelements might give application-specific guidance on what to do. Alternatively, the ROLE attribute of one or more of these elements could indicate to an XML application how this multidirectional link should be interpreted.

The related-term element for thesauri might be defined as follows in the DTD:

```
<!ELEMENT related-term EMPTY>
<!ATTLIST related-term
    XML-LINK CDATA #FIXED "LOCATOR"
    ROLE CDATA #FIXED "RT"
    HREF CDATA #REQUIRED
    TITLE CDATA #IMPLIED
    SHOW (EMBED|REPLACE|NEW) "REPLACE"
    ACTUATE (AUTO|USER) "USER"
    BEHAVIOR CDATA #IMPLIED>
```

This again enforces the role "RT", while leaving all other linking attributes with their default behavior.

Inline Extended Links

Extended links also have the three attributes INLINE, CONTENT-TITLE, and CONTENT-ROLE. Within an extended link, the INLINE attribute allows you to say that the linking element is one of the resources of the link. This is a relatively painless way of expressing two-way extended links, because the familiar approach of embedding one end of the link in a source document is still employed. The related-term-group element could be made into an inline extended link, with the inline related term being given as character data within the related-term-group element itself. These are the changes to the declarations for related-term-group:

```
<!ELEMENT related-term-group
        (#PCDATA | related-term)*>
<!ATTLIST related-term-group
        XML-LINK CDATA #FIXED "EXTENDED"
        INLINE CDATA #FIXED "TRUE"
        CONTENT-ROLE CDATA #FIXED "RT"
        ...>
```

The following is the example with the first of the related terms (pine) now given as the content of an inline extended link:

```
<related-term-group>pine
<related-term HREF="beech.xml"/>
<related-term HREF="oak.xml"/>
<related-term HREF="willow.xml"/>
</related-term-group>
```

This linking element can now be placed inside the entry for `pine`.

Notice that it isn't necessary to add any extra attributes to the `related-term-group` element, because the additional information is declared, in fixed form, in the DTD.

The example contains a mixture of locators (the `related-term` elements) and data content. As far as XML-LINK is concerned, only the data content (the word `pine`) counts as the inline resource for the link. The other elements are simply treated as part of the linking mechanism.

Addressing

As you have already seen, XML's HREF attribute specifications are designed to be interoperable with HTML. They consist of a URL, optionally followed by ? and a *query*, or followed by # (or ¦) and a *fragment identifier*. The interpretation of this fragment identifier depends on the type of resource that is referenced by the URL.

This strategy means that you can express links from XML documents to any non-XML resource (image files, HTML pages, Java applets, and so on) using exactly the same URL syntax that you would use from an HTML page. However, XML provides support for more sophisticated addressing within the target resource in cases when that resource is an XML document. Because XML's addressing strategy is interoperable with HTML's, you can use this special addressing from within HTML pages to address parts of XML documents.

Locator Syntax for XML Resources

XML interprets the general conventions for URLs in a scheme-specific manner when the target of the link is an XML resource.

The URL part, if present, is treated as a standard URL and identifies the *containing resource* that is the target of the link (that is, the document, normally). If no URL is given, the document in which the link is contained is taken to be the containing resource. This is exactly what HTML browsers do with HTML URLs.

Any fragment identifier is treated as an *XPointer*. If an XPointer is provided, the target resource is a *sub-resource* of the containing resource.

This fragment identifier is preceded by a *connector*, which can be one of the following:

■ The # connector is a standard HTML-style connector.

■ The ¦ connector is an XML-specific connector.

These two types of connectors indicate how and where the fragment is to be located and processed.

The # connector asks for all of the containing resource to be delivered to the client, which then has the job of locating the fragment for itself. (This is exactly the same behavior that you see for # fragments in HTML links.)

The ¦ connector means that the server does not necessarily need to deliver the whole containing resource to the client. An XML-aware browser could, for example, query the server to find out how large the containing resource is. If this resource is larger than a certain size, the browser could ask the server to locate just the required fragment and deliver only that part of the resource.

XPointers Made Easy

The simplest fragment identifier supported by XML involves putting a Name (in the specialized XML sense defined in Chapter 5, "The XML Approach") after the Connector, as in this example:

```
<LINK HREF="http://www.sq.com/overview.xml#sect1"/>
```

Here, the fragment identifier sect1 is a shorthand for the XPointer:

```
ID(sect1)
```

It specifies that the target sub-resource is the element in the containing resource (www.sq.com/overview.xml) with ID = "sect1".

This neatly kills two birds with one stone! From an HTML perspective, it looks the same as the following familiar syntax:

```
<A HREF="http://www.sq.com/index.htm#section1">
```

> Warning: The XML and HTML conventions are *not* exactly the same. In HTML, the target sub-resource is normally the <A> element with a NAME attribute equal to the specified value. In XML, the target is *any* element with an attribute of type ID whose value is equal to the required value. You should

> also be aware that XML attributes do not have to be called *ID* in order to be of type `ID`, although it is certainly considered bad form to give them any other name.
>
> HTML 4.0 now supports fragment identifiers that reference attributes of type `ID`, bringing it into line with XML practice. However, this is a recent change, and most HTML fragment identifiers will still reference `<A>` elements.

From an XML perspective, this shorthand encourages use of the ID mechanism for addressing. This is a good thing for two reasons:

■ The XML language specification guarantees that ID values are unique within each valid XML document. This rules out the possibility of two identically named targets within a single document (which is possible with the HTML approach).

■ Because IDs are arbitrary names, they are unlikely to be changed as the document is updated over time. This means that they are more likely to remain valid targets than the other addressing mechanisms, which involve various kinds of counting through the structure of the document.

You should recall one thing at this point from the general review of HTML and XML. XML elements are different from HTML because they always have a well-defined scope. This affects linking. When you link to a part of an HTML document, as in the following code, you are in effect jumping to a specific *point* within that document:

```
<A HREF="otherdoc.htm#section4">See also Section 4.</A>
```

This is often the point where Section 4 starts.

The following equivalent XPointer link to a specified part of an XML document points to an element with an ID equal to `section4`:

```
<LINK HREF="otherdoc.xml#section4">See also Section 4.</LINK>
```

You might reasonably expect this to be a *chunk*, consisting of everything in Section 4.

The fact that the fragment identifier references a well-defined chunk, rather than just a point within the document, makes it possible for you to grab the target of the link (Section 4) and deliver it as a document fragment:

```
<INCLUDE HREF="otherdoc.xml¦=section4"/>
```

It is also what makes the EMBED value for the SHOW attribute meaningful.

In most circumstances, this simple form of the locator syntax is all that you will ever need. As I have said, it is equivalent to the familiar fragment identifiers in HTML, except that it is based on unique ID values. These are certainly the most robust methods of addressing within an XML document, because they do not change simply from routine editing.

> Tip: Because elements with attribute values of type ID can be referenced by this easy form of XML fragment identifier, it is a good idea to sprinkle your XML documents with sensible ID values. In addition to making it easier for you to cross-reference within and between your own XML documents, this makes life easier for other Web users who want to make links into parts of your XML documents. If someone else wants to refer to a specific part of an XML document that you have placed on the Web, that person can use the *preferred* form of ID-based fragment identifier, but only if the element to be linked to has been given an ID—by you.

The Rest of the XPointer Syntax

Just in case you do need to use it, let's review the XPointer syntax in full.

The ultimate goal of an XPointer is to direct you to the correct element within the target XML document. However, doing this is a bit like directing someone to a single house in your town; it is difficult to give perfect directions in one try. You might start with a named landmark, give a direction, count streets, and then describe houses. Here is an example:

```
go to the Central Station
head west on Station Road
take the third tree-lined road on the left
it's the fourth house on the right-hand side
```

Each of these instructions is dependent on the traveler following the previous instructions correctly.

XPointers work in exactly the same way. They are a sequence of *location terms*, which are either absolute locations or locations relative to the previous one. XPointers describe elements within the document in terms of various properties such as their type or attribute values, or simply by counting them.

A fragment identifier can contain a single XPointer or two XPointers separated by the .. directive. If it has two XPointers, the fragment is assumed to be everything from the start of the first XPointer's target to the end of the second one.

> **Warning:** You can't assume that a fragment that is specified by a pair of XPointers will be a meaningful chunk of the document. It is very unlikely to be a single element, or even a whole number of elements. This limits what an XML application can expect to do with such fragments.

Thus, the XPointer equivalent to the previous directions might look like this:

```
go to the element with ID = "intro.notes"
find the second <DIV3> element within this element
find the fourth <P> within this <DIV3> element
```

This set of directions would be expressed as the following XPointer:

```
ID(intro.notes)CHILD(2,DIV3)(4,P)
```

To put this more formally, each location term is defined in the context of a location source, which is the place it starts from.

The XPointer syntax is based on an addressing system developed as part of the *Text Encoding Initiative* (TEI) guidelines. The TEI Extended Pointer scheme has been slightly simplified for use in XML. More importantly, the syntax has been adjusted so that XML's XPointers can sit comfortably inside URLs.

> **Note:** Specifically, commas have replaced spaces within XPointers, so that it is not necessary to put in escape sequences for spaces within the URL. Also, the .. construction allows a pair of XPointers (representing a span within the target document) to be placed in a single URL. In the TEI scheme, the ends of a span are declared in two separate attributes—FROM and TO.

Absolute Location Terms

Each XPointer starts with one of the following absolute location terms:

■ ROOT() confirms that the location source for the first location term is the root element.

- ■ HERE() states that the location source for the first location term is the linking element containing the locator. This can be used meaningfully only if the target is in the same document as the link.

- ■ ID(Name) states that the location source for the first location term is the element with the specified ID (as in the previous example)

- ■ DITTO() can be used only at the start of the second XPointer of a pair. It states that the location source for the first location term is the location that the first XPointer found.

- ■ HTML(NAMEVALUE) states that the location source for the first location term is the first element of type A that has a NAME attribute whose value matches NAMEVALUE.

By default, the location source for the first location term is the *root element* of the XML document that is the containing resource. This means that, strictly speaking, you never need to specify ROOT(). However, including ROOT() does make the intention of your XPointer clearer to a human reader.

Relative Location Terms

When you have a starting point (a location source) for your XPointer, you can use relative location terms to move around the target XML document. Each relative location term consists of a *keyword*, followed by one or more *steps*. The allowed keywords are as follows:

- ■ CHILD selects child elements of the location source.

- ■ DESCENDANT selects elements appearing within the content of the location source.

- ■ ANCESTOR selects elements in whose content the location source is found.

- ■ PSIBLING selects preceding sibling elements of the location source.

- ■ FOLLOWING selects elements that appear after the location source.

- ■ FSIBLING selects following sibling elements of the location source.

By declaring a keyword, you limit the possible targets of a location term to elements that have the required property in relation to the location source. There might be zero or more. For example, if you move to an element with no preceding elements at the same level, the PREVIOUS keyword always fails. The elements that do match up are called *candidate locations*.

The keyword is followed by one or more steps. Each step defines an instance, an optional element type, and an even more optional attribute type and value.

The instance counts the candidate locations. It can be a positive number (found by counting forward from the first candidate location), a negative number (counting backward from the last candidate location), or the special value "ALL", which means all candidate locations are selected. Here are some examples:

```
(4) - select the fourth candidate location
(-2) - select the second-to-last candidate location
```

The instance is followed by a comma and an *element* type, which can take the following values:

- The *CDATA value selects *pseudo-elements* containing only text.
- The * value selects any element type.
- The . value selects elements only.
- The Name value selects elements with the type Name from the candidate locations.

Here are some examples:

```
(4,DIV1) - select the fourth <DIV1> element from the candidate
locations
(-1,EXAMPLE) - select the last <EXAMPLE> element from the
candidate locations
(3,*CDATA) - select the third untagged span of text from the
candidate locations
```

The element type, if specified, can be qualified by an attribute name and value.

The attribute name can take the following values:

- The * value matches any attribute name.
- The Name value specifies the attribute type Name.

The attribute value can take the following values:

- The *IMPLIED value matches attributes for which no value was specified and no default exists.
- The * value matches any value.
- The Name value matches the value Name, normalized into uppercase and with spaces normalized.
- The "value" value matches the value that is quoted.

Here is an example:

```
CHILD(1,FS,RESP,*IMPLIED)
```

This example selects the first <FS> element with the RESP attribute left unspecified, which is a child of the location source.

String-Match Location Terms

All of the absolute and relative location terms that I have described have as their target one or more complete elements. In order to allow text within an element to be the target of an XPointer, the STRING() location term is provided. If used, STRING() must be the last location term in the XPointer.

The STRING() location term takes the following three arguments:

- A number that indicates which occurrence of the specified string is required.
- The string to be matched.
- A number that indicates how many characters to count forward from the start of the matched string.

All three arguments must be provided every time STRING() is used. For example, this XPointer points to the ninth character after the start of the second occurrence of the string "Location Term" in the whole document:

```
ROOT()STRING(2,"Location Term",9)
```

This character is the letter T at the start of Term.

This XPointer selects the character immediately following the fifth exclamation mark within the element with an ID value equal to a27:

```
ID(a27)STRING(5,'!',1)
```

This definition means that the target of a STRING() location term is always a single character. To mark a range of characters, such as the actual phrase "Location Term", you need to use a span. This XPointer points to the range of characters from the beginning (offset 0) to the end (offset 12) of the second occurrence of "Location Term" in the document:

```
ROOT()STRING(2,"Location Term",0)..ROOT()STRING(2,"Location
Term",12)
```

All of the character data within the location source is used when looking for a string match. Markup is ignored completely. The matching has to be exact; it is case sensitive, and all spaces have to be exactly as specified in STRING(). Therefore, the "Location Term" example given previously would match the string within

```
<p>It is a <emph>Location</emph> Term ...
```

However, the newline (which does not match the space in the STRING() location term) means that the following markup will not give a match:

```
<p>It is a <emph>Location</emph>
[Term ...
```

Extended Link Groups

Because XML supports extended (out-of-line) links—which do not have to occur within either, or any, of the documents they point to—you need some means of telling an XML application where to find them. XML achieves this with *extended link groups,* which simply list the documents that combine to form an interlinked group.

The GROUP element contains one or more DOCUMENT elements, each pointing to a resource (or a sub-resource, using the XPointer syntax) that is considered to form part of the document group.

For example, if an XML document contains

```
<GROUP>
<DOCUMENT HREF="http://www.mysite.org/links1.xml"/>
<DOCUMENT HREF="http://www.mysite.org/links2.xml"/>
</GROUP>
```

where GROUP and DOCUMENT have XML-LINK values of GROUP and DOCUMENT, then an XML processor would process the documents links1.xml and links2.xml looking for links that involve this document.

It is possible that the resource identified by DOCUMENT will itself contain GROUP elements that point to yet more linked documents. These could point to even more documents, including the one you started with. To avoid situations like this, which could lead to endless program loops in XML applications, the DOCU-MENT element has a STEPS attribute. This allows authors to indicate how many steps of Extended Link Group processing it makes sense for an XML link processor to carry out. In this example, the link processor is advised to process Extended Link Groups in the starting document, and those that it finds in links1.xml and links2.xml. It is advised that it should then stop.

```
<GROUP STEPS="2">
<DOCUMENT HREF="http://www.mysite.org/links1.xml"/>
<DOCUMENT HREF="http://www.mysite.org/links2.xml"/>
</GROUP>
```

Summary

This chapter reviewed XML's linking facilities. You learned how XML's linking builds upon the Web's current hypertext facilities by using URLs and interoperating with HTML hyperlinks.

However, XML links allow users to control the behavior of links much more closely, and they provide support for two-way and multidirectional linking through the concept of out-of-line links.

I reviewed the methods by which XML allows you to address any single element or span of elements as a link target within an XML document.

Finally, you learned how you can help an XML processor to find out-of-line links that involve the current document but are not physically stored within it.

CHAPTER 10

The XML Style Mechanism

by Richard Light

Chapter 2, "Enter XML," briefly discussed the XML style sheet language known as XS. XML needs a style language that goes beyond Cascading Style Sheets. In this chapter, I go into XS in a little more detail.

Just as XML is a "profile" of the SGML standard, so XS is an application profile of the DSSSL standard (Document Style and Semantics Specification Language, ISO/IEC 10179). XS's scope is to support the style sheet requirements of XML browsers and editors. It is meant to be a baseline specification; there is nothing to stop software providers from developing products that offer a more complete implementation of DSSSL, or that integrate non-DSSSL extensions.

> Warning: You should be aware that the formal adoption of the XS specification is still in the future. See Chapter 17, "Resolution of the XML Specification," for details. I have pitched my description of XS at a broad level that, in my judgment, still will apply to XML's final specification.

This book has been processed by a DSSSL-O (XS-like) style sheet. It was authored in SGML and a style sheet was written to convert it to RTF (Rich Text Format). It was a straightforward job to convert this RTF file to the Word format used in this book's publishing process. I use parts of that style sheet as examples in this chapter.

Style Sheets: Why Bother?

Start by considering why style sheets might be a good idea. If you can manage to produce HTML pages that look really cool without any extra help, why bother with style sheets at all?

Separating Style From Markup

One good reason for using style sheets is that moving style information to a separate style file can dramatically simplify your markup. If you look at the source of some typical HTML pages, you will see that the markup is packed with attributes whose only purpose is to specify how the element should be displayed on the screen:

```
<body
bgcolor="#FFFFFF"
text="#000000"
link="#054BBB"
vlink="#054BBB"
background="/Images/backshadow2.gif">
```

or:

```
<img src="/Images/bump.gif"
border=0
width=50
height=5
align=left>
```

Putting this information into the markup is bad for the following reasons:

- More work: If an element type has five display-related attributes, for example, you will have to fill these in each time you add an example of that element type.

- Potential inconsistency: If you want a consistent look and feel to your pages, it is your responsibility to ensure that you use the display-related attributes in a consistent manner. This also applies when you make changes to the style of your pages.

- Inflexibility: Page display instructions are built into the pages themselves, making it difficult to display them any other way. You cannot optimize the display of your pages so that they look good in every browser software your clients might use.

- Obfuscation: Having all that display information in the markup makes it harder to see the underlying structure.

If you strip out all the style-related attributes from the two examples, you are left with the following:

```
<body>
```

or:

```
<img src="/Images/bump.gif">
```

which is much clearer.

Obviously, the display-related information that was declared as attribute values within the element's start tag has to be provided somehow; this is where the style sheet comes in.

Multiple Styles = Multiple Products

Removing style information from your XML documents allows you to do even more things with them.

Your primary purpose might be only an HTML-style information delivery on the Web. Even within this routine type of application, you can gain benefits from multiple style sheets. As a service provider, you can offer the following:

- Large-print versions of your documents for the visually impaired

- Preview versions of long documents that provide an abstract and structured overview of the full text

- Public and private versions of documents, with confidential details available only to those who have the required access level

In each case, exactly the same XML document would be displayed. The differences would be controlled by the style sheets associated with that document. Without style sheets, you probably would be faced with creating different forms of each document by hand to support these different requirements.

As a Web client, you might also want to use XS style sheets to control the way incoming documents look.

XS and Generic XML Applications

After you move away from HTML-like documents and into custom XML applications, a style language becomes essential.

Users have become accustomed to HTML browsers that "know about" HTML markup, and these browsers do a decent, forgiving job of rendering HTML pages. This rendering is possible because the semantics of HTML markup are widely understood and agreed upon. Even so, in some areas of markup (such as tables) a page will look sensible only if a particular browser is used.

Generally, an XML browser cannot be expected to have the knowledge to display the elements found within a custom application. Therefore, the browser needs to be fed this information, and that requires a style sheet.

How Do XS Style Sheets Work?

An XS style sheet controls the process of formatting a valid or well-formed XML document. It applies formatting characteristics to portions of the data. However, it cannot finish the job of paginating the document onto a screen or printed page. That job is left to a *back-end processor*, which knows about the target environment and can implement the formatting instructions in a sensible way.

As discussed in Chapter 2, a *flow object tree* is what the style engine passes to the back-end processor. This flow object tree contains *flow objects*, which represent display elements (paragraphs, tables, table-rows, characters, and so on). The flow object tree is created by merging the source document with the style sheet instructions.

This discussion of the mechanics of style sheets is all getting a bit abstract. Probably the best way to understand how XS works is to jump right in and take a walk through the process. In this section I'll use the Sams.net style sheet to format this small but well-formed XML document:

```
<?XML version="1.0"?>
<p>Hello world!</p>
```

The Core Expression Language

Before starting, here's some background. All XS style sheets use a low-level language called the *core expression language*, which is based on the Scheme Programming Language. Scheme is itself a dialect of Lisp. Although you won't learn this language, a couple of basics might help you to follow the examples of XS code that I will present in this section.

Parentheses are used to indicate procedure calls. As an example, consider the built-in * operator that carries out multiplication. The procedure call

```
(* 3 5)
```

says multiply 3 times 5, and therefore returns the result, 15. This is rather different from the way that multiplication is expressed in many programming languages.

Literal values (which have a specific meaning in the XS language) are introduced by a single quotation mark:

```
'start
```

This is a different syntax from that used for ordinary strings, which can contain anything you like:

```
"[SAMSFT]"
```

The core expression language is really low-level stuff. You can think of the XS style language (which is defined using the core expression language) as a high-level application.

What's in the Style Sheet?

An XS style sheet consists of many types of declarations, definitions, and rules. However, you can get a long way with just the following two:

- Definitions: Define procedures, using the full power of the underlying *core expression language*.
- Construction rules: Express rules for constructing parts of the flow object tree when a certain element is encountered.

Here are the parts of the Sams.net style sheet that you need to format your paragraph: two definitions and one construction rule.

First comes the definition of the STANDARD-PARAGRAPH procedure:

```
(define (STANDARD-PARAGRAPH)
  (make paragraph
        use: p-style
     space-after: *para-sep*
     quadding: 'start
     (literal "[SAMSFT]")
     (process-children-trim)))
```

Next comes the *element construction rule*. It uses the STANDARD-PARAGRAPH procedure you have just defined in the preceding code:

```
(element P (STANDARD-PARAGRAPH))
```

Finally, the STANDARD-PARAGRAPH procedure contains the following line:

```
use: p-style
```

This line refers to a predefined paragraph style, which is defined as follows:

```
(define p-style
  (style
     font-size: *bf-size*
     line-spacing: (* *bf-size* *line-spacing-factor*)))
```

That's all you need from the full specification to get started. Now look at each component in turn.

Procedures

You first have an example of a procedure definition:

```
(define (STANDARD-PARAGRAPH)
  ...)
```

In general, these definitions take the following form:

```
 (define (PROCNAME [arguments])
  PROCEDURE-BODY)
```

The definitions associate the procedure PROCNAME with the code in PROCEDURE-BODY. PROCNAME can optionally have one or more arguments; this example doesn't have any.

You can set up any number of procedures in your XS style sheets. In general, it's a good idea to place the complex processing you need to do inside procedures, which means you can simplify the appearance of the construction rules for each element. For really complex processing, you can write procedures that call other procedures to any level of nesting.

Flow Object Classes

So what is in this procedure? The first line, which follows, says that you should construct a *paragraph flow object* to add to your flow object tree:

```
(make paragraph
```

A paragraph flow object is just one example of a *flow object class*. The XS specification defines the following 25 flow object classes as mandatory:

- sequence
- display-group
- simple-page-sequence
- paragraph
- paragraph-break
- line-field
- sideline
- character
- leader
- rule
- external-graphic
- score
- box
- alignment-point
- aligned-column
- table
- table-part
- table-column
- table-row
- table-cell
- table-border
- scroll
- multi-mode
- link
- marginalia

The purpose of some of these will be self-evident: paragraph, external-graphic, table-row, box. Others require a deeper study of the XS specification.

In general, flow objects, when formatted, give rise to *areas* in the result. They can be *displayed,* which means that they are a separate block (like this paragraph), or *inlined,* in which case they form part of the flow of text (like this piece of code within the paragraph).

One flow object class is worth discussing in its own right—the *character flow object class.*

You might have been wondering where the text of your document fits into this flow object tree. The answer is that it doesn't! Instead, by default, each individual character in the document causes a character flow object to be added to the flow object tree.

So, in this example, you start with a sequence of characters inside a p element, like this:

```
<p>Hello world!</p>
```

And you end up with a sequence of character flow objects inside a paragraph flow object. You might represent this in an XML-like way, as shown in the following code:

```
<paragraph>
  <character char="H"/>
  <character char="e"/>
  <character char="l"/>
  <character char="l"/>
  <character char="o"/>
  <character char=" "/>
  <character char="w"/>
  <character char="o"/>
  <character char="r"/>
  <character char="l"/>
  <character char="d"/>
  <character char="!"/>
</paragraph>
```

Characteristics

The next three lines of your XS specification specify (directly or indirectly) the *characteristics* of your paragraph flow object, like this:

```
use: p-style
space-after: *para-sep*
quadding: 'start
```

Each type (or class) of flow object has a large number of characteristics, any of which you can specify if you so choose. The paragraph flow object class, for example, has more than 60 characteristics.

The character flow object class has more than 40 characteristics. These characteristics allow you to specify, in minute detail, exactly how individual characters in your XML documents will be displayed.

Inheritance of Characteristics

However, it is not necessary to provide a mass of information in order to get anything to display! Apart from having sensible default behavior, XS supports the concept of *inheritance* of characteristics. This states that, in general, if a characteristic isn't specified for a flow object, the value specified by the nearest ancestor of that flow object will apply instead.

For example, if the characteristic font-size isn't specified for a character flow object (which it normally is not), the parent flow object is checked out. In this case, the parent flow object is your paragraph, which specifies the font size. (If the font size wasn't specified at all, a default font size of 10pt would apply.)

Characteristics of Your Sample Paragraph

The following are the definitions of the paragraph characteristics that you are using in your example:

- font-size: A length specifying the body size to which the font resource should be scaled.
- line-spacing: A length specification giving the normal spacing between lines in the paragraph.
- space-after: The space to be inserted after the paragraph.
- quadding: One of the symbols, start, end, spread-inside, spread-outside, page-inside, page-outside, center, or justify, specifying the alignment of lines other than the last line in the paragraph.

Returning to your STANDARD-PARAGRAPH procedure, the first line tells you to find a style called p-style and apply that style. When you unwrap the definition of p-style, you find that it contains specifications for two characteristics:

```
font-size: *bf-size*
line-spacing: (* *bf-size* *line-spacing-factor*)
```

These characteristics specify the font size and line spacing, but not in an absolute way. Instead, they use the variable *bf-size*, which is defined elsewhere in the Sams.net style specification:

```
(define *bf-size*
 (case *visual-acuity*
   (("normal") 10pt)
   (("presbyopic") 12pt)
   (("large-type") 24pt)))
```

Here you see more of the power of the core expression language. This means that if the variable *visual-acuity* is set to "normal", *bf-size* will be set to 10pt. If *visual-acuity* is set to "presbyopic", *bf-size* will be set to 12pt. And if *visual-acuity* is set to "large-type", *bf-size* will be set to 24pt. Therefore, by setting the *visual-acuity* variable, you can control the font size of the whole display!

The value that *bf-size* ends up with is used directly as the font-size characteristic of your paragraph. The line-spacing characteristic is calculated by doing a little math on the body font size. It is multiplied by the line spacing factor, which is defined as 1.1 so that the gaps between lines are slightly larger than the body font size. (110%, to be exact. XS supports real-number math.)

```
(define *line-spacing-factor* 1.1)
```

The second line specifies the space-after characteristic:

```
space-after: *para-sep*
```

Again, the space after the paragraph is given as a variable. *para-sep* is defined as half the body font size:

```
(define *para-sep* (/ *bf-size* 2.0))
```

The last characteristic to be defined for your paragraph is quadding, which has the built-in value 'start:

```
quadding: 'start
```

This means that the paragraph is left-justified.

To summarize, you have just specified that your paragraph flow object has the following characteristics, assuming that you set *visual-acuity* to have the value "normal":

```
font-size: 10pt
line-spacing: 11pt
space-after: 5pt
quadding: 'start
```

Element Construction Rules

"What next?" you might ask! The good news is that you've already done the hard part. Having specified the characteristics of your paragraph flow object in the STANDARD-PARAGRAPH procedure, all you need to do now is associate that procedure with the p element. You do this with the following *element construction rule*:

```
(element P (STANDARD-PARAGRAPH))
```

This type of construction rule is central to the whole XS style process. In this case, the arrival of a p element triggers this rule, which in turn starts up the process of formatting your sample paragraph.

Starting Up the Style Engine

In the previous section, you saw how a style sheet is developed and what it contains. In this section I will explain how an XS style sheet is actually used to format an XML document.

Processing the Source Document as a Grove

Before trying to process your well-formed sample XML document, the XS engine first turns the document into a *grove*:

```
<?XML version="1.0"?>
<p>Hello world!</p>
```

> **Note:** You might remember groves from Chapter 6, "Logical Structures in XML Documents."

In this simple case, you can just think of the grove as a slightly larger tree structure—an XML-document node containing a processing instruction (the XML declaration), and a single element node with property gi="p" containing 12 data character nodes with the char property equal to the character in question.

This grove is then traversed. By default, all elements, attribute specifications, and data characters are processed (and therefore are converted to flow objects), while all other types of nodes are ignored.

> Note: The decision to include only elements, attribute specifications, and data characters is quite significant. When an XML document is represented as a grove, *everything* in that document becomes a node in that grove, as long as it is part of the *grove plan*. By default, this includes things such as processing instructions and the entities associated with the document. This design ensures that such things do not appear in the formatted output.

Choosing the Most Appropriate Construction Rule

On encountering a node of class `element` in the source grove, the style engine finds the most appropriate construction rule for it. In this case, there isn't much choice! The following is your only element construction rule:

```
(element P (STANDARD-PARAGRAPH))
```

However, in general, it is possible to have a number of alternative construction rules, which pick out elements because

- They match a query.
- They have a specific unique `ID`.
- They have a specific ancestry.
- They have a specified `GI` (name).

In particular, it is often convenient to specify that elements that appear in a certain context are displayed differently. You do this by including the ancestor element's name in the element construction rule. Here you have three different sets of instructions for the `head` element, depending on whether it is inside a `div1`, `div2`, or `div3` element:

```
(element (DIV1 HEAD) (HEADING-WITH-PREFIX "a"))
(element (DIV2 HEAD) (HEADING-WITH-PREFIX "b"))
(element (DIV3 HEAD) (HEADING-WITH-PREFIX "c"))
```

These three more specific instructions for the `head` element take precedence over the following element construction rule that applies to `head` elements in any context. This procedure has the effect that, by default, `head` elements will appear italic and centered:

```
(element HEAD (ITALIC-CENTERED-PARAGRAPH))
```

Formatting the Sample Paragraph's Content

Now return to your sample paragraph, and see what happens next. So far, your STANDARD-PARAGRAPH procedure has created a paragraph flow object with certain characteristics specified (and with the rest given default values, or values inherited from its ancestor flow objects).

Now you come to the following two lines:

```
(literal "[SAMSFT]")
(process-children-trim)
```

The first line uses the built-in XS command literal, which adds the string "[SAMSFT]" to the start of your paragraph. Well, that's the effect, but remember that you are now working with flow objects, which don't have a place for character data. Therefore, your literal command actually creates eight character flow objects, one for each character in the string, and attaches them to the paragraph flow object. It is thus equivalent to the following, but a great deal more user-friendly:

```
(make character char: #\[)
(make character char: #\S)
(make character char: #\A)
(make character char: #\M)
(make character char: #\S)
(make character char: #\F)
(make character char: #\T)
(make character char: #\])
```

> Note: Each of these lines creates a *character flow object* and sets its char characteristic to the correct character. #\X is the correct way of specifying the character X in the core expression language.

Finally, you come to the following command:

```
(process-children-trim)
```

This is another built-in XS command, which processes the children of the p element after stripping leading and trailing spaces. Because your sample document is now treated as a grove, the children of the p element include all the data characters within it, as well as any child elements. Each character is a separate node in the source grove's tree structure.

You haven't issued any specific commands to say what you want done with these characters, and you don't have to. By default, data characters are output to the current flow object. Putting that more formally, nodes with a char property (data characters, to you and me) have a default construction rule that returns and copies the char property from the source node to the newly created character flow object:

```
(make character)
```

Ports

The reason that these data characters end up in your paragraph flow object, rather than somewhere else, is that the instructions to process them are nested inside the *make-expression* for the paragraph:

```
(make paragraph
  ...
  (literal "[SAMSFT]")
  (process-children-trim))
```

This means that the paragraph has two *content-expressions*.

I have cheerfully stated that all of these data characters (the literal string "[SAMSFT]" and the data characters "Hello world!" from the p element) have been added to the paragraph flow object. That's an intuitively obvious idea, but there is a name for it in the XS language.

In order to be able to add flow objects as children of an existing flow object, that flow object has to have a *port*. This is a place where a list of one or more flow objects can be attached. By default, a flow object has a single port, called the *principal port*. Besides the principal port, you can have additional named ports, but those are only for advanced XS users.

Not every flow object has a port; for example, character flow objects never do. A flow object that doesn't have a port is called an *atomic flow object*. Atomic flow objects are the "leaf nodes" of the flow object tree.

A Generalized Result

The result you have now produced—this flow object tree—is still rather generalized. To be sure, it describes the flow objects that are to be output, and it specifies some of their characteristics very precisely. However, it is not a real formatted page, or even a page description language such as PostScript.

This strategy of producing a generalized result is deliberate. XS expects to work with a back-end processor that knows about the physical target environment for your formatted document. XS leaves some decisions (such as line wrapping strategy) to that back-end processor, which is intended to give optimal formatting performance, while allowing the style sheet to specify the required result very precisely.

A Real Result!

Your XS engine is tied to a back-end processor that generates RTF. The result can be read directly into Word. So, in this example, you have used XS to produce a formatted result that is actually editable. If you had chosen instead to use a back-end processor that produced PostScript, you would have an unrevisable result.

Yes, you've done it! Your XS style sheet has now produced a formatted paragraph within a Word document:

```
[SAMSFT]Hello world!
```

> Note: You might be asking yourself what is the purpose of the string
> "[SAMSFT]". It is placed at the start of each paragraph so that a Word macro
> can convert the paragraph to one that uses Sams FT (Flow Text) style. This
> restyling of the text was the last stage in the conversion of this book from its
> SGML source to a set of Word documents that fit into the Sams editorial
> process.

Now review how you produced a formatted paragraph from a well-formed XML document:

- You wrote an XS style sheet, which said that p elements generate a paragraph flow object, containing the literal string "[SAMSFT]" followed by the data characters in the paragraph.
- You called the XS style engine and told it to apply your style sheet to your sample document.
- The XS style engine converted your sample document to a grove.
- The XS style engine then scanned the grove to produce a flow object tree, checking each node to see whether it had non-default instructions attached to it, and carrying out default processing if it didn't.

- The XS style engine found that the p element had an element construction rule, and obeyed it.

- This element construction rule generated a paragraph flow object, with some specified characteristics, containing 18 character flow objects that each inherit the font-size characteristic from the paragraph.

- When rendered on the page or screen, the paragraph becomes a displayed area, with no space before it and a 5pt space after it. It is left-justified, with an 11pt gap between lines.

- The character flow objects are added to the paragraph as inline areas, with a font size of 10pt.

- The complete flow object tree is passed to a back-end processor that produces a real formatted result—in this case, a paragraph within an RTF document.

Some Refinements

You have now been through the basic process of formatting an XML document with XS, and you might want to skip to the next chapter at this point. That's fine. What follows isn't necessary for a basic understanding of how XS works.

In this section, you look at how to refine your XS style sheets in various ways. However, this isn't, by any means, a full overview of what XS can do. (That would be another book!)

One mark of a good style sheet language is that it lets you specify precisely how you want your documents to look. Think about how you can take advantage of the markup in your XML documents to control the formatting process.

Different Types of Construction Rules

Your example used a simple element construction rule that applied to all paragraphs:

```
(element P (STANDARD-PARAGRAPH))
```

However, this isn't the only type of construction rule you can specify.

You can specify a default construction rule that will apply to any element that doesn't have a rule of its own:

```
(default (STANDARD-PARAGRAPH))
```

This line of code would (perhaps unwisely) make any "unmatched" element into a separate paragraph.

You've already seen that XS has a built-in feature that lets you test for an element's ancestor in an element construction rule:

```
(element (DIV1 HEAD) (HEADING-WITH-PREFIX "a"))
```

This element construction rule fires only if the current node is a head element with a div1 element as its parent. If it matches, it takes precedence over any rules for head that don't specify a parent element type.

To be even more specific, you can write *id construction rules* that will fire for only the one element that has the specified ID:

```
(id "figure.2" (SPECIAL-GRAPHIC))
```

This rule applies the procedure SPECIAL-GRAPHIC to the single element (if any) that has ID="figure.2". If this rule matches, it takes precedence over any element construction rule that might otherwise apply.

Clearly, this level of specificity is useful only in style sheets that are designed for a single document. If you want a more general means of controlling formatting based on your document's markup, you can make use of the XS style language within your element construction rules.

Using Attribute Specifications to Control Formatting

One obvious thing you might want to do is vary the formatting based on attribute values. This lets you put a degree of fine control in the user's hands. Attribute specifications can be picked up and used directly in the style sheet. You might, for example, provide an INDENT attribute that allows users to specify the initial indentation of each paragraph:

```
<p indent="10">
```

Your style spec could pick up the value of the INDENT attribute, and use it directly to specify the first-line-start-indent property for that paragraph.

> Note: Too much use of this facility would be counterproductive. It would be quite possible to end up in a position where users' markup was once again full of attributes specifying formatting—one of the problems we set out to solve! However, it is reassuring to know that XML will support user-specified formatting.

Take as another example the note elements in this book. Various types of notes make it into the book: straightforward notes and notes as tips and warnings. Some other notes you never see—comments I made for my own reference while writing. I use the TYPE attribute to specify what type of note each note element is, as shown in the following:

```
<note>A plain ol' note.</note>
<note type="warning">A warning!</note>
<note type="hidden">For my eyes only ...</note>
```

My style sheet to output the book for delivery to Sams.net has to take account of these differences.

This is what I came up with. It uses a procedure called STANDARD-NOTE, which is called up by the element construction rule for note:

```
(element NOTE (STANDARD-NOTE))
```

Sound familiar?

The STANDARD-NOTE procedure looks like this:

```
(define (STANDARD-NOTE)
  (if (attribute-string "type" (current-node))
    (if (string=? (attribute-string "type" (current-node))
"hidden")
      (empty-sosofo)
      (BOXED-PARAGRAPH (attribute-string "type" (current-node))))
    (BOXED-PARAGRAPH "note")))
```

This procedure says the following:

■ If the TYPE attribute is specified and its value is hidden, discard this note.

■ If the TYPE attribute is specified and its value is anything else, output this note as a boxed paragraph, with the value of the TYPE attribute as the heading.

■ If the TYPE attribute isn't specified, output this note as a boxed paragraph with "note" as the heading.

Even if you are a programmer, you might find the logic of this procedure a little less than obvious unless you are familiar with Lisp-type languages. Again, the point is not to provide a tutorial in the XS language, but to give you an idea of its possibilities. If you want to understand what is going on here, the following might help.

The `if` expression takes three arguments: a test, a consequent (`then`), and an alternate (`else"`). If the test is true, the consequent is evaluated and its value is returned; otherwise, the alternate is evaluated and its value is returned. For example, the following returns `yes` because the test expression is true (3 is greater than 2):

```
(if (> 3 2) 'yes 'no)
```

My `STANDARD-NOTE` procedure contains two `if` expressions; the second one is the consequent of the first.

`(empty-sosofo)` is a built-in command that stands for "empty specification of sequence of flow objects." It means, in effect, "discard this node and all of its child nodes." The ability to discard selected parts of the document's tree structure makes it possible, for example, to present an XML document with confidential information suppressed:

```
(define (CHECK-SECRET)
  (if (attribute-string "class" (current-node))
    (if (string=? (attribute-string "class" (current-node))
"secret")
      (empty-sosofo)
      (process-children))))
```

The Core Query Language

The XS language includes expressions that give you access to many of the properties of element nodes in the grove that represents your XML document. These are called, collectively, the *core query language*.

For example, the expression `(current-node)` returns the element you are currently trying to process. You can use that expression to access the properties of the current node:

```
(attribute-string "type" (current-node))
```

This node returns a string if the current node has a `TYPE` attribute whose value has been specified. Otherwise, it returns the value `false`.

You also can access the properties of the parent of the current node or any of its ancestors:

```
(gi (parent (current-node)))
```

This procedure call returns the `gi` (element type name) of the current element's parent.

Summary

In this chapter, I discussed a difficult topic: the XS style sheet mechanism.

I began by reviewing the arguments for having a separate style sheet mechanism, including the following:

- The simplification of markup when formatting instructions are removed from it
- The consistency achieved by applying formatting as a separate exercise
- The ability to produce multiple products from each XML document
- The need for some general means of controlling the formatting of generic XML

You saw how a simple `"Hello world!"` paragraph might be formatted by an XS style specification. In the process of doing this, you discovered that XS works by converting the XML document to be formatted into a grove. It then scans that grove and merges it with the style specification.

You found that the result is another kind of tree structure—a flow object tree—which is a nested structure of flow objects. Everything that will appear in the result, even data characters, is converted to a flow object. Each flow object has characteristics, which determine how it will be rendered in the formatted result.

The flow object tree is a slightly abstract representation of the paginated result you are after. It requires the cooperation of a back-end processor to turn it into a formatted result. Depending on the delivery format chosen, this can be a fixed (read-only) or a revisable result.

In your encounters with the XS language, you discovered that it has three levels:

- The core expression language—a dialect of Scheme, which is the basis for the whole language and provides some built-in low-level expressions
- The core query language, which provides access to information about XML document-type objects in the grove
- The XS style language proper, which provides high-level commands specifically designed to support the production of a flow object tree

Finally, I started to explore the immense power and flexibility that XS will offer—just as soon as we can get a grip on the XS language!

CHAPTER 11

The XML Processor

by Richard Light

As I discuss in Chapter 2, "Enter XML," the XML language draft describes a piece of software called the XML processor. In this chapter, I outline the jobs that the XML processor is required to do.

The XML-Lang specification says the following about the XML processor:

> "A software module called an XML processor is used to read XML documents and provide access to their content and structure. It is assumed that an XML processor is doing its work on behalf of another module, referred to as the application. This specification describes the required behavior of an XML processor in terms of how it must read XML data and the information it must provide to the application."

In this chapter, I go through the XML-Lang specification and summarize that "required behavior of an XML processor."

Types of XML Processors

Conforming XML processors can work at one of two levels.

A *non-validating XML processor* checks XML documents for well-formedness. This means that the XML processor does not always have to make use of the information in the DTD. However, in order to be conforming, a nonvalidating XML processor must be able to process XML DTDs correctly. It must be able to read the DTD on request in order to check that an XML document is well-formed.

A *validating XML processor* additionally checks that the documents are valid—that they conform to the rules in their DTD and to all the validity constraints specified in the XML-Lang specification. Clearly, the DTD must always be processed to achieve this.

General Ground Rules

There are some general conventions about error handling and the treatment of characters that apply to all XML processors.

Treatment of Errors

XML processors are expected to be good citizens in the XML community, which requires them to know the law and to report any misdemeanors they encounter. In other words, XML processors must have full knowledge of the XML standard. Where the standard says that something must apply, the XML processor is required to behave as described. Where the standard says that something might apply, the XML processor is permitted to, but is not required to, behave as described.

On encountering a *fatal error* in an XML document, an XML processor must report it to the application and discontinue normal processing. It can, however, pass undigested text to the application to help with error correction.

The only mention of fatal errors I can find is when a document violates the rules for a well-formed XML document. On the other hand, violating the rules for validity is a reportable error and is not fatal. This makes sense. A sensibly well-formed document gives you a fully tree-structured object that you can usefully process. Anything less is not really useable.

This strategy for error handling is radically different from the approaches adopted by both HTML and SGML processors (parsers). On one hand, the HTML philosophy is that any page should be processed without complaint whatever errors it might contain. On the other hand, SGML parsers will diligently report each and every error in an SGML document. In both cases, however, the processor will battle on through the document, attempting to recover from the errors it encounters whenever possible.

The XML approach to validity checking is similar to the SGML approach—violations of validity constraints will be reported to the application, and the processor will continue. However, the draconian approach to well-formed constraints in XML is quite new. By saying that an XML processor will stop processing, and so reject any XML document that is not well-formed, the XML-Lang specification is stating quite categorically that well-formedness is the price of admission to the XML world.

Character Processing

Where strings of characters have to be folded to a single case, the XML processor has to fold to uppercase (despite the normal convention for Unicode, which is to fold to lowercase). Uppercase is necessary so that XML can be compatible with SGML, which uses uppercase.

All XML processors must accept the UTF-8 and UCS-2 encodings of ISO 10646 as a minimum. They must be able to use the Byte Order Mark to distinguish between these two encodings. In addition, the XML-Lang specification suggests that it is advantageous for XML processors (and applications) to be capable of interpreting the widest possible range of character encodings.

XML processors must read and act upon any encoding declaration that appears at the start of a text entity. Encoding declarations are described in detail in the "Character Encoding in XML Text Entities" section in Chapter 7, "Physical Structures in XML Documents." It is recommended that XML processors be equipped with a variety of methods of deducing the encoding of an entity when it lacks a suitable encoding declaration. They should use

- HTTP header information
- MIME headers
- Information about the XML text entity provided by the operating system or document management software

If all of the preceding techniques fail to provide reliable information on the encoding of an XML text entity, the XML-Lang specification describes a method for auto-detecting the general class of encoding within an XML text entity that is not encoded in UTF-8 or UCS-2. This technique is based on the knowledge that an XML text entity must begin with an encoding declaration, which in turn must begin with the characters <?XML. When the general class of encoding has been recognized, the XML processor will be able to read the encoding declaration, because that is guaranteed to contain only ASCII characters. It will then know the precise encoding that applies to this XML text entity, and can reliably process it.

If an XML processor cannot recognize or process the encoding of an entity, it should tell the application and offer it the choice of either treating the entity as a binary entity (one that the XML processor does not try to process) or giving up.

A nonvalidating XML processor (which is just looking for well-formedness and is not taking much notice of the DTD) must pass all characters in a document that are not markup to the application. This includes all white space characters. In addition, a validating XML processor must spot where white space can be ignored (because it comes at the start or end of an element with element content only). It must signal to the application that this white space is not significant.

This strategy represents a departure from the precedent set by SGML and HTML processors, which do not pass through to the application any white space around markup that they consider to be insignificant. An XML application is guaranteed to receive every character that appears in the source XML document. The XML processor will tell the application that certain characters are not significant, but it is up to the application to decide whether to suppress them.

Treatment of Logical Markup

The XML processor must follow certain conventions when it is interpreting the logical structure of an XML document. (See Chapter 6, "Logical Structures in XML Documents," for details of XML's logical structures.)

The DTD

Where a document has both an internal DTD subset and an external DTD subset, the XML processor must read the internal subset first, which ensures that local declarations take precedence over global ones.

In deciding whether to read the DTD at all, a nonvalidating XML processor must take account of any required markup declaration (RMD) embedded in the XML declaration at the start of the document. The RMD will say which parts of the DTD must be processed in order to interpret the XML document correctly. If an RMD is not provided, the XML processor must read the whole DTD, if there is one, even when it is not trying to validate the XML document. (See Chapter 8, "Keeping It Tidy: The XML Rule Book," for a full description of the RMD.)

Comments

Where comments appear in the DTD or the document itself, the XML processor might, but is not required to, make it possible for an application to retrieve the text of comments.

Attributes

If an attribute list declares attributes for an element type that is not declared in the DTD, a validating XML processor might warn the user of this fact.

The XML processor might warn the user if there is more than one attribute list declaration for the same element type. This provides for interoperability with existing SGML parsers, which do not permit repeated attribute list declarations.

Again, these are not errors.

Whenever an XML processor encounters an attribute value, it must normalize the value before passing it to the application. Normalizing involves the following:

- Replacing line-end characters (or, on some systems, record boundaries) by a single space character
- Expanding character references and references to internal text entities

- Normalizing all strings of white space to single space characters and removing leading and trailing white space, if the attribute is not of type CDATA

- Folding to uppercase all attribute values of type ID, IDREF, IDREFs, NMTOKEN, NMTOKENs, and all enumerated or notation types

> Note: Normalization of attribute values applies only if the XML processor is reading the DTD; otherwise, all attribute values are treated as though they are CDATA.

The XML processor must deal with attributes that have no specified value. If the rules in the attribute declaration provide a default value, the default value should be passed to the application as though the user had actually specified that value. Otherwise, the XML processor must tell the application that no value was specified for that attribute.

> Note: Even though attribute default values are specified in markup declarations and therefore might be assumed to be of interest only to validating XML processors, nonvalidating XML processors are also required to supply default values.

Notations

When a notation is mentioned in an attribute value, attribute definition, or entity declaration, the XML processor must provide the application with the following basic details about the notation:

- The notation's name
- The notation's external identifier

In addition, the XML processor might choose to resolve the external identifier and provide the application with information (such as a filename) that lets the application actually call up a helper application to deal with the notation in question.

Conditional Sections

The following keyword at the start of a conditional section is a parameter entity reference:

```
<![%optional.extras;[
...
]]>
```

This parameter entity reference should be resolved before you decide whether to include the following conditional section:

```
<![IGNORE[
...
]]>
```

When processing an IGNORE conditional section, the XML processor must read the conditional section to detect nested conditional sections and to ensure that the end of the outermost (ignored) conditional section is properly detected.

Treatment of Physical Structures

The XML processor must be able to manage the physical entities that constitute an XML document. This section describes the conventions it should follow.

Document Entity

The XML-Lang specification makes no statement on how the XML processor is expected to locate the document entity, which will depend on the application environment in which the XML processor is running.

Entities

The XML processor might warn the user if an entity is declared more than once.

When trying to locate an entity that has a PUBLIC identifier, the XML processor might attempt to use the PUBLIC identifier to generate a URL for that entity. If this fails, the processor must use the SYSTEM identifier that accompanies the PUBLIC identifier. This guarantees that the XML processor will provide the application with the entity in some form (provided at least one URL is valid).

The XML processor is given very precise guidance on how to treat character and general entity references. It should do the following:

- Tell the application that the entity reference has occurred, and provide its name or number. For external entities, it also should provide their SYSTEM and PUBLIC identifiers. For binary external entities, it should provide the notation name and associated details of the notation.

- Remove the reference from the text stream that is passed to the application.

- For character references and internal (text) entities, insert the actual character or text in place of the reference. Any markup within that text is to be interpreted (except when the entity itself is there to "escape" markup characters).

- For external text entities, a validating XML processor must insert the entity's content as part of the document. For well-formedness, however, an XML processor can, but is not required to, include the external entity. This allows for XML browser applications, which might prefer to represent the entity as an icon, and allow the user to decide whether, and when, it should be retrieved.

All XML processors must recognize the five built-in entities that are used as markup delimiters in XML, regardless of whether they are declared:

- lt is mapped to <
- gt is mapped to >
- amp is mapped to &
- apos is mapped to '
- quot is mapped to "

> Note: A validating XML processor would additionally require that the built-in entities are declared if they are referenced, so this stipulation matters only to nonvalidating XML processors.

Parameter entity references (which are found only in the DTD) are always expanded as soon as they are encountered.

The XML-Lang specification contains some more detailed rules on the expansion of references for anyone who is actually planning to develop an XML processor. These rules apply only when the replacement text for an internal entity itself contains other references.

Parameter-entity references and character references in the replacement text of an internal entity are resolved immediately, while general-entity references are left unresolved. General-entity references encountered in the document are resolved, and their replacement text is parsed. This will cause any references in the replacement text to be resolved, unless they are general-entity references that "escape" markup.

From a user's point of view, one practical effect of these rules is that you need to use general-entity references or doubly escaped character references if you want to represent markup characters within internal entities. For example, the entity declaration

```
<!ENTITY example "<p>An ampersand (&#38;#38;) may be escaped
  numerically (&#38;#38;#38;) or with a general entity
  (&amp;amp;).</p>" >
```

will be parsed and stored with this value:

```
<p>An ampersand (&#38;) may be escaped
  numerically (&#38;#38;) or with a general entity
  (&amp;amp;).</p>
```

A reference in the document to &example; will cause this replacement text to be parsed again, resulting in a p element containing the following data characters:

```
An ampersand (&) may be escaped
  numerically (&#38;) or with a general entity
  (&amp;).
```

Summary

This chapter provided an overview of the XML specification by summarizing the features that an XML processor is required to have.

Using XML

CHAPTER 12

Morphing Existing HTML into XML

by Richard Light

Let's start the XML practicals by taking a fairly typical Web page written in HTML and converting it to XML. The reason for doing this is *not* to suggest that all HTML pages will require this treatment! Rather, it's a good way to explore the differences in approach between HTML and XML.

> **Note:** Surprisingly, a fair proportion of the markup that you need to change to make your Web page into a valid XML document is actually valid SGML. SGML provides a number of shortcuts that have been widely used in HTML markup. They aren't valid XML because XML deliberately chooses not to use these markup minimization techniques.

Listing 12.1 shows the sample Web page. It's not a real one, but every element in it is based on features commonly found in real pages.

Listing 12.1. The source of the sample HTML page.

```
<html>
<head><title>Morphing existing HTML into XML
<hr>
<a href="l12_1.htm"><IMG ALIGN=MIDDLE SRC="home.gif"
alt="[home page]"></a>
<a href="l12html1.htm"><IMG ALIGN=MIDDLE SRC="html.gif"
alt="[HTML]"></a>
<a href="l12xml1.htm"><IMG ALIGN=MIDDLE SRC="xml.gif"
alt="[XML]"></a>
<hr>
<h1>Morphing existing HTML into XML</h1>
<P>We will start our XML practicals by taking a fairly typical
Web page, written in HTML, and converting it to XML. The reason
for doing this is <i>not</i> to suggest that all HTML
pages will require this treatment! Rather, it's a good way to
explore the differences in approach between HTML and XML.
<p><b><tt>SGML short-cuts</b></tt> are probably to blame for much
of the incorrect HTML that we see [<a href="l12note1.htm">Note 1</
a>]
<p>We will:
<ul compact>
<li>make our web page well-formed</li>
<li>update the HTML DTD for XML and make our page valid</li>
<li>use XML features to enhance our page</li>
<p><tt>Page last updated July 8th 1997 by Richard Light
```

When displayed by a Web browser, it looks something like what is shown in Figure 12.1.

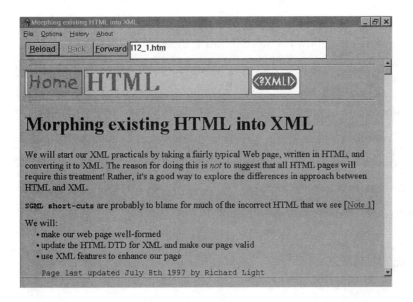

Figure 12.1.
A sample HTML page.

Toward Well-Formedness: From Tag Soup to Neatly Packed Suitcases

Your first objective is to make the sample page *well-formed*. This means that each element must have both a start-tag and an end-tag. It also means that the tags must nest neatly. (Remember the nested suitcases from Chapter 6, "Logical Structures in XML Documents.")

Non-Nested Tags

A common error is to treat HTML start-tags and end-tags as simply a means of switching features on and off. Therefore, users put them in the wrong order. For instance, the following code is not valid XML, because the b and tt tags do not nest properly:

```
<b><tt>SGML short-cuts</b></tt>
```

Having encountered the <b> start-tag, you are "inside" a b element when you insert a <tt> start-tag. Thus, you need to finish the tt element before you can finish the b element. Let's indent the markup to see that more clearly:

```
<b>
    <tt>
        SGML short-cuts
    </b> <!-- wrong!! -->
</tt> <!-- wrong!! -->
```

Switching the end-tags solves the problem:

```
<b><tt>SGML short-cuts</tt></b>
```

The tags now nest neatly.

```
<b>
    <tt>
        SGML short-cuts
    </tt>
</b>
```

Adding Implied Start-Tags and End-Tags

In this page, many end-tags and even a few start-tags have been omitted. You can do this in SGML (if your DTD allows the tags in question to be omitted), but never in XML. For example, both the start-tag and the end-tag for the body element are completely absent, and there is no end-tag for the html element that contains the whole page. As you have just seen when sorting non-nested tags, all the p elements also have a start-tag but no end-tag.

Listing 12.2 shows what the code looks like after you add all those missing tags.

Listing 12.2. An HTML page with all tagging explicit.

```
<html>
<head><title>Morphing existing HTML into XML</title></head>
<body>
<hr>
<a href="l12_1.htm"><IMG ALIGN=MIDDLE SRC="home.gif"
alt="[home page]"></a>
<a href="l12html1.htm"><IMG ALIGN=MIDDLE SRC="html.gif"
alt="[HTML]"></a>
<a href="l12xml1.htm"><IMG ALIGN=MIDDLE SRC="xml.gif"
alt="[XML]"></a>
<hr>
```

```
<h1>Morphing existing HTML into XML</h1>
<P>We will start our XML practicals by taking a fairly typical
Web page, written in HTML, and converting it to XML. The reason
for doing this is <i>not</i> to suggest that all HTML
pages will require this treatment! Rather, it's a good way to
explore the differences in approach between HTML and XML.</p>
<p><b><tt>SGML short-cuts</tt></b> are probably to blame for much
of the incorrect HTML that we see [<a href="l12note1.htm">Note 1</
a>]</p>
<p>We will:
<ul compact>
<li>make our web page well-formed</li>
<li>update the HTML DTD for XML and make our page valid</li>
<li>use XML features to enhance our page</li>
</ul></p>
<p><tt>Page last updated July 8th 1997 by Richard Light</tt></p>
</body></html>
```

Tidying Up Those Attributes

The rules for XML attributes state that all attribute specifications need to be quoted. Single or double quotes can be used. Numerical attribute values, in particular, tend not to be quoted in HTML. In this case, the alignment of the image

```
<IMG ALIGN=MIDDLE SRC="home.gif">
```

should be quoted

```
<IMG ALIGN="MIDDLE" SRC="home.gif">
```

Also, where an attribute has a single possible value, it is common practice to enter that value without quoting the attribute's name at all:

```
<ul compact>
```

SGML allows this, but for XML the attribute specification needs to be entered in full:

```
<ul compact="compact">
```

This is much less elegant—but then the HTML DTD was undoubtedly designed with this SGML shortcut in mind!

Converting Empty Elements to XML Format

All elements without any content—formally known as *empty elements*—need to be declared in a different way in XML. The special format used was invented for XML. (It's a novelty for people coming to XML from SGML.) Its advantage is that it marks an empty element quite unambiguously. With SGML conventions, you cannot tell whether an element is empty without looking up its declaration in the DTD.

You need to change the img element from

```
<IMG ALIGN="MIDDLE" SRC="home.gif">
```

to

```
<IMG ALIGN="MIDDLE" SRC="home.gif"/>
```

At this point you start paying a price—your HTML page is no longer valid HTML, because HTML does not recognize the XML convention for empty elements.

A Well-Formed XML Document

With all these changes, your sample page will now report as well-formed if an XML processor gives it the once-over. To celebrate this progress, add an *XML declaration* to the start of the page to make your intentions perfectly clear. The declaration states that you intend the page to be interpreted as a piece of XML.

The point of all the changes you have been making is that the logical structure of the page is now quite explicit. Notice that you haven't yet formally stated that this is actually an HTML document of any sort, yet an XML processor would be able to read this document and correctly deduce its markup from the start-tags and end-tags, empty elements, and clearly labeled attribute specifications that you have provided. It doesn't need the HTML DTD to do those things. That is the advantage that well-formedness provides.

Listing 12.3 shows how the whole page looks now.

Listing 12.3. The sample HTML page as a well-formed XML document.

```
<?XML version="1.0"?>
<html>
<head><title>Morphing existing HTML into XML</title></head>
<body>
<hr>
<a href="l12_1.htm"><IMG ALIGN="MIDDLE" SRC="home.gif"
alt="[home page]"/></a>
<a href="l12html1.htm"><IMG ALIGN="MIDDLE" SRC="html.gif"
alt="[HTML]"/></a>
<a href="l12xml1.htm"><IMG ALIGN="MIDDLE" SRC="xml.gif"
alt="[XML]"/></a>
<hr>
<h1>Morphing existing HTML into XML</h1>
<P>We will start our XML practicals by taking a fairly typical
Web page, written in HTML, and converting it to XML. The reason
for doing this is <i>not</i> to suggest that all HTML
pages will require this treatment! Rather, it's a good way to
explore the differences in approach between HTML and XML.</p>
<p><b><tt>SGML short-cuts</tt></b> are probably to blame for much
of the incorrect HTML that we see [<a href="l12note1.htm">Note 1
</a>]</p>
<p>We will:
<ul compact="compact">
<li>make our web page well-formed</li>
<li>update the HTML DTD for XML and make our page valid</li>
<li>use XML features to enhance our page</li>
</ul></p>
<p><tt>Page last updated July 8th 1997 by Richard Light</tt></p>
</body></html>
```

Toward Validity: Adding a DOCTYPE Declaration

As you see in the section "Well-Formed and Valid Documents" in Chapter 5, "The XML Approach," converting an HTML page into a well-formed XML document only achieves the first level of XML conformance. If you want to go further and make the sample page into a valid XML document, you need to declare the DTD to which the sample page conforms. In itself, that isn't difficult to do; you simply add a DOCTYPE declaration to the start of the document (but after the XML declaration):

```
<!DOCTYPE HTML SYSTEM "HTML2_X.DTD">
```

This states that the document type is HTML, and the DTD is held in the file `"HTML2_X.DTD"`. Let's note a couple of differences here.

First, the (external) DTD is declared using a SYSTEM name. You might be accustomed to seeing the HTML DTD declared as PUBLIC, as in this example:

```
<!DOCTYPE HTML PUBLIC "-//W3C//DTD HTML 2.0//EN">
```

It is pretty standard SGML practice to use a PUBLIC identifier to refer to the DTD that a document uses.

In SGML, a PUBLIC identifier (to be precise, a formal PUBLIC identifier) is carefully constructed. It tells you who is responsible (in this case, W3C). It tells you it's a DTD and it assigns a unique name to that DTD. The one thing a PUBLIC identifier doesn't do is tell you where to find the DTD itself!

XML takes a more pragmatic view. First, it doesn't attempt to control or interpret the value of the PUBLIC identifier. Second, it insists that you say where the DTD can be located by providing a SYSTEM identifier as well as a PUBLIC identifier. In the example, the SYSTEM name is a URL representing a local filename, but it could equally have been the URL of an "official" HTML DTD stored on W3C's Web site.

> Note: You can provide a PUBLIC name in XML only if it is followed by a SYSTEM name:
> ```
> <!DOCTYPE HTML PUBLIC "-//W3C//DTD HTML 2.0 FOR XML//EN"
> "HTML2_X.DTD">
> ```

The second difference is in the filename: `"HTML2_X.DTD"`. This is different from the filenames normally assigned to the HTML 2.0 DTD, and for a good reason. It refers to a different DTD. Before you can make your sample page into a valid XML document, you need an XML-valid DTD to check it against. The existing HTML DTDs will *not* work with XML, for several reasons that I cover in the next section.

Creating an XML-Valid HTML DTD

This section reviews the changes that need to be made to the HTML 2.0 DTD to make it XML-compatible. If your interest is solely at the level of document authoring, you might like to skip this section.

> Note: The updated HTML 2.0 DTD for XML is on the Web site that accompanies this book. It represents my own attempt to upgrade the DTD produced by W3C, and it has no official status. Hopefully, the W3C consortium will look at the issue of supporting HTML as an XML application, at which point W3C might come up with an official set of DTDs.

Omitted Tag Minimization Rules

In SGML you can omit start-tags and end-tags from your document and allow SGML-aware software to infer their presence, but not just anywhere. The HTML DTD contains *omitted tag minimization* parameters that state which tags can be omitted without causing an error. These consist of a pair of characters, one for the start-tag and one for the end-tag, which are either - to indicate that the tag must be present or 0 (capital O, not zero) to indicate that it can be omitted.

Anyway, this is all rather academic for XML; tag omission is outlawed. So all these omitted tag minimization rules must come out of the DTD. Otherwise, the DTD itself will give rise to parsing errors. For example, the element declaration

```
<!ELEMENT HTML O O (%html.content;)>
```

becomes

```
<!ELEMENT HTML (%html.content;)>
```

Grouped Element and Attribute List Declarations

In SGML, it is allowable to provide a single declaration for a whole set of element types or attribute lists. With parameter entities, this can lead to a very elegant declaration, such as the following:

```
<!ELEMENT (%font;|%phrase;) - - (%text;)*>
```

After %font; and %phrase; have been expanded, this declaration deals with no fewer than 10 different elements.

In XML, this isn't allowed. Every element type and attribute list must have its own separate declaration:

```
<!ELEMENT TT (%text;)*>
<!ELEMENT CODE (%text;)*>
<!ELEMENT SAMP (%text;)*>
<!ELEMENT KBD (%text;)*>
```

Inclusion and Exclusion Exceptions

SGML lets you declare that certain element types can *float* anywhere within another element. These are called *inclusion exceptions.* Conversely, element types can be barred from appearing within other elements by *exclusion exceptions.* Exceptions are declared after the element type's content model proper

```
<!ELEMENT (DIR¦MENU) - - (LI)+ -(%block;)>
```

states that block element types are not allowed anywhere within dir or menu elements. This prohibition will affect the li subelements and any children they might have.

XML doesn't allow such nonsense; all content models need to be complete and explicit. This requirement posed one of the two biggest problems that I faced in converting the HTML DTD for XML, because inclusions and exclusions at a high level in the document structure can affect the content models of many other element types.

In this case, I created a special element type, SIMPLELI, which has a different content model from LI, because block element types are not allowed within it. However, this introduces a new element type, which is not upward-compatible with the existing DTD. It also has no effect on the children of SIMPLELI elements, which could still introduce block element types. A simpler approach would be to remove the exclusion and accept that the XML DTD is less restrictive than the original.

Inclusions are potentially harder to deal with, because by ignoring them you are removing possibilities that are allowed by the current DTD. For example, the FORM element type has an exclusion and three inclusions:

```
<!ELEMENT FORM - - %body.content -(FORM) +(INPUT¦SELECT¦TEXTAREA)>
```

In this case, I changed the content model so that the inclusions can appear as immediate children of the FORM element type:

```
<!ENTITY % form.content "(%heading;¦%forms.block;¦HR¦ADDRESS
¦IMG¦INPUT¦SELECT¦TEXTAREA)*">
<!ELEMENT FORM (%form.content;)>
```

Again, this change will apply only to the immediate children of the FORM element.

In general, you will need to carefully reconsider the design of any SGML DTD that uses exceptions if you are trying to produce an equivalent XML-compatible DTD. It is not easy to produce a DTD with exactly the same properties, and you will probably need to choose between making the XML DTD more or less restrictive than the original.

& Connectors

SGML allows the element types in a content model to be separated by &, which means that they must all occur, but in any order:

```
<!ENTITY % head.content "TITLE & ISINDEX? & BASE? %head.extra">
```

XML doesn't support the & connector, so all the content models that use it must be rewritten. This necessity was the other significant headache I received in producing the HTML DTD for XML.

Here I decided that the TITLE element must be present and must appear once only, but the other element types are less critical. So I produced a content model where they can occur zero or more times, on either side of TITLE:

```
<!ENTITY % head.optional "ISINDEX | BASE | META | LINK
%head.extra;">
<!ENTITY % head.content "(%head.optional;)*, TITLE,
(%head.optional;)*">
```

This is not as precise as the original content model, but at least it is upward compatible.

Limited Attribute Types

XML supports fewer types of attributes than SGML. The HTML DTD uses some of the types that XML doesn't support. For example, you need to change

```
<!ENTITY % linkType "NAMES">
```

to

```
<!ENTITY % linkType "NMTOKENS">
```

and

```
<!ATTLIST PRE WIDTH NUMBER #implied
```

to

```
<!ATTLIST PRE WIDTH CDATA #implied
```

XML-Link Support

XML-Link provides a new method of indicating that certain attribute lists contain link information. It also adds value to these links with some additional attributes (ROLE, SHOW, and so on).

These additional attributes can all be neatly added in one place—to the linkExtraAttributes parameter entity:

```
<!ENTITY % linkExtraAttributes
"XML-LINK CDATA #FIXED 'SIMPLE'
ROLE CDATA #IMPLIED
SHOW (EMBED¦REPLACE¦NEW) 'REPLACE'
ACTUATE (AUTO¦USER) 'USER'
BEHAVIOR CDATA #IMPLIED
REL %linkType #IMPLIED
...
```

It is easy to add XML-Link support to HTML, because the designers of XML-Link took great care to make the attributes that control linking in XML upward-compatible with existing HTML practice. For example, they have adopted the HREF and TITLE attributes and have given them the same meaning as in HTML.

Another change I made that relates to linking was to convert the NAME attribute on the a element to an ID attribute. XML-Link gives preferential support to IDs by allowing a simple, HTML-like syntax when an element with an ID is the target of a link:

```
<a href="#backMatter">
```

This makes the full power of XML simple links available wherever links are used in HTML.

> Warning: As I have outlined, changing from NAME to ID gives you advantages in an XML environment, but it also has a price. The form that ID attribute values can take (they have to be an XML Name) is more restrictive than the form of a NAME (which can contain any character data you like).

For XML compatibility, the HREF attribute becomes mandatory for the a element type:

```
<!ATTLIST A
HREF CDATA #REQUIRED
ID ID #IMPLIED
```

```
%linkExtraAttributes;
%SDAPREF; "<Anchor: #AttList>"
>
```

Images

The img element type makes no attempt to check the presence of the image. I decided to redeclare IMG as an XML link that was automatically followed, with the resulting resource being embedded in the document:

```
<!ATTLIST IMG
XML-LINK CDATA #FIXED 'SIMPLE'
HREF CDATA #REQUIRED
ROLE CDATA #IMPLIED
SHOW (EMBED|REPLACE|NEW) #FIXED 'EMBED'
ACTUATE (AUTO|USER) #FIXED 'AUTO'
BEHAVIOR CDATA #IMPLIED
ALT CDATA #IMPLIED
...
```

Another method that achieves a similar result is to change its declaration so that the SRC attribute points to an *entity* rather than just being any old character data:

```
<!ATTLIST IMG
SRC ENTITY #REQUIRED
...
```

This is not strictly necessary for XML compatibility, but it does emphasize that the image is an integral part of the Web page, and not an optional link from it.

Note: This change means that all IMG elements in your sample page and the GIF notation now need to be declared in the internal DTD subset:

```
<!NOTATION GIF SYSTEM "lview.exe">
<!ENTITY logo.home SYSTEM "home.gif" NDATA GIF>
<!ENTITY logo.html SYSTEM "html.gif" NDATA GIF>
<!ENTITY logo.xml SYSTEM "xml.gif" NDATA GIF>
```

Predefined Entities

XML recognizes predefined entity references for five characters that are used in markup: <, >, &, ', and ". However, it then mandates that if these entities are declared in an XML DTD, they must take exactly the form specified in the XML standard:

```
<!ENTITY lt   "&#60;">
<!ENTITY gt   "&#62;">
<!ENTITY amp  "&#38;">
<!ENTITY apos "'">
<!ENTITY quot '"'>
```

Four of these characters are declared in the HTML DTD, but not in this form, so their declarations have been changed, and the fifth character (apostrophe) was added for completeness.

General Tidying Up

The following differences between the general syntax of SGML and XML affect this DTD:

- Comments: Inline comments, surrounded by pairs of hyphens, are not allowed within declarations in XML DTDs. Instead, they must be placed in "proper" comments before or (preferably) after the declaration.

- Parameter entity references: Where parameter entities are used, their name must be followed by a semicolon in XML. This is optional in SGML.

- Default attribute values: Where a default value for an attribute is given, it must be surrounded by a pair of quote characters.

- Conditional sections: XML does not allow spaces on either side of the keyword that introduces a conditional section:

  ```
  <![ %HTML.Recommended; [
  ```

  Therefore, these spaces had to be removed.

Declaring Embedded Entities

Now that you have an HTML DTD that is valid for XML, you can return to the sample Web page.

One difference between SGML and XML is that all the external resources used within the document must be declared in the DTD. What you have been updating is, strictly speaking, only part of your document's DTD—the *external DTD subset*.

The external DTD subset declares all the resources (such as entity references for common accented characters and markup characters) that any HTML document might contain. Now you want to declare the resources that are used by this particular document. For that, you have the *internal DTD subset.* You might remember that this appears inside square brackets, just before the end of the document type declaration:

```
<!DOCTYPE HTML SYSTEM "HTML2_X.DTD" [
<!-- internal DTD subset goes here -->
]>
```

Because you changed the img element type's SRC attribute in the DTD, you now need to declare your one image as a proper entity. This is done as follows.

First, put an entity declaration for the image file into the internal DTD subset. Because the image uses the GIF notation, which isn't yet declared in your DTD, you need a *notation declaration* for that too:

```
<!DOCTYPE HTML SYSTEM "HTML2_X.DTD" [
<!NOTATION GIF SYSTEM "/software/gifview.exe">
<!ENTITY image.home SYSTEM "home.gif" NDATA GIF>
]>
```

Now you need to amend the img element so that its SRC attribute specification points to this entity:

```
<IMG ALIGN="MIDDLE" SRC="image.home"/>
```

That's it! Your image is now a properly declared XML entity.

Health Check: Does It Validate?

By now, you should have a valid XML document. Let's check it and see. Using the RUNSP program to run the NSGMLS parser reveals one remaining error, which is shown in Figure 12.2. The error is that you have used a ul (unordered list) element inside a p (paragraph). This is not permitted by the original HTML 2.0 DTD or your XML version. (Did you know that? I didn't!)

You need to finish the previous paragraph with a </p> end-tag and remove the spurious /p end-tag from after the list. Then the whole page will be valid.

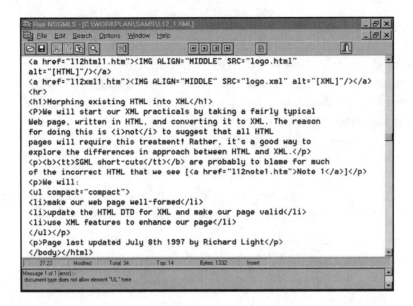

Figure 12.2.
Checking the sample page for XML validity.

Adding Custom Elements

If you now want to extend the HTML tagset, the internal DTD subset gives you a clean way of doing it. Suppose that you want to have person and date element types so that mentions of people and dates within your pages would be unambiguously marked up.

All you need to do is declare the additional elements in the internal DTD subset, like this:

```
<!ELEMENT person (#PCDATA)>
<!ELEMENT date (#PCDATA)>
```

Then you provide a place for the new elements to live, by redeclaring the phrase parameter entity to include them:

```
<!ENTITY % phrase "EM ¦ STRONG ¦ CODE ¦ SAMP ¦ KBD ¦ VAR
¦ CITE ¦ PERSON ¦ DATE ">
```

The rule is that declarations in the internal DTD subset override those in the external subset, so your local definition of phrase will take precedence. This means that person and date will be allowed anywhere that phrase-type elements are allowed in the DTD.

You can now mark up phrases that identify people and dates within your page:

```
<p><tt>Page last updated <date>July 8th 1997</date>
by <person>Richard Light</person></tt></p>
```

> Warning: Although it is technically possible to extend any XML DTD in this way for individual documents, you should bear in mind the potential larger-scale problems you might be creating. If several people or organizations are independently adding their own extensions to a base DTD, it is reasonably certain that they will add different element types with the same meaning (persName, for example). Worse, they might use a single element type to mean two or more completely different things! This all reduces the interoperability of the documents concerned. If a community is working with a single DTD, it is best to put in the extra work of coordinating extensions to that DTD on a central basis.

Entities: Creating Microdocuments

As I explain in Chapter 7, "Physical Structures in XML Documents," XML supports the concept of entities. In this section I suggest some ways in which entities might be put to good use within an XML-based Web site.

Consistent Page Headers

You can use XML's built-in entity support to make your Web site easier to manage. For example, all the header and footer stuff that goes at the top and bottom of every page could be stored in a file and referenced from each page as an external text entity. This has two major advantages:

■ You don't need to repeat the text in each page you create.

■ If you decide to change the style of your header, you can do it once, and every page on the site will automatically be updated.

The content of the external file will be the markup, optionally preceded by an *encoding processing instruction*:

```
<?XML· ENCODING='utf-8'?>
<hr>
<a href="l12_1.htm"><IMG ALIGN="MIDDLE" SRC="home.gif"
alt="[home page]"/></a>
<a href="l12html1.htm"><IMG ALIGN="MIDDLE" SRC="html.gif"
alt="[HTML]"/></a>
```

```
<a href="l12xml1.htm"><IMG ALIGN="MIDDLE" SRC="xml.gif"
alt="[XML]"/></a>
<hr>
```

This entity needs to be declared in the internal DTD subset:

```
<!ENTITY header.line SYSTEM "header.XML">
```

Then it must be referenced from the document itself:

```
<html>
<head><title>Morphing existing HTML into XML</title></head>
&header.line;
<h1>Morphing existing HTML into XML</h1>
...
```

This is a simple example; there are plenty of other potential uses for XML entities.

Combating "Link Rot"

Another idea is to use XML entities to keep all the links from your site in one place. This won't stop people from changing the URLs of their Web sites, but it will ease the administrative headache of ensuring that all your links to those sites are kept up-to-date.

Create a file that consists of nothing but entity declarations, one per link. Let's call this file "/resources/ext_links.ent":

```
<!ENTITY W3C.home
'<a href="http://www.w3c.org/">The W3C Consortium Home Page</a>'>
<!ENTITY W3C.XML
'<a href="http://www.w3c.org/Activity/XML/">The W3C XML Page</a>'>
<!ENTITY CIMI
'<a href="http://www.cimi.org/">The CIMI Consortium</a>'>
...
```

Declare this file and then include it in the internal DTD subset of each XML document:

```
<!DOCTYPE HTML SYSTEM "HTML2_X.DTD" [
<!ENTITY % external.links SYSTEM "/resources/ext_links.ent">
%external.links;
...
]>
```

Now you can use any of the entities you have declared as a shorthand for an a link within the text of your pages:

```
<p>For an overview of W3C's work see &W3C.home;. For
details of their work on XML see &W3C.XML;. ...
```

This will be processed as though you had entered the a element in full each time:

```
<p>For an overview of W3C's work see <a href="http://www.w3.org/"
>The W3C Consortium Home Page</a>. For
details of their work on XML see <a
href="http://www.w3.org/Activity/XML/">The W3C XML
Page</a>. ...
```

The advantage of this approach is that all your external links are now in one place, and each link is declared only once. So, if you find that a URL has changed, you need to update it only once. You can then be sure that any of your pages that are linked to that URL will continue to work.

> Tip: One useful idea would be to have a *test page*, containing references to all your external links. This would provide a straightforward (if tedious) means of testing that all your links still work, by going through the test page clicking on all the links. Alternatively, you could employ link-checking software to scan your test page.

Better Links

Your sample page contains a number of links that vary in their intentions. By using the built-in features of XML-Link, you can ensure that an XML processor is able to act sensibly on each of these links.

The three links that are wrapped around the images at the head of the page are standard URL links. They are *passive* links, which will be acted upon only if the client clicks on them. Not surprisingly, the default setting for XML's link attributes deals with this case, so there is no need to specify them. Just for the record, the first three links behave as though they were marked up like this:

```
<a href="l12_1.htm" SHOW="REPLACE" ACTUATE="USER">
...</a>
```

The link to the footnote is rather different. The target of the link is just a comment, not a separate page. In this case, the link can be marked up like so:

```
<a href="l12note1.htm" SHOW="NEW" ACTUATE="USER">Note 1</a>
```

The SHOW="NEW" attribute specification tells an XML browser to place the note in a new window. This allows the note to appear as a pop-up rather than take over the entire screen. As before, ACTUATE="USER" means that the note will appear only if the client clicks on the link.

Linking in a Header File

XML links give you two more ways of dealing with standard header and footer material, in addition to the technique described in the previous section.

The first method allows you to treat the header material as a self-contained XML "document" rather than a file containing some orphaned markup. However, this works only if the header material can be packed into a single element so that it can be a valid (or at least a well-formed) XML document. The body element is ideal for this purpose:

```
<?XML version="1.0"?>
<body>
<hr>
<a href="l12_1.htm"><IMG ALIGN="MIDDLE" SRC="home.gif"
alt="[home page]"/></a>
<a href="l12html1.htm"><IMG ALIGN="MIDDLE" SRC="html.gif"
alt="[HTML]"/></a>
<a href="l12xml1.htm"><IMG ALIGN="MIDDLE" SRC="xml.gif"
alt="[XML]"/></a>
<hr>
</body>
```

In this case, you can set up a link to the header information with the options SHOW="EMBED" and ACTUATE="AUTO":

```
<a SHOW="EMBED" ACTUATE="AUTO" href="header.xml"></a>
```

These options tell an XML processor that the header information is an essential part of the current document and that it should be inserted into the text at the point where the link is declared. However, it doesn't imply that the header information is actually a physical part of the page, in the way that embedding an entity reference does. This might affect the way that the header is treated by your XML-aware browser.

Linking in Part of Another Page

Instead of putting the header information into a separate file, you can use XML links in a slightly smarter way to "copy forward" the header information from the first page. If the header information is simply placed into the first page, but surrounded by an a element with a suitable ID, like

```
<a ID="header">
...
</a>
```

then subsequent pages can "pull in" the header information by using an XML link with the special ?XML-XPTR= connector:

```
<a SHOW="EMBED" ACTUATE="AUTO"
href="homepage.htm?XML-XPTR=header"></a>
```

This approach has the advantage that there is no need to manage the header information as a separate file. Admittedly, it means that your server will need to read the full home page to extract the header information, but in this case it is likely that it already did this when you first accessed the site.

Separating the Style Information

A fair proportion of the markup in your sample page is just there to ensure that the result looks right when the page is displayed. It is more in the spirit of XML to separate out the style information, so let's see what you can do with the example.

One obvious visual convention is the insertion of horizontal rules between each section of the document. In the absence of markup to show these sections unambiguously, you could simply place a horizontal rule before each h1 heading that you encounter. This means that you can take out the hr tags completely and, instead, have a style sheet entry for h1 (and h2, and so on) that looks something like this:

```
(element H1 (HEADING-WITH-RULE 16 "center"))
(element H2 (HEADING-WITH-RULE 14 "left"))
(element H3 (HEADING-WITH-RULE 12 "left"))
```

In this entry, the procedure HEADING-WITH-RULE outputs a horizontal rule, followed by the heading, using the quadding and point size specified (16pt centered for the h1 heading; 14pt left-justified for the h2 heading, and so on).

See Chapter 10, "The XML Style Mechanism," for a fuller description of the XML style mechanism.

Summary

In this chapter, you took a piece of HTML and learned how it would stand up as XML.

You found that the habit of using SGML-style markup shortcuts without SGML strength checking has led to HTML that routinely contains markup errors. Looking more closely, you found that even when these errors are removed, HTML won't be acceptable as XML because of these shortcuts. You spelled out everything and then managed to make the sample page a well-formed XML document.

The process of upgrading that well-formed instance to a valid XML document wasn't too difficult, but first you had a great deal of work to do on the HTML DTD itself. This revealed some differences between SGML and XML DTDs that will require some careful thought on the part of DTD designer folks.

After you made the sample HTML page into a valid XML document, you gave some thought to how you might leverage XML's built-in capabilities to make life easier for the XML-based Web site manager. You saw how entities could be used to hold information that occurs in several different pages and even to manage links more effectively. Then you explored how XML's linking facilities might be used to give closer control over the relationships between pages within a site. Finally, you looked briefly at how XML styles might be used to simplify the markup of the Web pages themselves.

Developing an XML Memo Application

by Richard Light

In the last chapter I discussed HTML in detail and showed how it might shape up as an XML application. Now I am going to discuss how to use XML for the job it is really designed to do—creating a custom application. I'll go over the following main tasks that must be performed for any XML application:

- Designing a DTD
- Deciding on a linking strategy
- Writing style sheets

I'll go through a concrete example to help you gain a better understanding of just how all this XML stuff fits together.

The XML Memo Application

The application that I use for an example is one for memos. Memos are a commonly found type of information resource and are made up of a reasonably consistent, simple structure. This simplicity makes it possible for me to try to cover all the bases of an XML application within a single chapter.

Memos are a suitable case for treatment by XML, because it is quite likely that a group of people might want to use a memo format to exchange and develop ideas. These people might be scattered around the world, using the Internet as their communications medium, or they might be employees of a single company, working within an intranet. In either case, the benefit of using XML is that it allows them to communicate their ideas using the framework they already have, without having to compromise the form of those ideas.

The Scenario

This is the situation. A group of people is discussing a topic of interest (such as how to write a book on XML!) and communicating their ideas via a memo format.

> **Note:** This task could equally be entrusted to a threaded e-mail discussion list. I will cover the extent to which XML provides a better (or worse) solution to this problem.

For the purposes of this design exercise, it doesn't really matter how the discussion group is physically organized. However, it helps to have an idea of the possibilities. Here is my vision of how the physical setup might go:

- Each member of the discussion group has an XML-aware editor that helps the member write correctly structured XML memos.
- Each person has access to a directory within a site where memos can be posted.
- This posting site is equipped with push technology that causes each new memo to be sent to every designated recipient.
- The posting site is also equipped with an XML-aware database.

A typical memo is shown in Figure 13.1. It contains the following features:

- Name of sender
- Names of recipients
- Date sent
- Main heading
- Optional subject keywords
- Text of memo

Although the memo contains only paragraphs, I will assume that the text of memos can contain the following features:

- Sections and subsections with optional headings
- Paragraphs
- Lists
- Images and diagrams
- Quotations from other memos

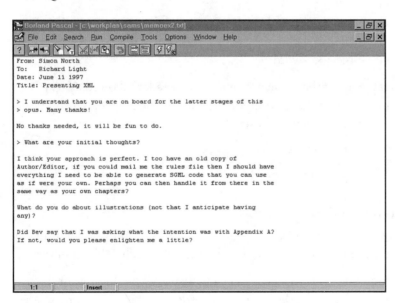

Figure 13.1.
An example of a memo.

Writing the DTD

The first step of the job is to design an XML DTD for the memo application. You might recall that in Chapter 8, "Keeping It Tidy: The XML Rule Book," I discussed the markup constructs that can occur in a DTD. Now it's time to put those theories into practice!

On one hand, this DTD needs to be flexible enough to cope with any memo. On the other hand, the DTD needs to be strict about those aspects of memos that are really vital. (The DTD can also be strict about aspects that really don't matter at all, but that is a different issue!) Start by doing an inventory of the types of information you need to support in your DTD.

Overall Structure

First of all, you have the following header information:

- Name of sender
- Names of recipients
- Date
- Main heading
- Optional subject keywords

You can start by saying that a memo consists of a header followed by text. The following is an element declaration for the memo element type, which says in XML-speak that the element consists of a header followed by text:

```
<!ELEMENT memo (header, text)>
```

Well, that's the beginning of your DTD!

Header Information

The header's contents include the five different types of information listed in the previous section. The following is a discussion of each of them in turn.

The "name of sender" clearly needs to be mandatory. You don't want to have unattributed memos in the discussion. So there must be at least one sender. But will there always be just one—or do you want to allow for the possibility of jointly authored submissions?

> Note: This is the first difficult DTD design decision. I'll say that joint authorship should be allowed. The effect of this decision on the DTD will become clear when you declare the `header` element type at the end of this section.

What will "name of sender" actually contain? It's a simple element, so the following contains only character data:

```
<!ELEMENT sender (#PCDATA)>
```

Next is "names of recipients." Again, you need to decide how many of these are allowed. There must be at least one recipient, and this time it's pretty obvious that you need to support multiple recipients as well.

In fact, the problem here is how to indicate neatly that a memo is to be broadcast to all the people who are on the discussion list. At this point, you must go beyond the issue of DTD design. Anything to do with the data content of an XML document is an application-specific issue. So you might have an application-specific convention such as the following:

```
<recipient>broadcast</recipient>
```

This convention is to be taken as an instruction to send the memo to everyone on the list. And that raises another issue. How do you control the values of both `sender` and `recipient` so that they are valid identifiers for people taking part in the discussion? The answer is that your XML application must take on the job of ensuring that this information is correct. There is no way that the XML DTD can do it for you. Its job is simply to declare and enforce the logical structure of your XML documents.

To finish off your work on the `recipient` element, just declare its element type as follows:

```
<!ELEMENT recipient (#PCDATA)>
```

Dates: Analysis Versus Attributes

The "date" raises some more issues. In itself, it's a simple concept, and it should certainly appear only once in all memos. In fact, you might expect the editing application to be able to add the current date for you. The issues arise over how the date might be used.

For the purpose of displaying the memo, you will want the date in a user-friendly form such as the following:

```
August 12th, 1997
```

However, from an information-management point of view, you might want to be able to find all memos that were written before a certain date, after a certain date, or within a range of dates. To be able to do this, you need the date in a searchable form. Here is an example:

```
19970812
```

How do you design a `date` element that meets both of these needs?

One approach is to analyze the date. This involves declaring subelements that each contain a component of the date:

```
<!ELEMENT date (year, month, day)>
<!ELEMENT year (#PCDATA)>
<!ELEMENT month (#PCDATA)>
<!ELEMENT day (#PCDATA)>
```

With these subelements, the example date would be marked up as follows:

```
<date><year>1997</year><month>8</month><day>12</day></date>
```

This analyzed form will support date-based searches, where the day, month, and year can be matched exactly, compared with a required range, or just ignored. You can ask, for example, for memos with a date containing a year equal to 1997, a month between six and nine, and any day you like. This would return all the memos from the summer of 1997.

For display, you would ask your style sheet to reorder the components of the date (`month`, then `day`, then `year`), convert the numerical month to a word (August), and add a suitable suffix (th) and a comma to the `day`. These steps require more work for the style sheet mechanism, but the approach is more flexible. Here in the UK, people prefer to see dates in the form `day month year`. A variant on the style sheet could deliver the same analyzed date to me in the following UK-friendly format:

```
12th August 1997
```

An alternative strategy is to use attributes to contain one of the forms in which the information is required. In this case, it is probably easier to have the friendly form of the date as the actual data content and give the searchable form as a `SORTFORM` attribute value such as the following:

```
<date sortform="19970812">August 12th 1997</date>
```

To provide a place to store both forms of the date, you need to declare both an element type and an attribute list for date, such as the following:

```
<!ELEMENT date (#PCDATA)>
<!ATTLIST date
SORTFORM CDATA #IMPLIED>
```

The default for SORTFORM is #IMPLIED. If you had specified #REQUIRED instead, users would be forced to enter a searchable form of every date, or the authoring software they use would have to generate a searchable form of each date and insert it for them.

Note: Note that the SORTFORM attribute is of type CDATA. Unlike SGML, XML doesn't have the NUMBER attribute type (that you find in the HTML DTD). It certainly doesn't have a special "ISO date" attribute type. Once again it is up to the application to ensure that this attribute is given sensible values.

The designers of XML are actively discussing this issue, and some method of defining types of element content is likely to be added to the XML-Lang specification in the future.

Which approach to designing a date element type is better? There is no right answer to that question. The analyzed approach involves more markup and more work in writing the style sheet, but it is more flexible and only involves entering the actual data once. The attributes approach is more pragmatic and is simpler to support, but it does involve double-entry of the data in two different forms, unless your authoring software can deduce one of those forms for you. For dates, double entry isn't really an issue, but it would be if the data was a person's name, such as the following:

```
<person sortform="Light, Richard B.">Richard B. Light</person>
```

For this memo application, I'm going with the attributes approach.

Defining the header Element Type

At this point, the decisions get simpler. You need to have a main heading that can be used both as a title when viewing the memo and as a potential key for threading. You can say that there should be only one main heading, and it will contain only data characters. Here is how:

```
<!ELEMENT main-heading (#PCDATA)>
```

Subject keywords also contain text. They are optional, and there can be any number of them. The following is for subject keywords:

```
<!ELEMENT subject (#PCDATA)>
```

Now you can pull together all of the header material. The following shows the preceding decisions on the element types that can occur within the header, and the number of times each can or must appear:

- Sender must appear one or more times.
- Recipient must appear one or more times.
- Date must appear exactly once.
- Main-heading must appear exactly once.
- Subject can appear zero or more times.

You can now declare the `header` element type as follows:

```
<!ELEMENT header (sender+, recipient+, date, main-heading,
subject*)>
```

> Note: Note that by using the , separator you are mandating the order in which the elements of the header can occur. In general, if you want to control the contents of an element, you have to do this. The other approach that XML offers is the ¦ separator, which allows you to specify alternatives. However, this makes sense only if you make the whole group repeatable, as in the following:
>
> ```
> <!ELEMENT header (sender ¦ recipient ¦ date ¦ main-heading ¦
> subject)*>
> ```
>
> However, in this case you cannot specify that there is exactly one `date`, and so on.

So far, your memo DTD looks like the following:

```
<!ELEMENT memo (header, text)>

<!ELEMENT header (sender ¦ recipient ¦ date ¦ main-heading ¦
subject)*>
<!ELEMENT sender (#PCDATA)>
<!ELEMENT recipient (#PCDATA)>
<!ELEMENT date (#PCDATA)>
<!ATTLIST date
SORTFORM CDATA #IMPLIED>
<!ELEMENT main-heading (#PCDATA)>
<!ELEMENT subject (#PCDATA)>
```

You now need to deal with the `text` element.

Structure of the Memo Text

Let's try to provide a framework for text that is reasonably flexible, yet simple. I've identified the following element types that can occur within the text of memos:

- Sections and subsections with optional headings
- Paragraphs
- Lists
- Images and diagrams
- Quotations from other memos

In the simplest case, you want to be able to place any of the preceding element types directly inside the text element. You don't know how many of each there will be or in what order they will occur. This is a definite case for the ¦ separator. The following is an example:

```
<!ELEMENT text (section ¦ p ¦ list ¦ image ¦ quote)+>
```

> Note: By using the + qualifier (one or more) rather than * (zero or more), you are insisting that text actually contains something, thus outlawing empty memos.

The following stipulates that each section consists of an optional heading followed by the same subelements:

```
<!ELEMENT section (head?, (section ¦ p ¦ list ¦ image ¦ quote)+)>
```

One important feature of this content model is that it allows section to be a subelement of itself. This is not a mistake; it is a powerful feature of XML called *recursion*. (I discuss this concept in Chapter 8 under the heading "Element Declarations.") It means that sections can nest within sections to any level required. When you have this generalized sort of design, it's a good idea to provide some attributes so that you can distinguish one section from another, as in the following:

```
<!ATTLIST section
    TYPE CDATA #IMPLIED
    LEVEL CDATA #IMPLIED>
```

> Note: Strictly speaking, the LEVEL attribute is redundant because a section element's level of nesting can always be calculated by software or worked out by a careful person.

Now you can say that paragraphs can contain text plus the other three types of information I have identified. Here is an example:

```
<!ELEMENT p (#PCDATA ¦ list ¦ image ¦ quote)*>
```

> Note: What you leave out of a content model can be as important as what you include. This example says that paragraphs cannot contain nested paragraphs, nor can they contain sections. This enforces an orderly approach to the structuring of your memos.

Parameter Entities as a DTD Design Aid

You can use *parameter entities* as a shortcut for commonly occurring structures. In the content models I have developed so far, the following pattern crops up repeatedly:

```
list ¦ image ¦ quote
```

You can declare that pattern as a parameter entity called common-elements, as follows:

```
<!ENTITY % common-elements "list ¦ image ¦ quote">
```

Now you can shorten all of the preceding element declarations into the following:

```
<!ELEMENT text (section ¦ p ¦ %common-elements;)+>
<!ELEMENT section (head?, (section ¦ p ¦ %common-elements;)+)>
<!ELEMENT p (#PCDATA ¦ %common-elements;)*>
```

Using a parameter entity like common-elements makes for greater consistency between element declarations, and it also makes your intentions clearer.

The use of parameter entities has an added advantage when you decide (as I think you certainly will) that you want to add another information type to the DTD. Having declared the new element type, all you have to do is to change the declaration for common-elements to include that element type.

The following element declaration is required if you decide to mark up people's names within the text:

```
<!ELEMENT person (#PCDATA)>
```

You would just add the following new element type to common-elements to finish the job:

```
<!ENTITY % common-elements "list ¦ image ¦ quote ¦ person">
```

Now all you have to do is to declare the following common elements within text, and your DTD is complete:

- Lists
- Images and diagrams
- Quotations

Using Attributes to Generalize Elements

Although there are different types of lists, they can be generalized to a single list element type. You can provide a TYPE attribute to distinguish bulleted lists, numbered lists, and so on. This can be an open-ended set of possible types (declared as CDATA) or a fixed set of possibilities. For simplicity, try a fixed set of list types. Each list will consist of one or more item elements. Here is an example:

```
<!ELEMENT list (item)+>
<!ATTLIST list
    TYPE (bullet¦number¦plain) "bullet">
<!ELEMENT item (#PCDATA)>
```

Declaring Notations in the DTD

Now you need to declare an element type for images and other visual material. The following shows how to declare an empty element that has a number of attributes to contain the information required to find and display the image:

```
<!ELEMENT image EMPTY>
<!ATTLIST image
    SRC ENTITY #REQUIRED
    DESC CDATA #IMPLIED
    ALIGN (TOP¦MIDDLE¦BOTTOM) "middle">
```

At this point you come up against the real world! The actual images included in the memos will all be in some *notation* that must be declared in the DTD.

You can choose to declare those notations up front in the DTD or leave the job to the users (in the internal DTD subset found at the start of their documents).

It makes sense to decide which notations are going to be supported within your memo application, and to pre-declare those in the memo DTD. If you decided to support GIF and JPEG images only, you would include the following notation declarations:

```
<!NOTATION GIF SYSTEM "http://www.viewers.org/gview.exe">
<!NOTATION JPEG SYSTEM "http://www.viewers.org/jview.exe">
```

If users choose to include images in any other format in their memos, they can then add declarations for the relevant notations in their internal DTD subsets.

Quotation: Setting Up Links

The final matter is quotations. These are perhaps the most interesting aspect of the XML memo application.

Most e-mail spends a lot of its time quoting previous e-mails in order to reply to the points made. The quoted text is physically copied and inserted into the reply.

A similar process is bound to happen with your memos. The sample memo is a reply to an earlier one, and it quotes two passages from the earlier memo. In turn, it generated a reply that quoted three passages from this memo. Can you use XML links to describe this sort of quotation? You certainly can, and moreover, XML linking offers you a choice of approaches!

The simplest approach is to make the quote element type into an XML simple link, as follows:

```
<!ELEMENT quote EMPTY>
<!ATTLIST quote
    XML-LINK CDATA #FIXED "simple"
    ROLE CDATA #IMPLIED
    HREF CDATA #REQUIRED
    TITLE CDATA #IMPLIED
    SHOW (EMBED|REPLACE|NEW) "EMBED"
    ACTUATE (AUTO|USER) "AUTO"
    BEHAVIOR CDATA #IMPLIED>
```

The attribute list declaration for the quote element type sets up quote elements so that by default they have SHOW="EMBED" and ACTUATE="AUTO". These SHOW and ACTUATE values mean that the quoted text will be fetched and physically inserted into the memo as part of the process of reading the memo.

What can be quoted? Any part of any previous memo, for a start. The standard XPointer syntax gives you the ability to quote any single element or span of elements from any XML document. XPointer links are easiest if the element being pointed at has an ID. This allows you to use the robust and simple ID addressing mode. The following example retrieves the element with ID="para3" from the document memo43.xml:

```
<quote HREF="memo43.xml#para3">
```

At a late stage in the process, the realization that attribute values of type ID are useful for linking suggests that perhaps your DTD should include an ID on every element (except perhaps the root memo element itself). The following is a parameter entity, a.global, which declares global attributes that can be included in the attribute lists of elements that already have attributes:

```
<!ENTITY % a.global "
ID ID #IMPLIED">

<!ATTLIST section
%a.global;
    TYPE CDATA #IMPLIED
    LEVEL CDATA #IMPLIED>
```

The following pattern of attribute list declaration can be used for element types that don't have any other attributes:

```
<!ATTLIST p %a.global;>
```

The linking requirement also suggests that it would be helpful if your XML-aware editor could automatically assign a unique ID to each element as it is created. Otherwise, authors of memos will have to add an ID to every element or try to second-guess which parts of their memos will be worth quoting!

Note: The strategy of assigning attribute values of type ID is particularly relevant where the XML documents concerned are liable to change over time. An element with a unique ID represents a stable target for a link, even when the document of which it forms a part is edited. However, in cases like the memo application, where a memo when written will not be updated, XML-Link's XPointers are quite capable of navigating to any specific part of a memo without needing to use IDs.

Of course, the generality of XML's links means that you can use the quote element to quote any part of any document that is available on the network, which might be a relevant part of a large report or policy procedure, encoded as part of a different XML application. It might be part of an HTML page. Or it could even be a Word document.

> Note: In the latter case, it would probably be wise to override the default behavior by specifying ACTUATE="USER", so that the user has to click on an icon to see the linked Word document.

These simple links have one major advantage over quotations in e-mail. They do not store the same information redundantly, perhaps several times over.

Advanced Linking: Out-Of-Line Links

Your simple quote elements can be improved upon. Like all inline links, they point only one way. Yet, in the broader context of your memo database, you want to be able to start from any memo and see what chain of argument flowed from it. You also want to be able to look back and see what arguments preceded it. In the case of your sample memo, there are three links forward (which are not obvious), as well as the two links back to the previous memo. Figure 13.2 shows your sample memo being browsed by an SGML application (Panorama Pro) that supports out-of-line links. The link icons show that this document indeed has five, not two, links; where two of them relate to the same paragraph, one points back to the original memo and one points forward to the reply.

> Note: Panorama Pro doesn't currently support XML XPointer links. The effect in Figure 13.2 was achieved using HyTime links, one of the technologies on which XPointers are based.

To achieve two-way linking, you need to move up from simple links to extended links. These out-of-line links will be automatically bidirectional, which means that a source memo will know when it is being quoted. This capability allows you to start from any memo and move in either direction, as required.

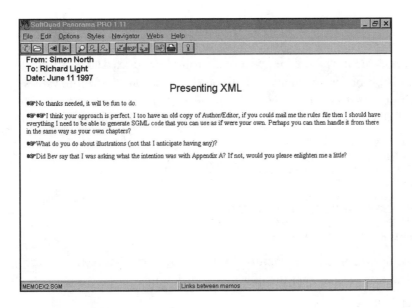

Figure 13.2.
A sample memo with out-of-line links.

You need a `quotation` element to hold the links, with the attributes of an `EXTENDED` element type, such as the following:

```
<!ATTLIST quotation
    XML-LINK CDATA #FIXED "extended"
    ROLE CDATA #IMPLIED
    TITLE CDATA #IMPLIED
    SHOW (EMBED¦REPLACE¦NEW) "REPLACE"
    ACTUATE (AUTO¦USER) "USER"
    BEHAVIOR CDATA #IMPLIED>
```

Note that the `SHOW` and `ACTUATE` attributes now have the standard defaults. I'll discuss why in a minute.

The `quotation` element will contain two types of `LOCATOR`. One will point back to the source memo, just as the simple `quote` link was doing. The other will point to the place where the source was cited. The types of `LOCATOR` are called `source` and `citation`. When declaring the `quotation` element type, you can allow any number of these locators by adding the following:

```
<!ELEMENT quotation (citation, source+)>
```

Links will now be expressed by a quotation element containing a citation and one or more source elements. In order to clarify their respective roles, the two LOCATOR element types can be given an appropriate and fixed ROLE attribute. They could also be given suitable default SHOW and ACTUATE attribute values. This attribute list declaration for citation ensures that references back will appear in full within the text (like your simple inline quote elements):

```
<!ATTLIST citation
    XML-LINK CDATA #FIXED "LOCATOR"
    ROLE CDATA #FIXED "citation"
    HREF CDATA #REQUIRED
    TITLE CDATA #IMPLIED
    SHOW (EMBED¦REPLACE¦NEW) "EMBED"
    ACTUATE (AUTO¦USER) "AUTO"
    BEHAVIOR CDATA #IMPLIED>
```

The following attribute list declaration for source ensures that references forward will appear as icons that the user has to click on:

```
<!ATTLIST source
    XML-LINK CDATA #FIXED "LOCATOR"
    ROLE CDATA #FIXED "source"
    HREF CDATA #REQUIRED
    TITLE CDATA #IMPLIED
    SHOW (EMBED¦REPLACE¦NEW) "REPLACE"
    ACTUATE (AUTO¦USER) "USER"
    BEHAVIOR CDATA #IMPLIED>
```

> Note: The containing quotation element doesn't have any special default behavior because its child LOCATOR elements need to behave in different ways.

The Link Farm

Where are these out-of-line quotation elements to live? If they form part of the memo in which the citation occurs, the source memo will feel no benefit. The source memo will have no means of knowing that it is participating in an out-of-line link declared in another memo. What you need here is a single document to act as a link farm for the memo database. A *link farm* is a single place where you can gather your links together and look after them (for example, by ensuring that they continue to connect resources that actually exist).

This document will contain nothing but quotation elements. It will have its own DTD, declaring quotation, source, and citation, as well as the following links cover element to group them together:

```
<!ELEMENT links (quotation)*>
```

So quotation elements and their child citation and source elements go into a separate document and do not form part of your memo DTD. The document might look like the following after a couple of entries have been added to it:

```
<?XML version="1.0"?>
<!DOCTYPE links SYSTEM "links.dtd">
<links>
  <quotation>
    <citation HREF="memoex2.xml#a1"/>
    <source HREF="memoex1.xml#p1"/>
  </quotation>
  <quotation>
    <citation HREF="memoex2.xml#a2"/>
    <source HREF="memoex1.xml#p7"/>
  </quotation>
</links>
```

The preceding code has two links from the sample memo "memoex2.xml". One is from the element with ID="a1" to the element with ID="p1" in document "memoex1.xml" (the original memo to which your example is a reply). The other is from the element with ID="a2" to the element with ID="p7" in the original memo.

Making the Memo DTD Links-Aware

The link farm document should be referred to by every single memo, in case that memo is part of a link. Back in your memo DTD, you need an *extended link group* with a single, fixed document locator pointing to the link farm. Here is an example:

```
<!ELEMENT links (memolinks)>
<!ATTLIST links
       XML-LINK CDATA #FIXED "group">
<!ELEMENT memolinks EMPTY>
<!ATTLIST memolinks
       XML-LINK CDATA #FIXED "document"
       HREF CDATA #FIXED "memo-links.xml">
```

The memo DTD should include a reference to this links file. A reference to the links file can be enforced for all memos by including a mandatory links element within memo. Here is an example:

```
<!ELEMENT memo (header, links, text)>
```

The following code ensures that each valid memo has the element structure in which the memolinks element contains the HREF link to the link farm as a fixed attribute value:

```
<memo>
<header> ... </header>
<links><memolinks/></links>
<text> ... </text>
</memo>
```

In addition, the memo DTD could use another low-level element that can act as an anchor for one end of these out-of-line links. In accordance with HTML practice, call it anchor. It can contain text (which will be underlined by an XML browser to indicate that it is one end of a link) and has an ID attribute, as in the following example:

```
<!ELEMENT anchor (#PCDATA)>
<!ATTLIST anchor %a.global;>
```

Now you need to update your definition of the common-elements parameter entity to include anchor, as in the following example:

```
<!ENTITY % common-elements "list ¦ image ¦ quote ¦ anchor">
```

That's all! There is no need to make anchor into a linking element. The actual linking will be done from the link farm by a citation locator element.

Note: Clearly it isn't the easiest job in the world creating these out-of-line links correctly by hand. It would be extremely useful if your XML editor could support creating links by letting you just highlight the two ends of the link, and then adding a correctly formatted entry to the link farm, which would require that the editor know about all aspects of XPointers, including where to find the links file.

Now you can drop the original quote element completely and rely on your out-of-line links in the link farm. However, please leave it in place for now.

The Full Memo DTD

Listing 13.1 shows the design for your memo application.

Listing 13.1. The memo DTD.

```
<!-- Memo DTD. First declare the parameter entities: -->
<!ENTITY % common-elements "list ¦ image ¦ quote ¦ anchor">
<!ENTITY % a.global "
    ID ID #IMPLIED">

<!-- The top-level memo element: -->
<!ELEMENT memo (header, links, text)>
```

```
<!-- Header information: -->
<!ELEMENT header (sender | recipient | date | main-heading |
subject)*>
<!ATTLIST header %a.global;>
<!ELEMENT sender (#PCDATA)>
<!ELEMENT recipient (#PCDATA)>
<!ATTLIST recipient %a.global;>
<!ELEMENT date (#PCDATA)>
<!ATTLIST date
    %a.global;
    SORTFORM CDATA #IMPLIED>
<!ELEMENT main-heading (#PCDATA)>
<!ELEMENT subject (#PCDATA)>

<!-- Fixed GROUP and DOCUMENT elements to reference 'link farm': -->
<!ELEMENT links (memolinks)>
<!ATTLIST links
    %a.global;
    XML-LINK CDATA #FIXED "group">
<!ELEMENT memolinks EMPTY>
<!ATTLIST memolinks
    XML-LINK CDATA #FIXED "document"
    HREF CDATA #FIXED "memo-links.xml">

<!-- Elements within the text of the memo: -->
<!ELEMENT text (section | p | %common-elements;)+>
<!ATTLIST text %a.global;>
<!ELEMENT section (head?, (section | p | %common-elements;)+)>
<!ATTLIST section %a.global;>
<!ELEMENT p (#PCDATA | %common-elements;)*>
<!ATTLIST p %a.global;>
<!ELEMENT list (item)+>
<!ATTLIST list
    %a.global;
    TYPE (bullet|number|plain) "bullet">
<!ELEMENT item (#PCDATA)>
<!ATTLIST item %a.global;>
<!ELEMENT image EMPTY>
<!ATTLIST image
    %a.global;
    SRC ENTITY #REQUIRED
    DESC CDATA #IMPLIED
    ALIGN (TOP|MIDDLE|BOTTOM) "middle">
<!ELEMENT anchor (#PCDATA)>
<!ATTLIST anchor %a.global;>

<!-- Notation declarations: -->
<!NOTATION GIF SYSTEM "http://www.viewers.org/gview.exe">
<!NOTATION JPEG SYSTEM "http://www.viewers.org/jview.exe">
```

Listing 13.2 shows the supporting DTD you have invented to hold your out-of-line links.

Listing 13.2. DTD for link farm.

```
<!ELEMENT quotation (citation, source+)>
<!ATTLIST quotation
    XML-LINK CDATA #FIXED "extended"
    ROLE CDATA #IMPLIED
    TITLE CDATA #IMPLIED
    SHOW (EMBED|REPLACE|NEW) "REPLACE"
    ACTUATE (AUTO|USER) "USER"
    BEHAVIOR CDATA #IMPLIED>

<!ELEMENT citation EMPTY>
<!ATTLIST citation
    XML-LINK CDATA #FIXED "LOCATOR"
    ROLE CDATA #FIXED "citation"
    HREF CDATA #REQUIRED
    TITLE CDATA #IMPLIED
    SHOW (EMBED|REPLACE|NEW) "EMBED"
    ACTUATE (AUTO|USER) "AUTO"
    BEHAVIOR CDATA #IMPLIED>

<!ELEMENT source EMPTY>
<!ATTLIST source
    XML-LINK CDATA #FIXED "LOCATOR"
    ROLE CDATA #FIXED "source"
    HREF CDATA #REQUIRED
    TITLE CDATA #IMPLIED
    SHOW (EMBED|REPLACE|NEW) "REPLACE"
    ACTUATE (AUTO|USER) "USER"
    BEHAVIOR CDATA #IMPLIED>
```

Encoding Your Sample Memo

Now that you have a DTD framework, you need to add XML markup to the sample memo. The job is pretty simple for the sample memo, because the text of the memo itself falls into paragraphs. The only complicating factor is that you need to strip out the quoted material and put in an anchor element as a placeholder for the references to the previous memo. Note also that you need to give these anchor elements, and every paragraph, a unique ID.

Listing 13.3 shows the full memo as a valid XML document.

Listing 13.3. Sample memo marked up as an XML document.

```
<?XML version="1.0"?>
<!DOCTYPE memo SYSTEM "memo.dtd">
<memo>
<header>
<sender>Simon North</sender>
```

```
<recipient>Richard Light</recipient>
<date sortform="19970611">June 11 1997</date>
<main-heading>Presenting XML</main-heading>
</header>

<links><memolinks/></links>

<text>
<p id="p1"><anchor id="a1"></anchor>No thanks needed, it
will be fun to do.</p>

<p id="p2"><anchor id="a2"></anchor>I think your
approach is perfect. I too have an old copy of
Author/Editor, if you could mail me the rules file then I
should have everything I need to be able to generate SGML
code that you can use as if were your own. Perhaps you can then
handle it from there in the same way as your own chapters?</p>

<p id="p3">What do you do about illustrations (not that
I anticipate having any)?</p>

<p id="p4">Did Bev say that I was asking what the intention was
with Appendix A? If not, would you please enlighten me a little?
</p>
</text></memo>
```

Writing a Style Sheet

It's particularly difficult to prepare a concrete example of an XML style sheet for memos, because no preliminary official draft to work from exists. You'll have to do what you can from the "NOT YET!" draft and hope that not too many changes will be made.

Recall from Chapter 10, "The XML Style Mechanism," that a style sheet takes an XML document and turns it into something completely different—a flow object tree. You might also recall that the style sheet is driven by constructor rules that say what to add to this flow object tree when each element type is encountered in the document. The flow object tree is an abstraction that requires some format-specific processing to render it onto a physical display medium (screen or paper).

In order to produce some concrete results, you need to write a style specification that can work with the Jade program. Jade works with XS-compatible style sheets and can produce output in a number of formats. One format is Rich Text Format, which is what you should generate. Figure 13.3 shows how one of your memos will look when you are done.

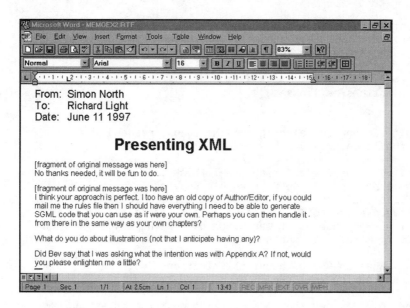

Figure 13.3.
A memo formatted by XS style sheet.

Note: At present, Jade does not have the means to produce an on-screen browsable version of XML documents. Software that does support this will clearly be a requirement if XS is to become a practicable style mechanism for XML documents.

Defining Styles

First you should define a number of styles that can be used throughout your style sheet. The following code defines the default font—Arial—for the whole memo:

```
(define memo-style
  (style
    font-family-name: "Arial"))
```

The following code defines three different font sizes (with suitable line spacing) for paragraph text, header lines, and the main heading (which is also centered and bold):

```
(define para-style
  (style
    line-spacing: 13pt
    font-size: 12pt))

(define header-line-style
  (style
    line-spacing: 17pt
    font-size: 16pt))

(define heading-style
  (style
    font-size: 24pt
    line-spacing: 26pt
    quadding: 'center
    font-weight: 'bold))
```

Declaring Procedures

You need to output the header information with suitable prefixes. In order to save yourself work, you should define a procedure called `para-with-prefix`, which takes a prefix as an argument and puts it before the text in the memo. The following is its declaration:

```
(define (para-with-prefix prefix)
  (make paragraph
    use: header-line-style
    (make line-field
      field-width: 50pt
      (literal prefix))
    (process-children-trim)))
```

The `para-with-prefix` procedure creates a paragraph. Within the paragraph it creates a *line-field*—an inline area—with a width of 50pt. It inserts the prefix into this line-field with the command (`literal prefix`) and then closes it. You are now back within the paragraph, and the command (`process-children-trim`))) simply outputs the data characters of the current element into the paragraph.

The purpose of the line-field is to line up the sender, recipient, and date, which follow the various prefixes.

Element Rules

Finally, your style sheet needs to have rules for the various elements in the memo DTD. Start off with a default rule that simply says to output the content of elements not specified elsewhere. Here is an example:

```
(default (process-children-trim))
```

The following declares the next step, a construction rule for the top-level memo element:

```
(element MEMO
  (make sequence
    use: memo-style
    (process-children-trim)))
```

The element construction rule for memo uses the style memo-style, which simply sets the font to Arial. By associating this font with a sequence at the highest level of the flow object tree, you are ensuring that all lower-level elements will inherit this property. Put simply, everything that is output will use the Arial font.

Now declare a construction rule for paragraphs, as follows:

```
(element P
  (make paragraph
    use: para-style
    space-before: 10pt))
```

The preceding code uses the para-style style, which was defined earlier, and enforces a 10pt space before each paragraph.

The following is a similar rule for the main heading:

```
(element main-heading
  (make paragraph
    use: heading-style
    space-before: 20pt))
```

Now declare construction rules for the three elements that occur in the header, as follows:

```
(element sender
  (para-with-prefix "From:"))

(element recipient
  (para-with-prefix "To:"))

(element date
  (para-with-prefix "Date:"))
```

This is where the effort of writing the para-with-prefix procedure pays off. It becomes very simple to display these three elements, each with a different prefix.

The fixed links element is not something you want to display, so suppress it as follows:

```
  (element links (empty-sosofo))
```

So far you do not have any means of displaying the quoted passages from previous messages. In place of the quoted passages, you can use the presence of an anchor element as a clue that quoted text should appear here and insert a fixed string saying so. The following is an example:

```
(element anchor
 (make paragraph
   (literal "[fragment of original message was here]")))
```

> Note: In order to display the quoted passages, you need an XML-aware browser that can resolve the XPointer links, which is not something that the XS style language has to do. The style language's job is simply to provide a means of rendering complete or partial XML documents when the application has managed to obtain them.

The Full Memo Style Sheet

Listing 13.4 shows the full style sheet.

Listing 13.4. XS style sheet for memos.

```
<!doctype style-sheet PUBLIC "-//James Clark//DTD DSSSL Style
Sheet//EN">

(define memo-style
  (style
    font-family-name: "Arial"))

(define para-style
  (style
    line-spacing: 13pt
    font-size: 12pt))

(define header-line-style
  (style
    line-spacing: 17pt
    font-size: 16pt))

(define heading-style
  (style
    font-size: 24pt
    line-spacing: 26pt
    quadding: 'center
    font-weight: 'bold))
```

continues

Listing 13.4. continued

```
(define (para-with-prefix prefix)
  (make paragraph
    use: header-line-style
    (make line-field
      field-width: 50pt
      (literal prefix))
    (process-children-trim)))

(default (process-children-trim))

(element MEMO
  (make sequence
    use: memo-style
    (process-children-trim)))

(element P
  (make paragraph
    use: para-style
    space-before: 10pt))

(element main-heading
  (make paragraph
    use: heading-style
    space-before: 20pt))

(element sender
  (para-with-prefix "From:"))

(element recipient
  (para-with-prefix "To:"))

(element date
  (para-with-prefix "Date:"))

(element sender
  (para-with-prefix "From:"))

(element recipient
  (para-with-prefix "To:"))

(element date
  (para-with-prefix "Date:"))

(element links (empty-sosofo))

(element anchor
  (make paragraph
    (literal "[fragment of original message was here]")))
```

> Note: The style sheet actually doesn't deal with all of the concepts in the memo DTD. However, there isn't space in this overview to deal with all the issues that this DTD raises, such as nested divisions and different types of lists.

System Requirements

Apart from the system requirements that I reviewed when looking at the initial scenario at the start of this chapter, it is clear that any real-life XML application will impose certain demands on its support software. Now look at these issues for editors and browsers that your simple memo application has raised.

Editor Requirements

In thinking through the design of an XML DTD for memos, you have come across a considerable number of areas where the XML editor can play an important role. (I assume, as a starting point, that the editor is able to interpret an XML DTD and that it will support the addition of XML markup in a user-friendly manner.)

The following are some requirements that were raised:

- Data validation (possibly in association with an external database)
- Insertion of the current date on request
- Automatic assignment of a unique ID to every element
- Automatic insertion of elements and attributes that are required by the DTD
- Capability of creating out-of-line links in a user-friendly manner

In addition, you might expect, in your memo application in particular, there to be a facility to create a reply to a memo, where the sender and recipient are automatically entered, the date is filled in automatically, and the main-heading is copied from the source memo. However, this job need not be carried out by the XML editor.

Browser Requirements

What about XML browsers? Here, the memo example doesn't really make any brand-new demands on the software, but it does emphasize the importance of the following aspects of the XML specification:

- Full support for XPointers (including traversal)
- Built-in support for XS style sheets
- Capability of using style sheets to render fragments of XML documents that are embedded within another document (possibly conforming to a different DTD)

Summary

In this chapter, you have put theory into practice by developing an XML application for memos. This application demonstrates the potential usefulness of XML's out-of-line links and XPointers.

You started by analyzing the information that could occur within a memo and then designed a DTD that is flexible enough to cope with a wide range of possible formats. During the course of this example, you found that you can use out-of-line links to represent the connection between replies and the part of the original memo to which they are a response.

You then marked up the sample memo according to this DTD. Finally, you devised an XS style sheet that will render the memos on paper or on the screen.

CHAPTER 14

Creating an XML Museum Information Application

by Richard Light

In this chapter I examine an industry-specific (or *vertical*) application of XML—museum information systems. Although museums do not at first glance have much in common with commercial or technical applications of XML, they have the following features that will apply to many areas of application:

■ The information that each institution holds about its collections is mission-critical and long-term; the objects in the collection are of little value and cannot be managed without associated information resources.

- The information associated with each object is variable in nature and can be very complex. It will routinely include a variety of formats and media.

- Each institution wants to have a documentation system that matches its own requirements and circumstances exactly.

- Conversely, museums regularly need to interchange information about objects, exhibition facilities, and so on.

- There is a regular need to deliver selected parts of museums' information to a variety of publics in an increasing number of delivery formats.

- Most museums have very little money to spend on computer-based documentation systems!

Interchanging Structured Museum Catalog Records

Museums have tended to cooperate rather than compete when it comes to defining logical data structures for their object records. In this section, I discuss an example of an interchange framework for structured museum catalog records, and I show how it could be implemented in XML.

Example: The SPECTRUM Standard

In the United Kingdom, for example, a single framework—the SPECTRUM standard—covers all the disciplines represented in museum work. To give you an idea of the range, these disciplines include the following:

- Archaeology
- Biology
- Decorative arts
- Fine arts
- Industrial archaeology
- Paleontology
- Social history

SPECTRUM describes the collections management processes that museum objects might be subjected to and the information associated with each activity.

It is a generalized framework that can be implemented in both manual and automated documentation systems. In the case of automated systems, museums are free to use whatever software they have available.

Figure 14.1 shows a sample page from SPECTRUM that lists some of the information that should be recorded when setting up an exhibit.

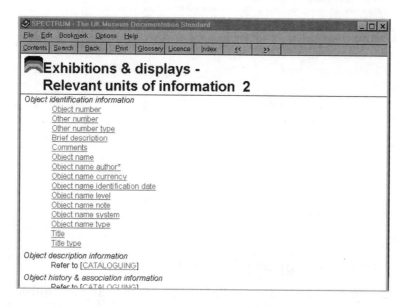

Figure 14.1.
SPECTRUM concepts for exhibits.

Figure 14.2 covers the detailed requirements for a single concept—Brief description. The requirements for this concept include the following:

- Definition: What the concept means
- How to record: Guidelines on the method to use when entering this information
- Examples: One or more concrete examples
- Use: How often, or in what circumstances, this information should be recorded
- Required in: The collections management procedures to which this information is relevant
- Alternatives: Other names that have been used for this concept within museum standards and systems

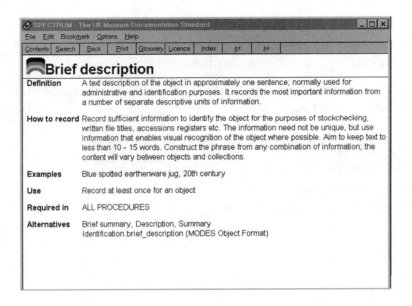

Figure 14.2.
SPECTRUM definition of the Brief description concept.

XML as an Interchange Format

Different museums have implemented SPECTRUM in different ways, which is fine while the information stays inside the museum. As soon as it needs to travel, however, a variety of implementations causes problems, which can happen quite often.

For example, one curator might be researching long case clocks for an exhibit that she is planning. She might request full information on the long case clocks in three other collections. Ideally, she wants to be able to receive this information in a form that is immediately useable within her own collection management system. XML can help in this situation.

By designing an XML DTD that reflects SPECTRUM's logical information structure, you can set up an interchange format for museum object information. Each museum will then have two jobs to do (or its software supplier will). They need to do the following:

- Write an export procedure that outputs records in the agreed XML format.
- Write an import procedure that reads the XML and converts it to the in-house format.

Armed with these export and import procedures, museums will be able to freely interchange object information. All the data each museum receives will be directly useable within its native collection management system. Using XML means that the requesting and delivery of this information can take place over the Internet, which removes the need for a dedicated communications network.

This scenario could be repeated in many other application areas. The key component, without which it won't work, is an agreed framework for information interchange. If that framework exists, it can be represented in XML.

This approach doesn't require that everyone who participates has to work to some impossibly high standard of recording, nor does it require that they change their current methods of doing business in any way. It simply mandates an interchange format for the information that they wish to share.

An XML DTD for SPECTRUM

Now take a minute to think about the design of the interchange DTD for SPECTRUM information. SPECTRUM is expressed in neutral terms. It will usually be implemented using a relational schema. To package up SPECTRUM information for interchange, you need to ensure that the packaging process doesn't lose any key information.

At the highest level, it makes sense to see the package as containing zero or more object records. The following code calls the package an `"object set"`:

```
<!ELEMENT OBJECT-SET (OBJECT*) >
```

To decide how to organize the information about each object, go back to SPECTRUM itself. There you find that the information categories are grouped by type. Figure 14.3 shows the "Object identification information" grouping, within which your Brief description concept is located.

The analysis gives you a simple two-level structure for object information. Most of the groupings, such as the following, can easily be mapped to level-1 elements within `object`:

- Record information
- Amendment history
- Object identification information
- Object description information
- Object production information

- Object collection information
- References

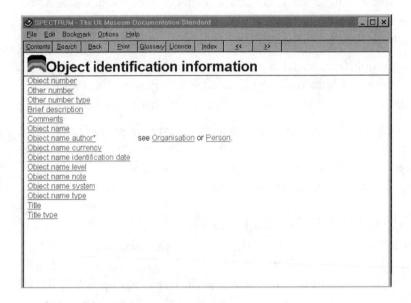

Figure 14.3.
SPECTRUM "Object identification information" concepts.

A closer examination of the following few concepts shows that they are complex structures that actually occur at level 2:

- Address
- Date
- Organization
- People
- Person
- Place

Because these occur frequently, they were placed in the level-1 list to avoid repetition. However, since they really belong at level 2, you don't need them in your level-1 content model.

The SPECTRUM headings give rise to the following model for `object`:

```
!ELEMENT OBJECT ((RECORD-INFORMATION
¦ AMENDMENT-HISTORY
¦ OBJECT-IDENTIFICATION
¦ OBJECT-DESCRIPTION
¦ OBJECT-PRODUCTION
¦ OBJECT-COLLECTION
¦ REFERENCES
...
¦ LOSS
¦ DISPOSAL)*)>
```

Note that the content model for `object` states that these groups of information are optional, repeatable, and can occur in any order.

This design approach means that any museum object record will be valid against this DTD, no matter how simple or complex it might be. Putting it another way, the DTD is descriptive rather than prescriptive.

You need to apply a similar approach for the level-2 elements. The following is the declaration for the `object-identification` element, within which your Brief description concept will appear:

```
<!ELEMENT OBJECT-IDENTIFICATION
  ((OBJECT-NUMBER
¦ OTHER-NUMBER
¦ BRIEF-DESCRIPTION
¦ COMMENTS
¦ OBJECT-NAME
¦ TITLE)*)>
```

You might have spotted that the list of subelements (six in all) is shorter than the list of 15 concepts in Figure 14.3. What has happened? If you check out the full list, you will see that the "missing" entries are all concepts that qualify a concept that you have included. For example, "Other number type" is defined as "A description of an Other number assigned to an object." In the "Use" section it says "Record once only for each Other number."

Using XML to Enforce the Rules

The SPECTRUM rule gives you a chance to be more prescriptive and to ensure that your interchange format supports SPECTRUM by enforcing any mandatory requirements it might lay down. How do you ensure that there is always only one "other number type" for each "other number"?

You can make other-number-type a subelement of other-number. This ensures that it cannot be delivered independently of other-number. There are two ways you can express the rule for other-number.

The first is to say that the actual "other number" appears as character data, with an optional "type" subelement. In XML this *mixed content* model has to be declared in the following way:

```
<!ELEMENT OTHER-NUMBER
(#PCDATA | OTHER-NUMBER-TYPE)*>
```

With this approach, a lender's number might be recorded as follows:

```
<other-number>PXM 92/35
<other-number-type>lender</other-number-type>
</other-number>
```

The second approach, which you could use if you wanted to ensure that each "other number" had exactly one "type," is to declare a TYPE attribute. The other-number element would then have a simpler content model and an attribute list, as in the following example:

```
<!ELEMENT OTHER-NUMBER (#PCDATA)>
<!ATTLIST OTHER-NUMBER
TYPE CDATA #IMPLIED>
```

With this approach, a lender's number would be recorded more simply as follows:

```
<other-number TYPE="lender">PXM 92/35</other-number>
```

If you felt that SPECTRUM is mandating an "other number type" for each "other number," you could easily achieve this by making the TYPE attribute #REQUIRED instead of #IMPLIED.

By the time you have finished analyzing the SPECTRUM framework, you will have a DTD with many more than two levels. For example, the object-name element will contain an object-name-author that will in turn contain a potentially detailed entry about a person or organization.

One advantage that XML brings is that you only have to declare the person element, with all its complex subelements, once. You can then use person as often as required within the overall structure, which avoids redundancy within the DTD. Next you should look at how you might avoid redundancy in the actual data records that are interchanged using this DTD.

Entity Relationships with XML-Link

Earlier, I demonstrated that some common concepts such as person, place, and date appeared "wrongly" at the top level in SPECTRUM and relegated them to their proper place within the structure. However, if you think about the reality of the information that is going to be transferred, it is clear that there will be some redundancy in this approach.

The same person—for example, a donor who has given many objects to the museum—can be mentioned within many of the object records. Each time he is mentioned, his details will be the same. Is there a way to avoid this redundancy? One method involves using XML-Link to support a simple type of entity-relational modeling.

Think back to how the information is probably stored in the museum's in-house database. Assuming it has a relational design, the details of each person (like the donor) will be normalized into a separate "table." The "acquired from" rows will link that person to each object that he donated, without any need to repeat the name, address, and so on. You can do that too in XML; in fact, there are two ways of doing it!

In both cases you need to separate (or *normalize*) the personal information. Then use XML's linking facilities to make the required connections.

You need a place in your data delivery structure to put the personal data, which will involve some changes to the top level of the DTD. One simple way of doing it is to rename object-set to something more neutral, such as SPECTRUM-set, and allow person as well as object entries within it, as follows:

```
<!ELEMENT SPECTRUM-SET ((OBJECT | PERSON)*)>
```

When declaring the person element, providing it with an ID attribute is important. An ID attribute will make it easy to use XML links to point at the person elements. The following is an example:

```
<!ATTLIST PERSON ID ID #REQUIRED>
```

The simpler of the two approaches will probably be adequate. The simpler approach involves one-way links from the object records to the relevant person entries.

You need to provide a person-link element type, as an alternative to a fully embedded person element. The person-link will have the standard attributes of an XML simple link, such as the following:

```
<!ELEMENT PERSON-LINK EMPTY>
<!ATTLIST PERSON-LINK
    XML-LINK CDATA #FIXED "SIMPLE"
    ROLE CDATA #IMPLIED
    HREF CDATA #REQUIRED
    TITLE CDATA #IMPLIED
    SHOW (EMBED¦REPLACE¦NEW) "EMBED"
    ACTUATE (AUTO¦USER) "AUTO"
    BEHAVIOUR CDATA #IMPLIED>
```

Note: The default values of the SHOW and ACTUATE attributes have been changed so that, by default, the linked personal details will be embedded automatically within the relevant object record.

The following declares a person authority record:

```
<person ID="BROWN_H">
<name><forename>Harold</forename>
<surname>Brown</surname></name>
...
</person>
```

The following uses a person-link to point to the person authority record:

```
<object>
<object-production>
<person-link ROLE="designer" HREF="BROWN-H"/>
...
```

The preceding code states that the person Harold Brown was involved in the production of the object in the role of a designer. In other words, he designed it!

Note: All XML links have the built-in ROLE attribute, which is the perfect place to put another SPECTRUM concept: Person's association. This is defined as "the way in which a Person is associated with a particular object."

The second approach to the creation of links involves XML extended links, which are more like the linking table in the relational database, because they simply make the connection between the object and the person. This has the important side-effect of enabling them to be traversed in either direction. As I said earlier, simple links are probably sufficient for this application, because you are primarily interested in objects. People only play a walk-on role, and the objects are the stars! However, if you were just as interested in the people as the objects, you might want to be able to go to Harold Brown's details and be able to link to all the objects he had been involved with. You can't do that with these simple links; they only point one way (from the objects to the people).

To avoid a review of Chapter 9, "Linking with XML," assume that you will use the standard extended link element extended, with child element locator. There is no need for a special element for the museum application. What you must do is allow extended elements to appear at the top level of the interchange structure, as follows:

```
<!ELEMENT SPECTRUM-SET ((OBJECT | PERSON | EXTENDED)*)>
```

You also need to add an ID attribute to the object element.

> Note: If you are planning to use XML linking extensively, it is a very good idea to make sure that all of your element types have an ID attribute. This just makes it easier to point to them!

Now you're all set. All you have to do is ensure that the object record has an ID:

```
<object ID="MYMUS-1992.345">
```

Then you create an extended element linking it to Harold Brown:

```
<extended>
<locator ROLE="designer" HREF="BROWN-H"></locator>
<locator ROLE="designed by" HREF="MYMUS-1992.345"></locator>
</extended>
```

Note that each locator has a different role. If you are starting from Harold Brown's record, he is the "designer" of the object at the other end of the link. If you are starting from the object, it was "designed by" the person at the other end of the link.

> Note: Locators are not very precise. They just point to the top-level element for the object and person. In principle, the object's locator could point to an element within `object-production` to locate the context more precisely. However, in the case of the biographical record this would require the creation of additional elements to hold details of the things Harold Brown made.

Delivering Authorities

In addition to exchanging information about objects, museums are consumers of another type of information—authorities— which contain lists of standardized terms and concepts with definitions (such as the Art and Architecture Thesaurus from the Getty Information Institute). They are central to museums' cataloging work. Use of an authority will greatly improve the consistency of a museum catalog, especially if the catalog is being created by a number of different hands.

Authorities pose a number of problems at a practical level. For a start, each museum software package has its own method of storing standard terms and making them available to the curator. Also, controlled terminology is continuously updated, which means that previously valid terms might now be obsolete. Finally, many museums using a standard source will create their own extensions (containing more specific terms or local dialect versions of standard terms).

XML provides a potential solution to these problems. Obviously, XML can be used as a standardized delivery format for authorities in the same way that it can be used to deliver object records. However, XML offers a new, more direct way of working with authorities on the Web.

Major providers of museum authorities are already putting their resources up on the Web in HTML format, which is fine for browsing by people, but not for use by software! If an XML version was created, client software could go to the Web site as required and download those parts of the authority that were actually requested by the curator, which would let the client prepare lists of possible terms, offer definitions, and so on, as if the complete authority were held locally.

XML also provides a method of linking in local extensions to a standard authority scheme. Assume that relationships between terms in the main authority are expressed as extended links such as the following:

```
<extended>
<locator ROLE="broad term"
HREF="http://www.gii.org/sports/sports.xml"></locator>
<locator ROLE="narrow term
HREF="http://www.gii.org/sports/baseball.xml"></locator>
</extended>
```

This extended link says that baseball is a narrow term of sports in some (mythical) GII classification system.

There is no reason a museum cannot set up its own set of additional links like this:

```
<extended>
<locator ROLE="broad term" HREF="http://www.gii.org/sports/
baseball.xml"></locator>
<locator ROLE="narrow term"
HREF="http://www.mymus.org/terms/Boston_softball.xml"></locator>
</extended>
```

Here you have a local variant on baseball, called Boston softball, whose authority record is stored in the museum's local site. As far as the museum staff is concerned, this is a perfectly valid narrow term to the official GII-sanctioned term baseball. However, because other museums do not have access to this museum's additional in-house links, they will not see this extra term.

XML for In-House Museum Use

Apart from its use for interchange, what value might XML have within an individual museum?

Textual Resources

Traditionally, museums have underplayed the information value of their textual resources, devoting their energies instead to creating and managing databased information, which means that major pieces of work, such as printed catalogs, are not saved in a form that can be reused. Part of the reason for this is that the final format from which a publication is printed (DTP format, usually) is too closely tied to that particular product to be reusable.

XML offers a holding format in which new publications could be authored and to which previous publications could be converted. XML links can be used to make sense of the connections between a museum's different resources. XML links could pick out, for example, j´+t the section of a complete collection catalog that talks about a particular object, and then link it to that object's database record.

Valid XML documents are also International Standard valid SGML. Museum information has to be managed as a long-term resource—so the future-proofing offered by SGML conformance makes XML an attractive proposition.

When in XML format, the museum's textual resources can be managed more easily and the intellectual capital they represent can be safeguarded. Existing information can be reused to produce new publications in a growing range of formats and media. For example, relevant sections from the museum's main printed catalog could be dusted off and included in a new interactive kiosk in the reception area that introduces visitors to the museum's holdings. The catalog for a new exhibit could be issued simultaneously in print and CD-ROM format, and placed, without any reworking into HTML, on the museum's Web site.

Multimedia Resources

Apart from textual material, museums tend to have a rich variety of resources that complement their collections. These include images, video, sound recordings, and a lot of primary written material that is in a variety of manual and computer-based formats. XML offers a means of tying all of these resources together in a coherent manner. Its use of notations gives flexibility because new data formats can be declared as a notation and linked in without difficulty.

Another use for XML is as a format to hold metadata. For example, a digitized image file does not usually contain within itself any information on its subject matter, or even on the precise technical circumstances of its own creation (resolution, bit depth, and so on). It is easy to create an XML-encoded record that contains this information with captions, copyright and reproduction rights information, and so on. The XML metadata can also contain links to several versions of the same image, each stored at a different resolution.

> Note: As of this writing, work is hotly under way on universal Web metadata frameworks based on XML.

Research

Curators, academics, and members of the public all carry out research on museum collections. When XML-encoded museum object records are more readily available, it will be possible to carry out very precise searches on the Web and retrieve relevant information in a usefully structured format.

When a researcher has retrieved a set of relevant material, he will be able to compile a meta-catalog containing descriptions of just those objects that interest him. The researcher can also write critiques and commentaries that compare and contrast the objects concerned. XML links can be used to reference the sources that are being discussed and to build up a personal web of relevant material.

When the critique is finished, it can also be placed on the Web, and other scholars can make reference to it from their own work. In this way, a network of scholarship can evolve organically.

From Database to Structured Infobase

One particular development shows how the arrival of XML might have a profound effect on what is viewed as information in museum cataloging. The development concerns a software package called MODES that is widely used by museums in the United Kingdom. Although it is a database, MODES uses an XML-like hierarchical structuring of fields within each record. Figure 14.4 shows a MODES record being edited: The indentation of the field codes shows their hierarchical relationships.

The hierarchical structure is designed to place information in a correct context, and to group together related items of information. The following example puts a method, person, and date element into the context of the production of the object, and furthermore says that they all relate to the same production process:

```
PRODUCTION
   METHOD        pencil & watercolour
   PERSON        draughtsman : Boyce, George Price (b1826 d1897)
   DATE           1864 (d)
```

Placing elements into context in this way is essential for effective retrieval. The MODES data structure ("DTD") for object recording uses the fields person and date in many different contexts. To find objects that were made in the 1860s, you need to be able to specify "DATE *within PRODUCTION*" as part of your search.

```
MS-DOS Prompt - MPLUS
Auto  ▼  □ ⓖ ⓑ 🖧 ⓗ 🖸 A
═════════════Editing (records) - press ^F1 to restore prompts═════════════
file: ART01        record: TWCMS : B7421
Enter command -    Last edited: by RBL on 30/4/1997 (4)        validation: X

 IDENTIFICATION
   SIMPLE_NAME        drawing
   TITLE              Windmill Hills, Gateshead
 PRODUCTION
   METHOD             pencil & watercolour
   PERSON             draughtsman : Boyce, George Price (b1826 d1897)
   DATE               1864 (d)
 IDENTIFICATION
   FULL_NAME          British & 19 century (late)
 DESCRIPTION
   PART:DIMEN:READING : height : 30.9 cm & 12 1/8 in
   PART:DIMEN:READING : width : 42.9 cm & 16 7/8 in
   INSCRIPTION
     TYPE3            inscription
     METHOD3          signed & dated & bodycolour
     POSITION         bottom right
     TRANSCRIPT       G.P. Boyce.1864.5.
   PART:ASPECT:DESC   medium : material : pencil & watercolour
   PART:ASPECT:DESC   support : material : paper (wove)
 CONTENT_ANALYSIS    landscape : moorland (with trees)
                                                          Val field
```

Figure 14.4.
MODES record for "Windmill Hills, Gateshead."

MODES as a Pseudo-XML Application

As part of a more general upgrade to Windows, MODES is now being re-engineered as a pseudo-SGML/XML application. What does this mean? It means that MODES will appear to the outside world as a native SGML or XML database, delivering information in either format on request. A MODES server, connected to the Web, will be able to return hits as valid XML documents.

However, MODES will continue to use its existing proprietary storage format within the database. This format will not support arbitrary XML or SGML DTDs; it will only support the particular record-oriented data structures that are required for museum-type applications.

Other types of databases might be able to adopt a similar strategy and develop an XML interface without altering their underlying data structure.

Requirements for XML Compatibility

In order to make MODES XML compatible, the following changes and additions were required:

- DTD generation: In order to serve up valid XML, a DTD is required. Most of the required information is in MODES' existing proprietary format file, and the rest (for example, notation declarations) is added from hand-written control files. The DTD is then generated automatically.

- Resolution of subfield separators: MODES uses : as a shorthand for a field separator, and it uses & to separate keywords within a field. These implied subfields need to be replaced by proper XML elements.

- Linking to image files: MODES has a complex and limited method of referring to external image and text files. Adopting the XML approach of entity references with notations is actually simpler and cleaner!

- Record IDs: In order to support record-to-record links, MODES automatically adds a unique ID to the top-level element in each record. This is derived from the unique database identifier, but some characters have to be changed and others removed to make the ID into a valid XML Name. References to related records are converted in the same manner.

- Mixed content: Not a requirement, but an opportunity! Currently, MODES lets you enter text in any way you want, followed by one or more subfields, but you can't mix the two. The XML-compatible version will support mixed content within any field.

New Possibilities

Adding XML support to MODES opens up new possibilities. Two of them are of major significance to how museums might use MODES.

First, support for mixed content means that MODES records could be written in a manner that is more like ordinary prose, without losing the advantages of a precise context for retrieval. Start by recasting the production example given earlier into XML, as in the following:

```
<PRODUCTION>
<METHOD><k>pencil</k><k>watercolour</k></METHOD>
<PERSON><role>draughtsman</role>
<name>Boyce, George Price (b1826 d1897)</name></PERSON>
<DATE>1864 (d)</DATE>
</PRODUCTION>
```

The elements that have been added in place of the : and & separators are in lowercase.

The following is how that `production` entry might be written as an ordinary sentence, yet still be fully marked up:

```
<PRODUCTION>Drawn in <METHOD><k>pencil</k>
and <k>watercolour</k></METHOD>
by <PERSON><name><forename>George Price</forename>
<surname>Boyce</surname> (b1826 d1897)</name>
(<role>draughtsman</role>)</PERSON>
in <DATE><k>1864</k> (d)</DATE>.</PRODUCTION>
```

> **Note:** The inverted form of the artist's name (Boyce, George Price) has been turned around, and subelements `forename` and `surname` have been added to retain this information. The inverted form was used in the first place so that personal names would sort, and can be searched for, by surname. There will always be a tension between the requirements of retrieval (which usually are of a consistent, formal presentation) and free text when you are trying to make one piece of structured text serve both purposes. Another strategy you can adopt is to hold the searchable form of a name as an attribute value where it is "hidden" when the data content is viewed, such as in the following:
>
> ```
> <person KEY="Boyce, George Price">George Price Boyce</person>
> ```

The second major opportunity that the XML-compatible version of MODES offers is in the area of linking. Up to now, MODES applications have been very object-centered, with information such as a donor's name and address being buried deep within each object's record and repeated each time that donor gives an object. This creates additional recording work and a maintenance headache. (If the donor relocates, you have a lot of records to update!)

With the improved linking offered by XML, this information can be held in a separate donor file. Each record will just contain a link to the donor's entry—no more redundancy. If the donor relocates, you have only one entry to update and all the references will automatically stay current. From a data maintenance point of view, this is as good as having a relational database.

This approach can also open up a new, broader way of managing museum information. Museums, and their public, have always been interested in the relationships of museum objects to the real world: who owned them, what events they commemorate, places they were used. It now becomes straightforward for MODES users to create separate files for historical people, events, and places of relevance to the collection, and to link them to the object records. Also, these need not be one-way links. XML extended links would let you start from the description of a place and navigate to all the objects in the collection that have associations with that place.

Best of all, because XML links work on the Web, there is no need for the museum to create all of these additional resources. If a commercial publisher has put a detailed gazetteer of the UK on the Web in XML format (or even in HTML), why not link to that? Also, links can go the other way. When the museum collection is established as an XML resource on the Web, other information providers will start to make links into its object records. Each information provider can concentrate on her own area of expertise and still contribute to an information base that is greater than the sum of its parts.

Summary

In this chapter I have taken a look around the world of museums to see what it reveals about the potential use of XML.

You learned about the issue of interchange—delivering structured information reliably across the Web. Museums routinely need to interchange information about objects in their collections. I showed how XML can support interchange among heterogeneous systems, but only if there is community agreement on the semantics of the information itself. In the case of UK museums, the SPECTRUM standard provides that framework. A second example of interchange I touched on is the delivery and updating of authority files, and how to tie local extensions into the standard authority scheme.

I examined in broad terms the advantages that XML might offer to an individual museum in its own work. I showed that it provides a much needed framework for getting better value from textual material. XML can also pull together the rich and varied types of information resources that a museum has to manage. And it can help researchers create meta-catalogs of the objects they are interested in describing and comparing.

Finally, I took as a case study the MODES cataloging software. This showed how an existing database can put on an XML face without having to change the way it actually works. You saw how the new XML-aware MODES will let museums adopt a more natural cataloging style. More generally, the example of museums showed how the development of XML-linked information resources can take you beyond single providers acting as publishers, to a situation where multiple providers interlink their resources to provide an ever-growing Web-based infobase.

CHAPTER 15

Automating the Web: Rapid Integration with XML

by Charles Allen

This chapter explores the use of XML to provide a practical and cost-effective means for diverse business systems to be rapidly integrated across corporate intranets, extranets, and the Internet. The following topics are covered:

- The transformation of the Web from an access medium into an integration platform
- Applets, plug-ins, agents, and channels
- Dynamic HTML and the Document Object Model (DOM)
- Electronic commerce
- XML as an integration platform

Weaving the Web

The emergence of XML promises to accelerate the evolution of the Web from an access medium to an integration platform, and from a medium for universal clients that allows end-users to interact with distributed systems to a platform for applications that can share and process data.

Indeed, the ultimate benefit of using Web technologies will be the integration of an organization's information systems with those of its suppliers, distributors, and customers.

The delivery of Web data in XML documents ultimately will make the Web more digestible; using XML metadata to describe and add structure to HTML-based Web content enables users to achieve much of this vision today.

Web integration is a broad topic because the Web is a big place. To help you get your bearings, I will lightly sketch the major features of the landscape before honing in on the most pertinent details.

Accessing the Web

The success of the Web has exposed the advantages of distributed information systems to a global audience. Access to an Internet terminal is practically access to the world; national and organizational boundaries now can be crossed with such ease that they often go unnoticed.

At its beginning, Web content was mostly static; HTML documents were delivered to browsers directly from the Web server's file system. Today, Web sites with dynamic content are appearing at an astonishing rate. Relational databases integrated with Web servers are responsive to user selections, transforming standard database queries into result sets presented as HTML documents.

Transactional applications, such as mainframe-based order processing and banking systems, are also being connected to Web servers to give users real-time data in HTML formats.

The use of standard formats and protocols to provide access to corporate information and documentation has transformed both how organizations are perceived and the way that organizations knit themselves together. In the process, the Web browser has morphed from an occasionally informative accessory into an essential platform for organizations of all sizes and shapes.

There is no doubt that ubiquitous access promises to increase productivity on some fronts; at the same time, however, the Web's almost exclusive focus on end-users threatens to reinforce manual inefficiencies in business processes.

It is common, for instance, for users to transcribe data from Web browser windows into existing corporate applications, especially when the Web data is coming from remote business units or external organizations. The rapid spread of dynamic Web data thus threatens to spawn armies of clerical clickers.

Web servers today serve data to countless browsers; the goal in automating the Web is to have them serve data, or functions, to diverse applications. In other words, Web servers should be accessible as middle-tier application servers.

Serving the Web

The proliferation of database and transaction-based applications on the Web necessarily implies a proliferation of software platforms that connect corporate data sources to the infrastructure of the Web. Approaching the subject of practical Web integration over standard Web protocols, don't limit yourself to the more enlightened publishers who rapidly adopt XML as a means of preserving structure in Web data.

The only technologies you can count on Web server platforms to share in the near term are HTTP, HTML, and SSL. The use of XML metadata to define functional services over these standard protocols will enable developers to exploit this common ground.

As you are now well aware, HTML was designed for presentation, not exchange, of information. It is only natural that proprietary workarounds to HTML's limitations have appeared at several stages in the process of delivering content to end-users.

On the server side, products have appeared that interpret proprietary tags or HTML *extensions* at runtime. Such extensions enable richer content management frameworks, providing templates for the conversion of heritage and relational data into HTML documents, and for the application of advanced formatting and styles. This technology is contributing directly to the appearance of mountains of mission-critical data on the Web.

The benefits of server-side HTML extensions are primarily in flexible site management and rapid deployment. The costs are that valuable detail is lost in the process of merging templates with business data into standard HTML documents, and that a greater burden is placed on servers.

Database Read/Write and Transaction-Based Browser applications that utilize HTML lose detail regardless of their server-side implementation.

In the long run, XML will help in all of these areas. Today, however, the most sophisticated Web server platforms must still cater to a browser-based audience that is dependent on HTML. The result is that Web content creators are primarily concerned with formatting, not data structure.

The following product price list, for instance, has lost important information about the names and relationships of the database tables where the data originated:

```
<TABLE>
  <TR><TD>Hammer      </TD><TD>12.00</TD><TD>50</TD><TD>Tom's Tools
  </TD></TR>
  <TR><TD>Screwdriver</TD><TD>8.00 </TD><TD>60</TD><TD>Handyman
  Hardware</TD></TR>
  <TR><TD>Pliers      </TD><TD>10.00</TD><TD>35</TD><TD>Get A Grip!
  </TD></TR>
</TABLE>
```

To establish a functional relationship between a non-browser client and the data that is contained within such HTML, it is necessary to reintroduce structure via metadata files that map specific elements of the document to field names or program variables.

Not much is gained if the burden of providing such metadata is laid at the door of content providers. The architecture must be flexible enough to enable any organization to provide the metadata necessary to automate interactions with the resources provided by any other organization's Web servers.

Before discussing exactly how this can be accomplished, I want to explore a little further the challenges presented by the technology of the Web today.

The Desktop Dilemma

I have discussed how proprietary server-side extensions have attempted to address some of the shortcomings of the Web. On the client side, plug-ins, Java applets, and ActiveX are playing a similar role by enabling important functionality at the expense of introducing proprietary data formats that limit either cross-platform deployment or the capability of other applications to process Web content.

Delivering client applications dynamically over the Web seems to solve many of the most troubling deployment issues introduced by client/server architectures.

As long as the focus is on delivery of user interfaces, however, business-to-business integration will continue to be dependent on human middleware.

When Jon Bosak of Sun stated, "XML gives Java something to do," he was in part suggesting that XML should be used instead of proprietary message formats to communicate with server-side functionality. If this were the case, the benefits of Java (or any other client technology) could be realized for end-user applications delivered via the Web without sacrificing further integration opportunities.

There is good reason to be optimistic that this vision might soon be realized. Already a number of XML parsers are available in Java, and Sun's involvement in the development of both technologies makes it very likely that an XML parser could soon be packaged as a standard Java utility. This would have the effect of making XML the message format of choice for communications between Java clients and Web-enabled servers.

In this regard, XML promises message formats and data sets that do not tie content and service providers to particular vendors' authoring, scripting, or publishing tools. XML could even be used to define languages and formats to deliver the full richness of today's browser plug-ins. Microsoft has already suggested that XML be used as one possible Data Object delivery format for Data Binding in Microsoft's version of Dynamic HTML.

Where plug-ins, applets, and ActiveX components with proprietary transports are used to deliver end-user interfaces, it is still possible that some portion of the available functionality could be encapsulated, although numerous issues with security and firewalls would limit the portability of any such efforts. Another concern is that there is an administrative overhead to each new data format that needs to be integrated.

The bottom line is that in a world of many-to-many relationships, organizations that are not focused on selling directly to individuals will be limiting their long-term potential for integrating their supply chains if they deploy application interfaces consumable only by people.

Agents and Channels

Agents were the first Web citizens to automate interactions with Web servers. The earliest agents were Web crawlers that sucked down HTML documents and ripped them apart to enable free-text searching of their contents by search engines. Today, agents can auto-submit multiple URLs to numerous search engines and directory listing services. The more sophisticated ones know how to check whether submissions were successful.

Some agents are even aggregating classifieds from multiple corporate Web sites or enabling real-time price comparisons for commodity items such as books and CDs (although such price comparisons are actively resisted by vendors who don't want their services to be commoditized).

In many cases, agents utilize some form of script or metadata file to describe the forms to which they auto-submit information and the structure of the documents from which they cull meaningful data. Metadata and script files enable agents to rapidly learn about resources that vary widely in layout and functionality. Because HTML does not describe the data that it contains, such files must be crafted and managed by people.

The trouble is that no standard language exists for describing the functional resources of the Web. Although there are numerous agent applications, there is still no generic agent platform formalizing the means of automating interactions over the Web.

Push channels are a more recent instance of Web automation. At present, competing push vendors require that both publishers and subscribers have proprietary software installed. Microsoft has defined a Channel Definition Format (CDF) in XML that would enable push channels to overcome these limitations and become interoperable across different push technologies. It remains to be seen, however, whether CDF will succeed as a standard. There is already reason to think that CDF functionality could be subsumed into a much broader metadata standard.

The arrival of push technologies has introduced alternative delivery mechanisms for Web content, moving the Web beyond the browser. Both agent and push technologies, however, are still almost exclusively focused on the end user.

Although some agent technologies exercise HTML forms, and some channel technologies provide structure to the information offered on Web sites, no attempt has been made to address the metadata requirements for business systems to utilize the Web for secure and robust integration of remote functionality. XML is well suited to the task.

Automating the Web

In the August 1997 edition of *Wired* magazine, Tim Berners-Lee was quoted as saying, "The objective is an automatable Web. It could have a very revolutionary effect."

The revolution is upon us. The use of XML as metadata can provide sufficient information about existing Web content to enable non-browser applications to automate interactions with Web servers. In other words, it is not necessary for Web content to exist as XML in order to use XML to automate the Web today.

In fact, in order to integrate business systems over the Web, it would not be sufficient to have only data that describes itself; it would also be necessary to have metadata that describes the behavior of services hosted by Web servers.

As you know, documents written with XML are extremely amenable to automated processing. For instance, an XML document containing patient information might be dragged from a browser and dropped into a desktop application, which could then utilize the markup to extract appropriate data fields and update hospital records.

Transactional and database read/write applications on the Web, however, are typically driven by forms implemented in HTML. To check a company's stock price (inevitably delayed by 15 minutes), a stock symbol is submitted via a form on one document, and the relevant data is returned into a second document. If data is unavailable, or a symbol is invalid, a third or fourth document structure might be used to return appropriate error messages.

An automated Web wouldn't require a person to drag and drop documents from one application to another. In order to create a fully automated stock quote service, metadata would have to describe both the method for submitting input criteria into a form in one HTML document and the mechanisms for retrieving relevant output information from all documents that could conceivably be returned. In other words, a functional behavior across two or more documents would have to be defined.

Web servers use various proprietary APIs and CGI-bin scripts to integrate disparate databases and legacy systems. Application functions from innumerable legacy systems, databases, and middleware infrastructures are thereby united in a common platform, accessible via both the same protocol (HTTP) and the same data format (HTML).

The addition of XML metadata to define interfaces to Web-enabled application services would provide the basis for a common API across legacy systems, databases, and middleware infrastructures, effectively transforming the Web from an access medium into an application-integration platform.

My organization, webMethods, has employed XML to implement a Web Interface Definition Language (WIDL) directed at these needs. The remainder of this section examines WIDL's workings as an example of how XML can be used to automate the Web.

Describing the Functionality of the Web

In much the same way that Channel Definition Format (CDF) seeks to provide a metadata language that allows Web sites to be described as content for push channels, the Web Interface Definition Language seeks to enable the functionality of Web sites to be described to remote systems.

The concept of an Interface Definition Language (IDL) is not new. IDLs exist for many middleware technologies. For instance, an IDL for CORBA (Common Object Request Broker Architecture) describes interfaces to CORBA objects that live in a distributed environment.

The Web Interface Definition Language describes business objects on the Web, defining an API to services (such as CGI scripts) that reside behind Web documents.

Processing Documents

At the highest level, WIDL describes the location (URL) of services, the input parameters to be submitted (via GET or POST methods) to each service, and the output parameters to be returned by each service. This last requirement implies a capability to reliably extract specific data elements from Web documents and map them to output parameters.

Two candidate technologies for data extraction are *pattern matching* and *parsing*. Pattern matching extracts data based on regular expressions, and it is well suited to raw text files and poorly constructed HTML documents. There is a lot of bad HTML in the world! Parsing, on the other hand, recovers both document structure and the relationship between document objects.

From an administrative point of view, pattern matching is more labor intensive for establishing and maintaining relationships between data elements and program variables. Regular expressions are difficult to construct and more prone to breakage as document structures change. For instance, the addition of formatting tags around data elements in HTML documents could easily derail the search for a pattern. An object model, on the other hand, can see through such cosmetic changes.

Patterns must also be carefully constructed to avoid unintentional matching. In complex cases, patterns must be nested within patterns. The process of mapping patterns to a number of output parameters thus can become quite onerous.

It is possible to achieve the best of both worlds by using pattern matching when necessary to match against the attributes of objects accessible via an Object Model. Using a hybrid model, pattern matching within objects provides for the extraction of target information from preformatted text regions or text files.

Variable Assignment

JavaScript introduced a Page Object Model that provided access to a small set of elements on a page within a browser. More recently the World Wide Web Consortium (W3C) has established a working group to specify a standard Document Object Model (DOM) that makes it possible to address all the elements of both HTML and XML documents.

A convenient way to access document objects is with an object reference. Here again is the example price list:

```
<TABLE>
  <TR><TD>Hammer     </TD><TD>12.00</TD><TD>50</TD><TD>Tom's Tools
  </TD></TR>
  <TR><TD>Screwdriver</TD><TD>8.00 </TD><TD>60</TD><TD>Handyman
  Hardware</TD></TR>
  <TR><TD>Pliers     </TD><TD>10.00</TD><TD>35</TD><TD>Get A Grip!
  </TD></TR>
</TABLE>
```

An object reference of `table[0].tr[].td[0]` returns an array of item names. Using object references makes it simple to provide a mapping between elements extracted from Web documents and the output parameters defined by WIDL. The XML element to achieve this is defined as follows:

```
<VARIABLE   NAME='products'
            TYPE='string[]'
            REFERENCE='doc.table[0].tr[].td[0].value' />

<VARIABLE   NAME='prices'
            TYPE='string[]'
            REFERENCE='doc.table[0].tr[].td[1].value' />

<VARIABLE   NAME='quantity'
            TYPE='string[]'
            REFERENCE='doc.table[0].tr[].td[2].value' />
```

```
<VARIABLE   NAME='vendor'
            TYPE='string[]'
            REFERENCE='doc.table[0].tr[].td[3].value' />
```

In this example, each column of the price list is mapped into an array variable, demonstrating how XML metadata can be used to reintroduce structure into HTML documents.

Interfaces and Services

An interface is a collection of services. Services, in turn, consist of variables that are submitted and variables that are returned. In specifying WIDL, we thus needed to define XML elements for interfaces, services, and variables (both input and output), as well as appropriate attributes for representing the information necessary to automate interactions with Web servers.

Taking the example of the stock quote service I discussed earlier, a program that automates the Web processes a 'stocks' WIDL to understand that in order to access a 'stockQuote' service, it must submit an input parameter 'symbol' using the 'post' method to 'http://quote.yahoo.com'. WIDL also defines object references to map received Web content into output parameters, such as 'companyName', 'stockPrice', 'percentChange', and 'volume'.

Additionally, WIDL supports object-oriented interfaces, allowing for the definition of multiple instances of 'stocks'.

Given the preceding criteria, the XML for an implementation of the 'stocks' interface is written with WIDL as follows:

```
<WIDL NAME='yahoo' TEMPLATE='stocks'>

<SERVICE NAME='stockQuote' URL='http://quote.yahoo.com'
METHOD='post' INPUT='quoteInput' OUTPUT='quoteOutput' />

<INPUT NAME='quoteInput'>
<VARIABLE NAME='symbol' />
</INPUT>

<OUTPUT NAME='quoteOutput'>
<VARIABLE NAME='companyName'
REFERENCE='doc.table[2].tr[1].td[2].value' />
<VARIABLE NAME='stockPrice'
REFERENCE='doc.table[2].tr[2].td[2].value' />
<VARIABLE NAME='percentChange'
REFERENCE='doc.table[2].tr[3].td[2].value' />
<VARIABLE NAME='volume'
REFERENCE='doc.table[2].tr[4].td[2].value' />
</OUTPUT>

</WIDL>
```

WIDL is parsed in the same manner as Web documents to extract the relevant information about the services it provides. For instance, an array of available services for a given WIDL file is retrieved with this simple object reference:

```
widl.service[].name
```

The URL and method for each service, the input and output variables, and the object references for output variables are retrieved in a similar fashion.

Automated Applications

After defining a WIDL file for a given Web service, you can generate application-level functions or methods that are insulated from the specifics of the implementation of each service. A generated function must include a reference to a WIDL file, a service name, and input and output variable names; it does not need to include the specifics of where a service resides (URL), the method used to invoke the service (POST or GET), or object references used to retrieve data into output variables.

The specifics of a service's implementation are dynamically retrieved from the WIDL file at runtime, thus separating the administration of service definitions from a service's invocation in application code, and insulating applications from changes in Web-hosted functionality.

Resolving attribute mappings at runtime enables centralized change management of WIDL files as well as the use of naming services to provide location transparency. In other words, both the location and structure of Web documents can change without affecting applications utilizing their services. Application functions can even be remapped to equivalent functionality elsewhere on the Web.

From the 'stocks' WIDL, it is possible to generate a Java class 'stockQuote.java'. Java developers can simply include this class in their applications, accessing the stockQuote service with a single line of code:

```
stockQuote myQuote = new stockQuote("SUNW");
```

The Java class encapsulates an understanding of how to locate and interpret the 'stocks' WIDL, pass the input parameters to the appropriate Web service, and return the expected data to the calling program.

If for some reason the Yahoo stock service is unavailable, the WIDL can be used to transparently redirect this request to the CNN Financial Network.

Conditions and Error handling

A significant feature of WIDL is *condition processing*. Web-hosted applications return errors in different document formats than those used to return successful data responses. When unexpected document formats are returned as the result of a service request, object references return either null values or meaningless data.

In the case of the stockQuote service, a symbol of `'XXX'` might return a document containing the message `'invalid symbol'`.

The following simple condition element can handle this situation elegantly:

```
<CONDITION   TYPE='FAILURE'
             REFERENCE='doc.h1[0].value'
             VALUE='*invalid symbol*'
             REASONTEXT='invalid symbol' />
```

In other words, the condition element compares the value of an object reference to a known error condition. If the condition is met, the service fails with a message of `'invalid symbol'`.

Success conditions are also established using this mechanism:

```
<CONDITION TYPE='SUCCESS' OBJECT='doc.h1[0].value' VALUE='price' />
```

In this case, the service can be considered successful only if the specified object reference returns a value of `'price'`, indicating that the expected document has been returned.

Finally, conditions are used to divert a service to an alternate set of object references for output variables. This functionality is required when a Web application returns different document structures based on submitted input criteria. Different SKU numbers, for instance, often refer to items that are presented in pages with varying layouts.

XML Documents

Interfaces to services returning data in XML formats are described in WIDL in the same manner as services returning HTML documents. The main differences are that object references are less obscure and less likely to be impacted by major changes in document presentation, and that the process of constructing WIDL files is simplified by the presence of DTDs describing data schemas.

E-Commerce Extrapolations

Many companies make the mistake of equating electronic data interchange (EDI) with electronic commerce. EDI is a set of standards to facilitate business-to-business ordering and fulfillment processes, whereas electronic commerce embraces online querying of supplier databases and the real-time integration of supply chains over extranets and the Internet.

Electronic commerce, or *e-commerce*, in fact addresses a much broader exchange of information that facilitates ordering and fulfillment processes. But e-commerce on the Web is threatened by the proliferation of incompatible platforms that introduce proprietary protocols for communications between buyers and suppliers. Vendors of such platforms attempt to leverage buyer and supplier relationships to sell their solutions on both sides of the network. It's very rare, however, for an organization to possess the clout to force all buyers or suppliers to conform to one e-commerce infrastructure.

The many-to-many reality of buyer-supplier relationships mandates that a common ground be found. When restricted to standard Web protocols, e-commerce systems today can provide only browser-based access to transactional systems.

In many ways, e-commerce confronts obstacles similar to those experienced by middleware vendors attempting to integrate systems from different business units within the same organization. Crossing organizational boundaries with middleware technologies often introduces political tensions because software components must be purchased, installed, and integrated with diverse systems on either side of a network. In most cases, such integration efforts can be successfully driven only by executive vision.

Middleware Without the Middle: Middleware for the Masses

The use of XML metadata as an enabling mechanism for business-to-business integration over standard Web protocols facilitates a move from manually driven information links to automatic application links.

XML metadata requires only that a system be Web-enabled in order for it to be integrated over standard Web protocols. Hundreds, if not thousands, of vendors offer products to Web-enable existing databases and legacy systems, effectively removing the middleware dilemma. Because proprietary technologies are not required on both ends, there is in fact no middle. Buyers and suppliers of all sizes can use the Web-enabling technology of their choice, leveraging any investments they might have already made.

Flexible deployment is perhaps the most important attribute of an XML-based IDL for the Web. Instead of requiring all e-commerce–enabled sites to provide WIDL for their services, WIDL files can be centrally or independently managed by a buyer, a supplier, or a third party, or by a combination of buyer, supplier, and third party.

The next step is a service-based view and brokerage of Web functionality that enables a new level of integration.

Consumer-focused agent technologies are already aggregating services such as online ordering of books and CDs. CommerceNet, a consortium of industry and technology leaders promoting Internet-based commerce, envisions an economy of online services and virtual markets linked via an open Web platform that enables them to utilize and add value to each other's services.

An XML-based IDL such as WIDL provides the platform for a standards-based approach to the aggregation of functional services into vertical application domains, such as package tracking, healthcare, and financial services.

The Transformation of the Web

Web servers were originally designed to feed HTML to browsers for human consumption. Because the Web has been almost exclusively designed for the end-user, businesses have capitalized on Web technology to make business systems accessible via Web browsers.

Today, businesses are moving aggressively to capitalize on the integration of business systems made possible by intranet and Internet technologies. Although the Web infrastructure provides basic connectivity, it does not provide a standard integration platform. Web sites have been unable to intercommunicate without extensive hand-coding.

An open market requires support for many-to-many buyer-supplier connections. Integration via proprietary technologies threatens to limit the number of connections and therefore the openness of markets. Vendors, especially small vendors, cannot afford to maintain multiple proprietary technologies, which only increase complexity and exacerbate problems in management of information systems.

XML metadata in the form of an Interface Definition Language for the Web can deliver a practical and secure mechanism for the integration of business systems over standard Web protocols.

Summary

The World Wide Web is providing millions of end-users with *access* to ever-increasing volumes of information. Although the Web initially served static documents to browsers, dynamic content has rapidly emerged to provide end-users with interactive information services including package tracking, travel reservations, and online purchasing.

On corporate intranets and extranets, the Web browser has enabled *access* to business systems, but in many cases it has reinforced manual inefficiencies because data must be transcribed from browser windows into other application interfaces. Understandably, the technology behind public content sites and corporate applications has been focused almost exclusively on the presentation of data. HTML extensions and hacks, which embed ancillary information in proprietary tags or comments, are workarounds that have enabled dynamic data to be merged with HTML templates for display purposes. Inevitably, data structure information is lost in the process.

Browser plug-ins and applets have extended browser functionality, but they have introduced numerous proprietary message and document formats. In a world of many-to-many relationships, a standard for cross-organizational messaging and data transfer is sorely needed.

XML will address all of these concerns. XML preserves data structure information and provides a standard message format. Furthermore, XML metadata is now being employed to define Web content for push channels, and there is an active project within the W3C to use XML syntax to define a far broader standardized, portable, metadata format for Web content. XML is poised to transform the Web.

This chapter has presented the view that XML metadata in the form of an Interface Definition Language (IDL) also can be used to define functional interfaces to business objects on the Web.

Interactions normally performed manually in a browser—such as entering information into an HTML form, submitting the form, and retrieving HTML documents—can be automated by capturing details such as input parameters, service URLs, and data extraction methods for output parameters. Mechanisms for condition processing also can be provided to enable robust error handling.

An IDL for the Web would transform the Web into a standards-based integration platform, removing many barriers traditionally associated with middleware technologies, and fueling the growth of business-to-business electronic commerce over Web.

PART IV

The Future of XML

CHAPTER 16

XML Software

by Simon North

Because the XML specification is still in its draft form, you probably do not expect very much software to be available. It is therefore a pleasant surprise to be able to say that although there aren't hundreds of software packages out there, there are still quite a few, and some of them are extremely good. Many of the packages are either free (and a tribute to the generosity and open-spirit of their authors) or can be used on an evaluation basis.

Trying to create a definitive list is, of course, an almost impossible task because a new package can be added overnight. The most definitive source of information concerning new software is probably Steve Pepper's now quite famous "Whirlwind Guide to SGML Tools and Vendors," which can be downloaded free of charge from `http://www.infotek.no/sgmltool/`. However, many other sources of information are available. For full details, see Appendix B, "Bibliography."

XML-Specific Software

The software programs and packages described in this section are true XML applications, not packages that were originally created for a different purpose.

Jumbo

Jumbo (Peter Murray-Rust, Director of the Virtual School of Molecular Sciences, Nottingham University, England NG7 2RD, `peter.murray-rust@nottingham.ac.uk`) is a set of Java classes designed for viewing XML applications. This package was originally intended for use with a homegrown SGML variant called Chemical Markup Language (CML). Described by its author as "HTML with chemistry added," CML allows molecular structures, analysis spectra, crystal structures, and many other aspects of molecular chemistry to be modeled and displayed without forcing the user to become involved in too much SGML code. Jumbo was one of the very first XML applications. The viewer can be used as a standalone application (under a Java interpreter) or as an applet under a Java applet viewer or any Java-enabled Web browser. Full details of Jumbo can be found at `http://ala.vsms.nottingham.ac.uk/vsms/java/jumbo`. The package, including a full set of examples, is available free for personal use only. (You can add new examples, but you cannot redistribute the classes without the author's permission.) It can be downloaded from `http://www.venus.co.uk/omf/cml`.

Lark

Lark (Tim Bray, Textuality, 321-3495 Cambie Street, Vancouver, British Columbia, Canada V5Z 4R3, `tbray@textuality.com`) is an XML processor written in Java. Lark does not validate XML documents and actually is missing quite a lot of XML support, but it is fairly well documented, and as a tool for exploring the design of XML processor application program interfaces (APIs), it is an interesting and very valuable contribution. The Lark distribution, including the source code for eight of the 10 Java classes, can be downloaded for free from the Textuality Web site at `http://www.textuality.com/Lark/`.

LT XML

LT XML (Language Technology Group, Human Communication Research Centre, University of Edinburgh, 2 Buccleuch Place, Edinburg, Scotland EH8 9LW, `http://www.ltg.ed.ac.uk`) is a set of command-line utilities for processing well-formed XML documents. The utilities included are, among others, `sggrep` for performing regular expression searches on XML and SGML files, `sgmltrans` for translating XML files into some other format, and `sgrpg` for querying and transforming XML files. The package also includes a C language API. LT XML currently runs under only UNIX (although a 16-bit MS-Windows version is promised soon) and is available free to individuals, researchers, and development teams for non-commercial purposes. To obtain the package, fill in the research license agreement at `http://www.hcrc.ed.ac.uk/software/researchxml.html`, and an e-mail message will be sent to you giving the address of the ftp site from which it can be downloaded.

MSXML

MSXML (Microsoft XML Parser in Java, Microsoft Corporation, One Microsoft Way, Redmond, WA 98052-6399, USA, `http://www.microsoft.com/`) is an XML parser written in Java. The parser loads XML documents and builds a tree structure of element objects that can be manipulated through a simple set of Java methods. MSXML does not yet fully support all of XML. (Support for `XML-SPACE`, `XML ENCODING`, the `RMD` (required markup) declaration, and conditional sections has not yet been implemented.) However, it does make a good base on which to build applications. MSXML is subject to a Microsoft license agreement, but it can be downloaded for free from `http://www.microsoft.com/standards/xml`.

NXP

NXP (Norbert's XML Parser, Norbert H. Mikula, Department of Informatics, University of Klagenfurt, Austria, `nmikula@edu.uni-klu.ac.at`) is a full, validating XML parser written in Java. NXP is free and can be downloaded from `http://www.edu.uni-klu.ac.at/~nmikula/NXP/`.

RI.XML

RI.XML (Sean Russell, University of Oregon, Eugene, OR, USA, `ser@javalab.uoregon.edu`) is an XML parser written in Java. Although it is still in development, and thus very poorly documented, the package can be downloaded for free from the Web site at `http://jersey.uoregon.edu/ser/software/XML.tar.gz`.

TclXML

TclXML (Tcl XML Toolkit, Steve Ball, Australian National University, Canberra, Australia, `tcltk@anu.edu.au`) is a Tcl add-on that allows you to parse XML documents and DTDs. The package also includes "pretty-printer" commands for printing out Tcl list or Tcl linked tree representations of the parsed XML document. To use TclXML, you need Tcl version 8.0b1 or later. The package is free and can be downloaded from `http://tcltk.anu.edu.au/XML/`.

XDK

XDK (XML Developers Toolkit, Copernican Solutions, Inc., 1313 Fifth Street SE, Suite 11, Minneapolis, MN 55414, USA, `support@copsol.com`) is a C++ and Java developer's kit including both validating and well-formed parsers and APIs for validating, loading, and accessing XML documents. There are no availability details for this tool yet, but you can check the Web site at `http://www.copsol.com/products/xdk/index.htm`.

XMLLINK

XMLLINK (Bert Bos, W3C, `bert@w3.org`) is a set of various Java utility programs (xmlpipe, xmltest, xmllink, xmllink2, and xmlxptr) for parsing and processing XML documents. It also includes *typechk*, which type checks XML documents based on the SQL-like typing proposed by Tim Bray. These and a few other interesting programs can be downloaded free of charge from `http://www.w3.org/XML/notes.html`.

XMLVIEW

XMLVIEW (Chris Stevenson, `chris@grace.ssabsa.sa.gov.au`) is an XML viewer Java applet written using the Java Developers Kit (JDK) version 1.1. This means that it can be used with the JDK, with the Symantec Appletviewer, or with Hot Java 1.0, but not with Web browsers because they do not yet support this version of the JDK. The package is free and can be downloaded from `http://www.users.on.net/zhcchz/java.html`.

SGML-Based Software

It is possibly a little unfair to all the other software vendors to selectively list just a few SGML packages here. However, there are a lot of SGML tools (160 packages at the last count, and 83 major software companies—not including the more than 30 independent developers responsible for some very excellent public domain and shareware packages). In principle, any SGML software package should eventually be able to deal with XML documents (which was one of the XML design goals, after all). However, rather than list all the packages, I have listed details of only those packages that already support XML or have announced that a version of their software that supports XML will be available in the near future.

This means, for example, that I have explicitly excluded packages such as Microsoft's Internet Explorer because version 4.0 currently supports only CDF (covered in Chapter 18, "Potential Applications of XML"), and it is anyone's guess when version 5.0 (which should fully support XML) will be released.

Be warned that as XML becomes more and more accepted, you can expect existing SGML packages to be very quickly converted to handle XML, so the list of available software packages can change very quickly.

ADEPT*Editor

*ADEPT*Editor* (ArborText, Inc., 1000 Visitors Way, Suite 100, Ann Arbor, MI 48108-2700, USA, info@arbortext.com) was originally an excellent native SGML editor. An XML version is expected. ADEPT*Editor is available for MS-Windows, UNIX, and IBM OS/2. For details, check ArborText's Web site at http://www.arbortext.com.

Astoria

Astoria (Chrystal Software, Inc., 10875 Rancho Bernado Road, Suite 200, San Diego, CA 92127-2116, USA, info@chrystal.com) is a document component management system. Initially intended for the storage of parts of SGML documents, it is suited ideally for the management and dynamic creation of XML documents. Astoria is available for UNIX and MS-Windows. For details, check Chrystal Software's Web site at http://www.chrystal.com.

Balise

Balise (AIS-Software, 35 Rue du Pont, 92200 Neuilly sur Seine, France, `emailinfo@ais.berger-levrault.fr`) is a software development kit initially intended for processing SGML code. Because it already supported Unicode (double-byte) characters, the transition to XML is probably the easiest for any SGML tool vendor. An XML well-formed document (WFD) scanner is promised in 1997. Balise is available for MS-DOS, MS-Windows, UNIX, and DEC/VMS. Limited-function evaluation versions are available on request. Check their Web site at `http://www.balise.berger-levrault.fr`.

DynaTag, DynaText, and DynaWeb

DynaTag (Inso Corporation, 31 St. James Avenue, Boston, MA 02116, USA, `saleschi@inso.com`) is a markup tool designed for the conversion of other formats into SGML, HTML, and XML. *DynaText* is an SGML formatting and display package. *DynaWeb* is an SGML-oriented Web server. This package is used by Sun Microsystems to dynamically convert SGML and XML into HTML for publishing on the Web (as covered in Chapter 18).

For details of these products, check the Inso Corporation Web site at `http://www.inso.com`.

Other Software

The software packages described in this section are not strictly XML packages, but they are either directly or indirectly involved with the XML developments.

DSC

DSC (Henry S. Thompson, Language Technology Group, Human Communication Research Centre, University of Edinburgh, 2 Buccleuch Place, Edinburg, Scotland EH8 9LW, `ht@cogsci.ed.ac.uk`) is a DSSSL expression, style, and transformation language syntax checker. The package currently runs under only UNIX (SunOS 4 and 5 and FreeBSD 2.1), is free, and can be downloaded by ftp from `ftp://www.cogsci.ed.ac.uk/pub/ht/dsc-1.0.tar.gz`.

Jade

Jade (originally known as "James Clark's Awesome DSSSL Engine," James Clark, London, England, `jjc@jclark.com`) is an implementation of the DSSSL style language. (This package and a back-end for the conversion of SGML into

Microsoft RTF were used not only to process the SGML code in which this book was written and to provide the Microsoft Word files required for printing, but also to process the SGML code in which the XML specification documents are written.) Supposedly, Jade currently supports only SGML and HTML documents, but it should have no problem handling XML. (James Clark is the technical lead on the XML Editorial Review Board.) It almost certainly will be the first package to support the XML style language (XS) when its definition has been completed. Jade is public domain (free) software. Compiled binary executables are available for MS Windows 95 and NT, and source code is available for UNIX (but the GNU `gcc` compiler version 2.7.2 is required). They can be downloaded from `http://www.jclark.com`.

Symposia

Symposia (Grif S.A., Immeuble "Le Florestan," 2 Boulevard Vauban, BP 266, 78053 St. Quentin en Yvelines, France, `sales@grif.fr`) was a combined HTML browser and editor, co-developed with INRIA (the French National Institute for Research in Computer Science and Control). A beta test version of this tool that supports the XML language (but not XML linking), called *Symposia doc+,* was released in July 1997. (An online demonstration can be viewed at `http://www.grif.fr/newsref/xmldemo.html`.) Symposia doc+ is available for MS Windows and UNIX. A 30-day evaluation version of Symposia doc+ is available free and can be downloaded from the Web site.

WebWriter

Stilo WebWriter (Stilo Technology Ltd., Empire House, Mount Stuart Square, Cardiff, Wales CF1 6DN, `info@stilo.com`) was originally a WYSIWYG HTML editor. An XML version was demonstrated at the SGML Europe 97 Conference in Barcelona, Spain, and it should be released in July 1997. The XML version will allow you to author XML documents and DTDs; you can author XML documents with or without a DTD, and you can even generate a DTD dynamically from the document that you have created. A time-limited evaluation version can be downloaded from Stilo's Web site at `http://www.stilo.com`.

Summary

This chapter gave you more than 10 dedicated XML packages and several more packages that started out as SGML or even HTML applications. That is a surprisingly large number, considering that the XML standard has not yet reached its final form. Some of the packages might sound a little "rough and ready," but don't let appearances fool you. Obviously, you can expect that the package released by Microsoft reaches a certain standard (although what exactly that standard is might be a topic for some discussion), but some of the packages (such as NXP) are so central to XML that they were used during the formulation of the XML standard to try to determine whether certain actions were feasible. Such an approach says a lot about the software, but it also emphasizes the very practical spirit that underpins all the XML activities.

CHAPTER 17

Resolution of the XML Specification

by Simon North

The XML specification is not yet finished, nor is it complete. In this chapter, I review the current status of the specification and look at the features and facets that are either being worked on now or will need to be worked on in the near future.

Let's start by quickly tracing some of XML's inheritance from SGML and see how it has shaped XML's approach to what are really problems shared by them both. Following this, you'll browse through some formal and informal activities that are either part of or contribute to the completion of the specification of XML. To bring things full circle, I conclude by returning to SGML and looking at how XML is reshaping SGML's future, which in turn has a direct effect on XML's future.

> **Note:** I quickly skim over some pretty complex topics in this chapter. Wherever possible, I've tried to limit the technical depth to just what is necessary. The full (technical) details of each of the topics covered in this chapter are generally publicly available on the Internet. For a full list of the URLs, see Appendix B, "Bibliography."

SGML on the Web

Years before XML was even thought of, there was an initiative called "SGML on the Web" whose intention was exactly that—to get SGML onto the World Wide Web alongside (or, for preference, instead of) HTML. The movement never really was much of a success and, now that XML has arrived, it has either finally succeeded, or will probably never succeed, depending on how you look at it. (An SGML purist might well consider XML to be an SGML sell-out, while a realist might welcome any means of getting SGML onto the Web.)

The original "SGML on the Web" initiative might have either renamed itself "XML," or it might have ceased to exist; however, the factors—and the people—involved in the development of XML and the problems that have to be overcome have remained much the same. XML has, therefore, also been able to inherit some of the earlier work on "SGML on the Web" (or at least to benefit from the earlier thought that has been given to the problems). One of these inheritances is a modular approach to the development activity (adopting the standard software development approach of "divide and conquer" by splitting a big problem into a lot of little ones).

The "SGML on the Web" approach divided the problem into four separate areas, some of which you can see returning in XML's specification:

- Syntax: This is part 1 of the XML specification.
- Linking: This is part 2 of the XML specification.
- Style: This has been distributed as an intended part 3 of the XML specification, but it has not yet been submitted to the W3C as a formal proposal.
- Chunking: For "SGML on the Web," this was delegated to the SGML Open Consortium.

The XML syntax and linking mechanisms have already been covered in Part II of this book, as has a little of XML style. The specification of XML will not be complete until the part on style has been finalized and a chunking mechanism has been worked out. In the first part of this chapter, we'll first look at XML style, then look at chunking, and finally consider some of the other contributions to completing the XML specification.

XML Style

In May 1997, Jon Bosak, the co-editor of the XML language specification, made a personal draft of a projected style section for the XML specification publicly available on the Internet. (See Appendix B for the URL.) The fact that this document bears the thought-provoking title "XML Part 3: Style [NOT YET]" might lead you to believe that what you are about to read is a rough draft that has been very quickly thrown together. Not so; in fact, nothing could be further from the truth.

The XML style specification (commonly known as *XS* for short) is, in fact, a minor reworking of the DSSSL-o application profile. DSSSL (pronounced *dissel*), which stands for Document Style Semantics and Specification Language (which you'll learn a little more about later in this chapter), is a language for specifying the formatting of an SGML document. (It is actually an awful lot more than this, as you'll learn later, but for now this description will suffice.) Whereas SGML has had a rough time getting accepted, DSSSL has had an incredibly difficult time, even though it has been around for a lot less time than SGML. It is no exaggeration to say that DSSSL is extremely complex. To be able to do anything serious with DSSSL, you need a fair familiarity with not just the programming language LISP, but also with a specific dialect of LISP called Scheme. Needless to say, you could probably cram the world's supply of Scheme programmers into one room. Add to this the fact that there is almost no documentation for DSSSL other than the drafts of the ISO standard (although in June 1997 a volunteer project to create a DSSSL handbook was started on the DSSSL Internet mailing list, which is detailed in Appendix B) and, as far as large-scale adoption is concerned, you have a recipe for disaster.

The complexity of DSSSL (compounded by the fact that it describes two languages and not just one—the transformation language and the style language) very quickly led to an attempt to create a "cut-down" version called *DSSSL-Lite*, even before the standard was published. (Voting on the draft of the DSSSL standard started in August 1994; the final standard was published in April 1996.) The DSSSL-Lite idea, in turn, gave rise to an Internet variation of DSSSL called DSSSL-o (short for DSSSL-online) that was published in December 1995 and then reissued in August 1996 to include a few corrections resulting from changes in the final version of the DSSSL standard.

It has been said that DSSSL is to SGML, as XS is to XML, as CSS (cascading style sheets) is to HTML. I don't intend to go any further into any of these topics here, other than to say that the jury is still out on the matter of XS. There are, as yet, no commercial DSSSL packages, precious few noncommercial ones, and no XS packages at all. (Not one SGML package supports DSSSL yet, despite various promises years ago, and none of the XML tools have made any mention yet of support for XS.) On the other hand, a few packages support CSS, and CSS capability is either already present or is being built into most of the major Web browsers. Microsoft has committed to supporting CSS, and Netscape is both directly supporting a slightly different version of CSS in its latest browser releases and indirectly committed to supporting CSS through its new JASS (JavaScript Style) technology. It is an unarguable fact that XS is far more powerful than CSS could ever be (without radical change), but the best technical solution is not always the winner. We must wait to see how XS develops and what the market decides about supporting it.

Chunking

The Internet was still very new when people started to think about publishing SGML documents on it. Even then, people realized that it was going to be necessary to publish composite documents (documents constructed out of pieces of other documents or, as we see quite often on the modern Internet, extracted from some other source such as a database and then assembled "dynamically" as circumstances require). This implied that there had to be a means of not just combining multiple documents into a single unit, but also of breaking SGML into pieces (that is, *chunks* or *fragments*).

Several initiatives have been concerned with methods for splitting up SGML documents into pieces and combining the pieces into documents again. The following sections cover the four most important methods and, to help trace the development of the common thread that unites them, I cover them in order of seniority, from oldest to newest.

Fragment Interchange

Long before XML was even an idea, the SGML Open Consortium (a fee-paying group of SGML software vendors and other interested parties) was asked to look at ways in which a fragment of an SGML document could be successfully parsed without access to the complete document. The matters that had to be settled were what information would be necessary to identify the document fragment or provide whatever other context information might be needed (such as automatic numbering), a notation in which to describe that information, and a means for linking that information with the fragment.

The result is SGML Open Technical Resolution 9601:1996, published as a draft in November 1995 and released in its final form in November 1996. The technical resolution describes an SGML specification that identifies the context of a piece of an SGML document (the name of its SGML declaration, its DTD, and its location in the hierarchical tree of SGML elements of the document it came from). The "packaging" of the description with the fragment itself is quite simply done using the same MIME Multipart/Mixed identification scheme used for e-mail messages made up of several parts.

Although it is a reasonably simple and quite elegant solution, the technical resolution is very much an SGML solution and, sadly, one that has not yet been implemented (and probably never will be).

So much for 1995/96's answer; on to the next one!

Web Collections

As its name suggests, whereas the SGML Open Technical Resolution was an SGML approach, the Web Collections angle is very definitely an Internet approach, or rather an HTML approach.

Having gone through several versions, the original (pre-XML) version of the W3C working draft (February 1996, and the October 1996 IBM Haifa revision) intended to extend HTML by adding specific tags to identify collections of documents and to specify the points in the collective document at which the individual comments are to be included. On the face of it, the scheme was quite workable, except for the fact that although they were able to suggest using the HTML <META> tag and adding a *tag ID* to URLs to provide most of the identification information needed, they were unable to suggest a workable scheme for including informative data (*meta-data*) for "sets of sets" such as lists, without defining a completely new set of tags.

The Web Collections idea would probably have stalled at that point if XML had not blown new life into it. In March 1997, a new proposal was submitted to W3C (with the editor's chair passing from IBM to Microsoft). This version is like an idea reborn; Web Collections is suddenly a full-scale XML application that promises to be expressible within HTML documents or in standalone documents.

Taking full advantage of XML's extensibility, the Web Collections syntax calls for a set of new elements to identify the collective document and the HTML pages that are included in it. To provide the "packaging" information, the authors propose creating a new MIME type (similar to the suggestion made in the pre-XML days) by using URLs in property element attributes (something that SGML couldn't do, but XML can) and by using XML's <LINK> element and its REL attribute to describe the relationship between the documents.

The proposal is still in a very rough draft form, but it shows a great deal of promise and, by using XML, there seem to be few, if any, technical problems in its path.

PICS-NG

PICS New Generation, or *PICS-NG* for short, represents yet another approach to the problem of collating XML documents and fragments of documents. This initiative comes from a totally different, even unexpected corner.

The Platform for Internet Content Selection was originally formed in 1995 as a response to the increasing amount of "bad press" that the Internet had been getting on account of too much pornography allegedly being accessible to children on the Web. At the time, it looked as though the Web faced a simple choice: censorship or self-regulation. PICS is an attempt at self-regulation. On a purely voluntary basis, the author of the home page (or whatever first page a visitor will see) adds a <META> element within the <HEAD> element in the HTML code to describe the nature of the content of the Web site (or more precisely, to state whether the content is unsuitable for minors). Then, using PICS-aware software, parents and teachers can monitor, or even block, access to sites with undesirable content.

It isn't a very large step to conclude that the kind of identification (labeling) done as part of PICS can also be put to other uses: to add digital signatures to HTML documents for cataloging purposes, and by letting a group of documents "point" to the same description set through a common URL, to allow multiple documents to be logically associated. In early 1997, a proposal was circulated to extend PICS in just this way and make it a more general, application-neutral method of describing content. The May 1997 proposal, submitted to the W3C working groups concerned with these matters, formalized the syntax, worked out a few of the concepts a little further, and extended the original to turn it into an XML application.

There is still a lot of work to be done on this proposal; currently, the XML syntax is somewhat experimental, and a number of issues still need to be worked out (such as the matter of inheritance). There seems to have been little thought paid to the possibility of handling partial documents, even though the use of XML to provide the extra element tags needed to describe the content gives an obvious pointer in the direction in which this could be achieved. It will be interesting to see whether or not the relevant working groups pick up on this and in what direction they take it.

MCF

The *Meta Content Framework Using XML* (*MCF* for short, and less affectionately known in some circles as "The Netscape Proposal" because Netscape provided one of the editors) is one of the most recent additions to the list of candidates for fractional and composite HTML/XML documents, the proposal to W3C being dated June 1997.

MCF starts off with the novel proposition that one man's metadata is another man's core data; it is simply a matter of context and does not justify an artificial distinction. The foundation of MCF is twofold: a set of labels (somewhat more extensive than any of the other schemes, but fundamentally the same in both purpose and function), and a mathematical model called a Directed Labeled Graph (DLG). Although there has been some criticism of this mathematical model, it certainly gives the MCF proposal the strongest theoretical foundation, even though this does seem to be at the cost of simplicity. I won't go any deeper into the model, but full information about it is available on the Internet, including a tutorial. One thing that makes MCF worth watching is that, unlike the other candidates, XML is wonderfully suited for computer manipulation, including database storage.

XML-Data

If MCF is Netscape's proposal, XML-Data is Microsoft's proposal. Beginning its life as a Microsoft position paper in June 1997, XML-Data was formally submitted to the W3C on June 26, 1997.

Turning its back on graph-based based methods (that is, MCF) as being incomplete, XML-Data defends the tree structure as the best way of modeling data and metadata and proposes the concept of a *schema* to contain the meta-information. Essentially, the schema is just XML data, but with a slight twist. To make an XML schema more compact, the XML-Data proposal suggests an extension on the normal element definition mechanism that exploits the fact that whole groups of elements are often very similar. To handle this, XML-Data introduces a generic mechanism whereby after the first element has been defined, all the other elements following it can use the same definition and *extend* it (in much the same sense that a Java class is extended) to add or modify attributes locally. Suppose you have a book and an article (both are types of publications); the schema for this could be as follows:

```
<xml:schema ID="PubsSchema">
  <elementType id="book">
    <relation href="#TITLE"/>
  </elementType>
  <elementType id="article" extends="#book">
    <relation href="MAGAZINE"/>
  </elementType>
</xml:schema>
```

XML-Data has a few advantages over the other methods: It is compatible with CDF (as covered in Chapter 18, "Potential Applications of XML") and PICS-NG, and it is consistent with the XML linking specification. It also has a very strong argument in its favor because, through the use of lexical data types, it even attempts to lay down a constraint mechanism for ensuring that the data contained inside elements is expressed in a well-defined format. (This kind of "data typing" is quite difficult to do in SGML and is next to impossible in HTML without recourse to external aids such as JavaScript. See the section "XML Typing," later in this chapter.)

With the considerable weight of Microsoft behind it and the impetus that CDF could give it, XML-Data will most certainly be an initiative to follow closely.

XML Processor API

Jon Bosak, the chair of the W3C Editorial Review Board (ERB), which is ultimately responsible for the XML specification, has been quoted innumerable times saying that "XML gives Java something to do." Well, this will be true when the programmers have worked out how.

Seriously though, one of the strengths of XML (and also one of the many reasons that HTML is proving inadequate) is that behind both SGML and XML lies a profound wish to live out the dream of "write once, publish many times." Tailoring the delivery of information to an Internet-based audience requires adaptability as well as extensibility, and to achieve that it requires a firm and powerful base. XML is ideally suited for this purpose and is ideally suited for computer processing to achieve it. Indeed, a lot of the restrictions that XML imposes on established "normal" SGML use are aimed at taking away the ambiguities in the language that make the software needed to process it so complex and, therefore, so expensive.

In order for XML to be machine processable, a standard must be set, or at least an application programming interface (API) must be agreed upon so that programmers can write common, interchangeable software and ensure that their software will work correctly with that of others.

At the moment, two quite contrasting initiatives are aimed at defining an API for XML: one a commercial effort, and the other a public domain effort driven by the authors of some of the leading free XML-related software.

I don't intend to go into any of the fine details of either development; rather, I will merely skate over their surfaces, highlighting the interesting points. Rest assured, though, that neither programming language experience nor understanding will be required.

DOM

The Document Object Model (DOM) started its life as an HTML-based idea under the aegis of the W3C. Somehow, however, it never publicly progressed any further than a very sketchy set of requirements. Then, in March and April of 1997, Microsoft started to show signs of cranking up its publicity machine for the pending release of version 4.0 of the Internet Explorer (IE) package. This package started life as a simple Web browser, but has since exploded into a multipurpose Internet client package (like Netscape Communicator, which is a Web browser, an e-mail package, and a Usenet reader). With version 4.0, Internet Explorer has completely cast off its humble beginnings and is threatening to become almost a complete user interface on the scale of Microsoft Windows itself.

Part of the IE 4.0 press package currently in circulation speaks very loudly of Microsoft's *Dynamic HTML* but says that this is the DOM proposal that has been submitted to the W3C and is based on XML. The charter for the W3C DOM working group, in which both Microsoft and Netscape are actively involved, includes support for HTML, SGML, and CSS. It can therefore safely be said that the DOM will support XML. So far, however, there has been no mention of XML in the material published online by Microsoft for IE 4.0 (other than the adoption of the Channel Definition Format, which is based on XML), and the descriptions of the syntax for object manipulation use methods that do not significantly differ from those already in use based on JavaScript. This is not to say that the results are not novel. Quite to the contrary, Dynamic HTML allows, among other things, the content of HTML pages (text and graphics) to be altered on the fly as well as the style attached to the HTML code to change (even interactively). It also allows HTML elements to be very precisely positioned (and moved, which enables animation) using local processing, without returning to the server for additional information or processing.

The closest that Microsoft seems to have come to a commitment in the direction of combining the existing W3C Document Object Model with XML is a "white paper" on XML that it published on its XML standards Web pages on June 23, 1997. Here's a direct quote:

> "In addition to providing a file format for representing data, XML needs a standard API for programmatic manipulation of data. Microsoft is working with the W3C to define a standard set of properties, methods, and events for programmers and script authors to use. This *object model* provides a simple means of reading and writing data to and from an XML tree structure. These methods enable programmers everywhere to treat XML as a universal data type for encapsulating and transferring data. Because the object model for XML matches the Document Object Model for HTML...."

Given how active Microsoft is in other XML matters, and given how active Microsoft is on the Internet standardization front, it's likely that soon a Microsoft-originated API for XML documents will appear. In particular, although Microsoft has said that IE 4.0 will only partially (through CDF, as discussed in Chapter 18) support XML, "future versions" will *fully* support XML. (IE 5.0 is predicted for a 1998/1999 release.)

XAPI (-J)

In June 1997, John Tigue, a programmer at DataChannel, voiced a growing concern that the rapidly increasing number of XML software packages each had a different way of looking at XML data. To try to initiate some kind of standardization, he made an informal suggestion on the XML developers' mailing list (a public e-mail forum for anyone active in, or just interested in, XML software developments) for a standard XML API for Java. Java was a natural choice because the majority of the currently available XML software is written in Java (as covered in Chapter 16, "XML Software"); the collective feeling was that Java would be achievable and, therefore, would be a good first step, leaving other languages for some later date.

What began as a loose, informal suggestion caught on like an infection, and within a few days the authors of the leading XML shareware and free software were pledging their support and offering to modify their packages to comply with an agreed proposal. That is how the XML API (XAPI) for Java was born (XAPI-J).

It is still very early as far as this activity is concerned, but things are developing very quickly. The parties involved have implicitly agreed to try to make an inventory of their individual approaches—often publicizing complete details of their software's code—and find some common ground for all their applications. The discussions are continuing, but the openness and willingness (even enthusiasm) of the people involved is a promising sign of great things to come.

XML Typing

One final piece to the XML resolution jigsaw puzzle really deserves a mention, but it has not yet gained sufficient momentum nor has it captured enough interest to develop much further. That piece is a public discussion document written by Tim Bray (one of the two XML specification editors) titled "Adding Strong Data Typing to SGML and XML."

It is a long-standing complaint in SGML circles (and it will probably become one in XML circles) that, although it is quite possible to enforce a rigid structure, there is no way to control or check the actual content of the elements. (Strictly speaking, some content validation can be enforced and achieved in SGML, but it very quickly makes the DTD so unwieldy as to be impossible for a human being to use.)

Tim Bray's proposal is to define SQL's strong type declarations as reserved attributes that can be attached to XML (and SGML) elements. (The Structured Query Language is the *de facto* standard for database query languages.) Using these data types (character, character string, integer number, real number, floating-point number, date, time, and timestamp), it would be possible to constrain the content of the elements to a form and format that would be far more usable for electronic data interchange and database-related applications. (XML's tree structure makes it ideally suited for representing the structure of relational databases, but it suffers severely from the lack of data typing.)

This proposal will almost certainly (even inevitably) be taken further; the only real question is when it will happen.

The SGML Technical Corrigendum

What does an *SGML Technical Corrigendum* (*TC*) have to do with XML? Well, to be honest, on the face of it, not a lot—except for one major problem: The whole of the XML syntax specification is based on the assumption that this TC will be accepted; if it is not, some clauses might have to be changed. You already know that XML is a subset of SGML; let's briefly look at the history of SGML and see what the TC entails.

The SGML Standard

Originally formalized as an ISO standard in October 1986, SGML has had a pretty quiet time until now, as far as international standards are concerned. An amendment to the standard was published in July 1988 to clean up a few ambiguities and typographic errors, and then it remained untouched until the Technical Corrigendum (TC) for Extended Naming Rules for SGML was published as Annex J to the standard in December 1996. (This TC is optional in SGML, but it is incorporated into XML. For a full description of the contents of the TC, see Appendix A, "Differences Between SGML and XML.")

It is normal practice to review a standard every five years, but for various reasons SGML escaped this normal revision procedure. There are, in fact, many reasons for the delay; however, apart from the great time and effort involved in reviewing the whole of this quite large and extremely complex standard clause by clause, most delays are related to standards associated with, or dependent on, SGML. Without going into too many of the technical details of these standards, it might still be interesting to skim over some of the major highlights.

HyTime

HyTime (ISO/IEC 10744 Hypermedia/Time-based Structuring Language) is a very important application of SGML that actually takes SGML several steps further and gives it the facilities it needs for representing, addressing, and linking both static and dynamic information in an unlimited number of formats and media, whether already defined or yet to be invented. (Some of HyTime's linking mechanisms have been incorporated into XML, as discussed in Chapter 9, "Linking with XML.")

Using HyTime, it is possible to link into and from individual frames in a film, time fragments of a digital sound recording, or even individual notes in a symphony.

First published in November 1992 (and still, rumor has it, not understood by more than a handful of "gurus"), the formalization of various theoretical models that underlie hypermedia such as addressing, linking, and accessing has had a very strong influence on the thought behind SGML and its future. The influence of HyTime on SGML has, in fact, been so profound that when the HyTime Technical Corrigendum was completed in early 1995, the SGML community realized that it described facilities that could be used by normal, non-HyTime SGML documents. It became pretty obvious that SGML needed some kind of modification to incorporate these.

DSSSL

Although HyTime was becoming formalized, a separate standard called DSSSL (ISO/EIC 10179 Document Style Semantics and Specification Language) had been living a fairly separate life, secure in its position as a means of describing the formatting and "other transformations" of SGML documents.

As long as it constrained itself to just the formatting, DSSSL seemed to live a fairly secure life, but that was only part of its purpose. DSSSL was also intended to provide a language in which a general transformation specification could be written that could transform documents from one SGML to another (for example, from "full" SGML to HTML). It was here that the problems really started.

HyTime versus DSSSL

The kind of addressing and linking that HyTime made possible as well as the kind of processing applied by DSSSL both required a formal way of looking at and describing the results of parsing an SGML document. Initially there was simply no agreement between the two approaches, and this caused major problems.

Over the next few years a lot of heads must have done some serious thinking and a lot of hard work; then, in 1995, the concept of *groves* (which was also incorporated into XML, as discussed in Chapter 7, "Physical Structures in XML Documents") first saw the light of day. With the publication of the proposal for a TC for DSSSL in November 1996, HyTime and DSSSL actually started to agree with each other about certain essential points.

> Note: These points of difference between DSSSL and HyTime were quite complicated and absolutely fundamental to their processing models. They involved a lot of extremely technical questions that sometimes seemed to the outsider to be involved with trivia (such as the handling of white space). At the heart of it was the problem that DSSSL and HyTime could parse an SGML document and produce two quite different trees of its structure. Fortunately, we don't need to concern ourselves with that here!

Revising SGML

Revision of the SGML standard did not seem to make much sense while the future form of HyTime and DSSSL was still being finalized. The HyTime and DSSSL standards have now been revised. (Revision 2 of the HyTime standard was approved in early May 1997 and should be published later this year; the DSSSL standard, distributed for voting by ISO members in August 1994 and published in January 1996, was the subject of a TC in November 1996.)

With all this settled, and with the specter of XML looming large, it became obvious that the time for a revision of SGML had truly come and that it had better happen quickly. Serious work has now started on the revision of the SGML standard, with the intention of publishing it by the end of 1997.

One of the most important changes is the incorporation of Appendix A of the HyTime standard into the body of the SGML standard. This includes the following:

- **Lexical types**: Rules for identifying and describing the parts of SGML's language—delimiters, elements, and so on.
- **Architectural forms**: Rules for creating and processing SGML elements.

- **Property sets and groves**: Named sets of properties that can be recognized by applications. (See Chapter 7.)
- **Formal system identifiers**: The formal definition of the notations used in system identifiers that can then be used to specify access to the "storage objects" and the entities in them.

While all this hard work was going on (and it really is a recurrent theme throughout SGML's and XML's joint history), the World Wide Web had been happening, and HTML had become the "killer" SGML application. These changes to the SGML standard had already been planned, and they are quite radical and far-reaching changes.

With so much going on, it would surely seem like a small effort to adopt some of the changes suggested by XML; however, the ISO standards procedure can take years. (Two years is not an unreasonable length of time for passing a draft standard through a vote by all the member countries.) If ever a saying typified the Web, it is quite simply "the Web won't wait."

The answer is a Technical Corrigendum for the SGML standard that allows a lot of the ISO's formal approval procedure to be either bypassed or accelerated. The TC introduces changes that will give SGML some of XML's strengths and, on the other hand, will make XML an official "conforming" SGML application.

The TC consists of two annexes to the SGML standard—*Annex K: WebSGML Adaptations* (a "normative" addition; in other words, not mandatory for compliance with the SGML standard), and *Annex L: Application Requirements for XML* (an "informative" addition).

Annex L is really (in its version 1.0 form) nothing more than a pointer to the XML syntax specification and a paraphrasing of the list of restrictions imposed on SGML by XML contained in Appendix A of the XML specification. (These differences are listed and explained in Appendix A of this book.) In the rest of this chapter, I concentrate on Annex K.

Annex K: WebSGML Adaptations

Until Annex K is adopted and implemented into SGML, the existing SGML tools will be largely unable to handle XML instances. The XML Syntax standard includes its SGML declaration (in Appendix A of the standard), which makes most of XML's features valid in SGML, but not all of them. The SGML "WebSGML Adaptations" basically lay out the instructions for modifying

SGML (mostly through changes to the SGML declaration), but they also introduce to SGML some of the basic concepts that make XML so powerful.

> **Caution:** A word of caution before you go any further! The Technical Corrigendum as described here is only a proposal (project JTC1.18.15.1) that was submitted for ballot on June 9, 1997. The closing date for voting by the members of the working group (Working Group 8 of Subcommittee 18, which is a part of ISO/IEC Joint Technical Committee 1—even though there is only one joint TC) is September 22, 1997; only then can anyone outside the working group know what the future form of the TC will be. On May 8, 1997, the French and Norwegian representatives (Michel Biezunski and Steve Pepper, respectively) submitted a proposal for a phased introduction of the TC. Without guessing what the reaction to this proposal might be, I can say that it does give some indication that the future of the TC is not necessarily guaranteed.

You might be wondering if the changes might not even happen. Undoubtedly they will happen, but it's more a question of "when" than "what." Let's look at what these changes are. I won't go into full details of all the changes because some of them require a pretty good knowledge of SGML to make them comprehensible, and I won't even mention all of them because some are only of passing interest. (The proposal is freely available on the Internet if you want to check out all the fine details. See Appendix B.) Instead, I'll concentrate on those changes most relevant to XML, and you'll see for yourself how XML and SGML seem to be doing their best to find some middle ground with SGML on the Web and XML as a recognized SGML application.

New Definitions

The very first change to SGML—one that a lot of SGML diehards would probably never have even dreamed of—is the adoption of XML's concept of *well-formedness*. Not to make it too obvious, though, SGML has adopted its own terminology to define three different types of SGML documents:

- **Type-valid documents**: These are just the same old SGML documents they always were—that is, documents that have an SGML DTD associated with them to which they conform.

- **Tag-valid documents**: These are documents that are fully tagged but do not need a DTD. There may be a DTD, but the document can be parsed with or without it.

■ **Fully tagged documents**: These are documents in which every element has a proper start tag, end tag, and name (called a *generic identifier*), and the name of every attribute is present in the start tag in every attribute specification.

In addition to these new types of documents, the TC introduces new concepts concerning the storage of elements. The following new concepts also can be used to define the kind of processing required, but they are primarily storage oriented:

■ **Integrally stored documents**: These are documents in which every marked section and every element ends in the entity in which it started (which is necessary for XML to allow parsing to continue after failing to resolve an entity reference).

■ **Reference-free documents**: These are documents that have no entity references other than delimiter references, although they can contain attribute values that refer to entities. (This is needed for systems that cannot resolve entity references or, if the document is tag valid, for systems that cannot parse DTDs.)

■ **External-reference–free documents**: These are documents that have no *external* entity references, although they can contain attribute values that refer to entities. (This is needed for systems that cannot resolve external entity references.)

■ **Entity-declaration–free documents**: These are documents that have no entity references at all. (If the document is tag valid, it can be parsed by systems that cannot parse DTDs.)

Taking all these definitions together and relating them to XML, a well-formed XML document would, in these new SGML terms, be *tag valid* and *integrally stored*.

SGML Declaration Changes

Many of the changes affected by the TC are concerned with the SGML declaration that often precedes the SGML DTD. If the default SGML declaration is acceptable (the "Reference Concrete Syntax"), an SGML declaration is not needed. Where an SGML declaration is used, it allows you to define the *lexical* structure of a document (the DTD provides the description of the *syntactic* structure), what characters can appear in the document, how they are to be recognized, and what their functions are.

In the following sections, I'll give you a brief overview of some of the most important changes and additions. Don't forget, though, that the TC is still a proposal and can still change.

SGML Declaration References

One of the other most important changes brought about by the TC (next to not having a DTD) will be the fact that a subdocument will be able to contain an SGML declaration.

To implement this, an alternative form of the SGML declaration is permitted (known as an *SGML declaration reference*, which references an SGML declaration body). SD is added as a new public text class to identify an SGML declaration body.

Capacities and Quantities

The CAPACITY parameter in the SGML declaration limits the total number of certain objects that can appear in an SGML document (such as the total number of elements and the total number of entities). The TC introduces a new keyword, NOLIMITS, to indicate that there are no capacity limits. (In the SGML declaration for XML, the quantities are all set to 99999999 to get around the capacity limits.)

The QUANTITY parameter in the SGML declaration limits the total length of certain objects that can appear in an SGML document (such as the length of element names). The TC introduces a new keyword, NOLIMITS, to indicate that there are no quantity limits except BSEQLEN (the length of a blank sequence recognized as a short reference), which has the quantity specified for it in the reference quantity set (960 characters). However, specifying QUANTITY NOLIMITS does not necessarily mean that a system will be able to support unlimited quantities!

Assertions

The TC adds two new *assertions*, which are statements about the kind of processing that a document requires. These assertions are the *check validity assertions* and the *check entity constraint assertions*.

The check validity assertions are declared using a new VALCHECK parameter that allows a document to assert whether it is type valid, tag valid, or both. Here's the syntax:

```
VALCHECK, (TAGVALID?, TYPVALID?)
```

The SGML parser will report an error if an assertion is untrue; therefore, if an otherwise conforming type-valid document incorrectly asserts that it is tag valid, the document is no longer considered to be conforming. Had the assertion not been made, the document would have been conforming.

The check entity constraint assertions are declared using a new ENTCHECK parameter that allows a document to assert whether it satisfies specified constraints. The syntax of this assertion is

```
ENTCHECK, (INTEGRAL?, (NOREF ¦ NOEXTREF ¦ NOENTDEC)?)
```

where INTEGRAL specifies that the document instance is integrally stored, NOREF specifies that the document is reference free, NOEXTREF specifies that the document is external reference free, and NOENTDEC specifies that the document is entity declaration free.

The SGML parser reports a markup error if an assertion is untrue. If an otherwise conforming SGML document incorrectly asserts that it is integrally stored, the document will be treated as being nonconforming; on the other hand, if the assertion was not made, the document would have been conforming.

Empty Start and End Tags

The TC defines a new delimiter role called a NESTC, which is a "NET-enabling start tag close."

This brings SGML into line with XML, making XML's use of the special end tag for empty elements acceptable. In SGML, if NESTC is / and NET is >, an empty img element with a null end tag would look just like it would in XML:

```
<img/>
```

Hexadecimal Character References

The TC adds a new hexadecimal character reference open (HCRO) delimiter that can be used to represent a numeric character reference by a hexadecimal string. Again, this brings XML into line with SGML, or vice versa, making XML's hexadecimal declarations (&#x) legal.

Attribute Minimization

A new attribute minimization keyword is added to the SGML declaration, which has the following syntax:

```
(ATTS, (DEFAULT?, NONAME?, NOQUOTE?))?
```

In this syntax, DEFAULT enables attribute value defaulting, NONAME allows some attribute names to be omitted, and NOQUOTE allows some attribute values to be specified directly.

This legalizes XML's looseness in not necessarily naming attributes.

Attribute Definitions

The syntax for ATTLIST is revised to provide the functionality of the syntax

```
<!ATTLIST "#NOTATION"?
  (name ¦ name group ¦ #IMPLICIT ¦ #ALL )
  attribute definition* >
```

where name is either an element type name or a notation name (depending on whether #NOTATION is specified), name group is one or more names in parentheses, and #IMPLICIT refers to all implicitly defined element types (or notation names). It is the equivalent of a name group. Finally, #ALL is all element type names or notation names.

With the #ALL keyword, the attribute definitions are associated with all element type names (or notation names). Definitions associated with #ALL can be overridden by attribute declarations for specific element types or notations, including definitions specified with #IMPLICIT (all implicitly defined element types or notations).

An attempt to redeclare an attribute that was previously declared for all element types (or notations) is no longer to be treated as an error; only the earliest declaration will count (just as for entity declarations). But, on the other hand, multiple attribute lists that do not contain the same attributes are allowed and the final result will be a collation of all the attributes. This does, for example, allow an element's attributes to be supplemented by additional declarations (possibly included, for example, in linked documents).

Implied DTDs

In order to be able to parse SGML documents (or XML documents for that matter) with or without a DTD, it is not enough to simply persuade SGML that a DTD is not needed. The DTD is very heavily ingrained into SGML thinking, and as far as existing SGML applications are concerned, the old system (in which having a DTD is absolutely necessary) must still work. When you add to this the need to be able to deal with documents that do not necessarily declare a DTD (the way an SGML document would), the need to be able to handle partial documents, and XML's requirement to have one "root element" that is the beginning of the structural tree of the document, it is fairly obvious that SGML needs to have some way to imply the DTD from a document. Two mechanisms help to achieve this: a new "imply document type name" declaration in the SGML declaration, and a new keyword in the SGML document.

IMPLYDEF Declaration

When IMPLYDEF DOCTYPE is specified in the SGML declaration and there is only one document instance and no document type declarations, the document type declaration associated with the SGML document is assumed to be this:

```
<!DOCTYPE #IMPLIED SYSTEM>
```

This facility is used to imply the applicable DTD. When parsing without a DTD, there is no need to imply one.

This IMPLYDEF declaration (now that you've started implying things) can also be specified with the ELEMENT, ENTITY, %ENTITY, NOTATION, and ATTLIST keywords; thus, the corresponding statements can also be used without an explicit declaration.

The implied definitions are as follows:

- ELEMENT: - - ANY
- ENTITY, %ENTITY, NOTATION: SYSTEM
- ATTLIST: CDATA #IMPLIED for each attribute definition

When IMPLYDEF ENTITY is specified, a default entity declaration is not permitted.

IMPLIED Keyword

The TC allows a new #IMPLIED to be used as an alternative to the document type name in a DOCTYPE declaration or the source document type name in a LINKTYPE declaration. Here's an example:

```
<!DOCTYPE #IMPLIED SYSTEM "some.dtd"> <book> .... </book>
```

When this keyword is used, the document type name will be assumed to be the element type name of the document element.

If #IMPLIED is specified, the document instance must begin with the start tag of the document element.

Internet Domain Names

The last change I'll mention here is probably one of the last finishing touches to make SGML truly ready for the World Wide Web. In the future, it will be possible to use Internet IP domain names that contain only minimum data as public text owner identifiers. To do so, the formal public identifier must begin with `IDN//domain.name`.

This almost brings SGML into line with XML, allowing it to use some Internet URLs as identifiers for public text. This doesn't go quite as far as XML, which is able to use "standard" Internet URLs (as defined by IETF RFC 1738). Just as with XML, however, the resolution mechanism for this is yet to be established.

Summary

In what must have seemed like quite a circuitous journey, we have traced the history of a wide variety of standards in this chapter. We started with SGML and how it more or less gave birth to XML. We looked at some of the problems that the combination of SGML and the Web had raised, and we followed their inheritance into XML where, hopefully, they will find their resolution. Then, browsing through activities related to XML, we looked at the supporting initiatives that will complete the definition of XML and make XML "ready for prime time."

Finally, coming almost full circle, we looked in some depth at the modifications that are being proposed for the SGML standard itself; modifications that will make XML documents valid SGML instances, thus opening the door in both directions: to the Web for SGML and to "industrial use" for XML.

CHAPTER 18

Potential Applications of XML

by Simon North

Although this chapter is called "potential" applications of XML, some of the applications that you learn about in this chapter are not potential applications at all; they are true working implementations (such as Channel Definition Format). Others are concrete applications that are firmly founded on XML but are either not yet complete or have not yet been released to the public (for example, Sun's AnswerBook and Math Markup Language).

Of the true "potential" applications of XML that you'll meet in this chapter, some (such as Health Level 7 and Handheld Markup Language) are in such an early stage of development that it is not even certain that they will become XML applications rather than applications of full SGML (or even HyTime). In one case (Topic Map Navigation), the reverse is true; even at this early stage we can safely say that it is an XML application, although we can really only guess what the final form of that application will be.

Whatever their state of development, the applications that you'll meet here give an interesting, even exciting, glimpse of some of the things that can and will be done with XML. No mean feat for a standard that isn't even complete!

CDF

The Channel Definition Format is currently hovering somewhere between being a proprietary Microsoft standard and an open WWW standard. The market has not yet made its choice, although some of the leading companies have committed themselves to supporting it. Whatever the market finally decides, CDF is an example of an XML application that has already arrived. It is here now, on the Internet, built into the latest release of Microsoft's Internet Explorer (version 4.0). If you haven't already seen it, you probably will see it soon.

Push Media

Ever since 1993, when "The Internet" really started to mean something to people outside academic and military circles, companies have been desperately looking for a business model that would serve as the foundation for true Internet commerce.

During the last few years there have been many attempts, ranging from closed systems such as CompuServe and America Online (AOL) to so-called *content providers* such as the ill-fated Microsoft Network (MSN).

When you surf the Web, the normal procedure is to start your Web browser (which is, statistically, most likely Netscape's Navigator/Communicator or Microsoft's Internet Explorer). You then enter the address (URL) of a Web page or pick an address that you have saved in your Bookmark or Favorite Places list. Needless to say, this is a pretty active process where you are in complete control. The experience can be made a more recognizable one (in terms of broadcasting) by adding advertising to the pages you visit in the form of *banners*, but the economics of charging for their positioning and use has raised problems that have not yet been resolved.

A new variant on banner advertising is beginning to appear now in the form of so-called *interstitials*. Interstitials are small advertisements that are displayed when you move from one Web page to another. The basic idea behind this type of Internet commerce remains as familiar as the billboards that line our streets and highways.

A business model that the media industry does recognize is traditional broadcasting. Translate that idea into World Wide Web terms and it becomes what Microsoft has aptly called *webcasting*.

Instead of browsing from Web site to Web site and from Web page to Web page within that site, you take out a *subscription* to a particular content provider. Instead of *pulling* Web pages to yourself, you allow someone else to *push* those pages to you when they decide. After you have made your subscription choices, you can sit back and passively enjoy the information as it is *webcasted* or *pushed* to your screen, almost as if you were watching television.

This is not to say that these services are bad; indeed, their success is a strange testimony to their merit. In a little more than a year, the original (and best known) providers such as Pointcast and Ncompass have been quickly joined by more than 30 other companies (including AOL, CompuServe, and MSN). Push media can now provide you with up-to-the-minute sports, news, entertainment, and financial information at a speed and efficiency level that very few television companies will be able to match. It will be up to us to decide whether we want to open our desktops to yet another source of potential information overload, or whether we will welcome it as an opportunity to cut down on information overload by publicly electing to receive certain types of information in preference to others.

It probably comes as no surprise that, with so many different companies competing for a place in this new market, there is no standardization among them and the methods they've adopted. No two webcasters are able to deal with each other's information.

For a while, it looked as though things were going to continue like this until, on March 9, 1997, Microsoft submitted a formal proposal to the W3C (the World Wide Web Consortium, one of the nearest things the WWW has to a standards body). Then on March 12, 1997, Microsoft made a public press announcement about its new Channel Definition Format (CDF) specification.

The Channel Definition Format

The Channel Definition Format (CDF) specification is an XML application that defines collections of frequently updated information, called *channels*.

The CDF XML Document Type Definition (DTD) is not yet complete; the latest release is version 0.31, which was updated on May 28, 1997. However, the basics of the DTD are reasonably stable and are already supported by version 4.0 of Microsoft's Internet Explorer.

The heart of the CDF XML DTD is the Channel element, which can contain a number of other elements that describe the information it contains and defines how and when the information it contains is to be updated:

```
<!ELEMENT Channel (Abstract, Channel, Item, Log,
                   Login, Logo, Logtarget, Schedule, Time)* >
```

It would be far beyond the scope of this book to go into the full details of the CDF XML DTD here, but it is worth looking at some of the highlights. The elements that the CDF DTD defines allow a channel to do a wide variety of things with your computer's screen display. Here are some examples:

- The <Usage> element can specify whether the information is to appear in the browser window as a screen saver or as a desktop component on Microsoft Internet Explorer's Active Desktop (introduced in version 4.0).

- The <Abstract> element identifies a *tooltip* text that will be displayed on the right of an icon when the cursor is placed over the channel icon.

Detailed information concerning the Channel Definition Format can be downloaded from Microsoft's standards Web pages and from its Internet Explorer Web pages. (See Appendix B for the URL addresses.)

Sun's AnswerBook

The quantity of technical documentation supplied with large computer systems has always been daunting. In some cases, it has even become totally overwhelming. Long-time (ex-mainframe) computer users would be familiar with the terms "Big Grey Wall" and "Big Red Wall," recalling the sight of a set of Digital Equipment's system documentation arranged in a copious bookshelf in some air-conditioned computer room. The cost of authoring, producing, and shipping such massive amounts of paper documentation has become a major overhead for systems such as these, not to mention the gargantuan effort of trying to maintain it.

It was, therefore, a fairly obvious step to start to move documentation away from paper and distribute it electronically. Sun Microsystems was a pioneer in this area, at one point even offering customers a free CD-ROM player if they would agree to accept their documentation on a compact disc instead of in paper form. Sun was prepared to offset the (then significant) cost of a CD-ROM drive against the major savings it would make in printing, storage, and shipping. With the move from the SunOS operating system toward Solaris, Sun has been moving almost completely away from paper documentation, so that the current recipient of a modern Sun workstation would actually receive a fraction of the amount of paper that a PC (or even a Macintosh) purchaser would have to browse through.

Sun's online documentation application, called AnswerBook, has been a great success. Based on PostScript versions of the printed documentation, the AnswerBook tool is easy to use and extremely useful. It provides the kind of hyperlinking that has since become familiar to anyone using a browser to view HTML pages on the World Wide Web (WWW), and it allows you to make the same kind of bookmarks and annotations that are familiar to any Microsoft Windows Help users.

Not content with relying on past successes, in 1994 Sun (which is, after all, the company that invented Java) started to appreciate that, despite the massive commitment that had been made in time and resources, AnswerBook was beginning to reach the end of its usability and would not be able to compete for very long with the developments that were happening on the Web. Sun therefore began to look seriously at alternatives to the current implementation of the AnswerBook software and to consider solutions for the future.

In the early 1990s, Sun experimented with HTML as an alternative, but it very quickly became obvious that, while HTML was a very good format for publishing and distribution, it was a very poor format for authoring, storage, and maintenance. The step "up" from HTML to SGML was a fairly natural one, and one made by a lot of other companies both before and since. SGML is, however, a time-consuming and initially very costly technology to adopt and, even for Sun, the argument for moving to SGML had to be convincing before it could be "sold to management."

The adoption of SGML and the move away from proprietary products to open systems was a natural move—a move very typical of the state and spirit of the software industry of the late 90s. SGML was the perfect enabling technology to meet the majority of Sun's goals for its documentation—but not all of them. SGML provided the means for the documentation to be written and managed in a controlled and controllable environment. SGML's validation mechanisms (using a custom Solbook DTD) ensured that the input was directly able to be stored and processed. However, looking to the future, Sun wanted to do certain things with its documentation that even pushed the limits of what was capable with SGML, such as link management.

The team tasked with finding and implementing a replacement for AnswerBook realized fairly early in their activities that an SGML solution was going to be expensive. It was going to take a lot of time and effort and they weren't going to be able to manage it on their own. The conclusion was that if they were going to commit to this project, there was no point in settling for half measures. The resulting goals were ambitious. The team that set out to rebuild Sun's online documentation identified not just the creation of the documentation as its terrain, but also included its management and delivery as well in its goals, which are as follows:

- To take the documents from the technical writers and package them in such a way as to make them available to all users (ideally with as little processing as possible).

- To support hyperlinking within and between separate "books" independently of where the books (that is, files) are physically located.

- To support context-driven searches.

- To support the manipulation by the users of the contents of book collections, enabling installation wherever they want.

- To enable the documents to be viewed outside the Solaris environment.

- To enable anyone to publish his or her own books within the environment.

During the period that the development team must have been making its initial design decisions, the Internet exploded, HTML arrived, and the WWW became the phenomenon that it now is, with Java rapidly following. It must not have taken much to persuade the team to experiment with publishing its documentation in HTML. A lot of computer and software manufacturers experimented with HTML. However, HTML (as you have already seen) is simply not powerful enough, and many of the goals that the team had set simply could not be realized with HTML. Java offered a way to compensate for some of the missing functionality, but very quickly the team was faced with adopting proprietary solutions once more. Worse, it was all very well to transform the SGML it was using to author and process the documentation downward into HTML, but it seemed such a loss to discard all the structural information in favor of something so very presentation-based as HTML. If nothing else, it was going to make the generation of dynamic tables of contents and indexes an extremely messy job. (How do you ensure that purely presentation-oriented markup such as font changes and boldface do not get carried across?)

At this point, it is worth noting that the same Jon Bosak who is chairman of the W3C SGML editorial review board (ERB) that approved the XML standard is employed by Sun Microsystems as an Online Information Technology Architect. With this in mind, it hardly seems a coincidence that the online documentation team embraced XML from the beginning as the answer to all its goals. Using dynamic (Java-driven) SGML to XML conversion, Sun can now publish its documentation via the Internet—but it has gone much further than this.

Via Sun's dedicated documentation Web server (currently at `http://docs.sun.com`, although it has not yet been widely publicized), the AnswerBook2 team is already publishing HTML and XML versions of the Solaris manuals converted dynamically from the SGML versions contained in the SolBook database. It is almost certain that when XML browsers make a serious entry into the marketplace, Sun will not hesitate to consider moving away from HTML.

Before leaving Sun's XML implementation of its online Solaris documentation, one experimental aspect of the software, though it is not directly XML-oriented, deserves special mention because it gives an interesting hint of some of the things that can be achieved with XML in the future.

Given that XML is able to store its hyperlinks outside the documents that are being linked, Sun has thought of an ingenious method of ensuring that a book will always be available. (Sun's goal is location-independent linking.) Using a variation of the SGML Open Catalog (which is used to manage SGML external entity references), Sun is trying to implement an external catalog that will describe the locations to which links can be resolved. Imagine you are reading a manual online and you click on a hyperlink to a different manual. This catalog would be consulted and the manual you have asked for would be located on your workstation. If it wasn't present locally, the software could be directed to look on the local network for the manual. If the manual couldn't be found on the local network, the link resolution mechanism could ultimately be directed all the way back to Sun's documentation server in Mountain View, California, where a copy would always be found.

Taking this a few steps further, this link resolution mechanism will allow Sun to accommodate some other intriguing situations:

- When a book is moved to a different server, all the links to it still work.
- When I'm reading in one language and a link takes me to a manual that isn't available in that language, I can automatically be switched to another preferred language if that is available.
- If I want to have my documentation installed locally to have it available as quickly as possible, I can still link to the very latest information on the Internet without necessarily even noticing that I've moved offsite.

The last word surely belongs to the team members themselves:

> "We are actively supporting the delivery of XML today and here come the applications. Do you think that Microsoft and Netscape own the WWW market? Think again....XML is!"
>
> *Eduardo Gutentag and Jeff Suttor, from a paper presented at the SGML Europe '97 conference in Barcelona, Spain, May 1997.*

MathML

The markup of mathematical formulae and equations has had a long and complicated involvement with electronic distribution. Long before the World Wide Web was even dreamt of, scientists were accessing databases containing mathematics marked up in TeX.

Somehow, however, mathematics and HTML have never quite managed to live together. The extension of HTML has been "on the way" for so long that even devotees have started to wonder whether it will ever happen. Proposals have been made, drafts have been circulated and discussed, and there was even a WWW browser (called Athena, which was available for the UNIX operating system only) that was able to interpret the HTML codes for basic mathematical equations. The syntax was rather simple, and the codes that it offered were a little limited, but given a little patience and some persistence, it was quite feasible to be able to include basic equations, matrices, and integrals, even if they did get a bit long for even relatively simple formulae, like this:

```
<MATH>{&int<SUP>a</SUP><SUB>b</SUB><LEFT>{f(x)<OVER>1-x} dx}
</MATH>
```

The HTML codes for mathematics were present in the March 1995 draft of HTML 3.0. In the discussion documents for HTML 3.2 (code named *Wilbur*), they had vanished. In the January 1997 W3C Reference Specification recommendation for HTML 3.2 (code named *Cougar*), it is as if they had never been there! Instead, in a small working draft called "additional named entities," a set of mathematical symbol entities are proposed for characters that can be represented as *glyphs*, as they appear in the Adobe Symbol font. Large symbols such as brackets, braces, and integration signs can then be built out of these glyphs by using their numerical codes:

```
&#189;&#913;&#178;
```

This is the code for the expression "one half alpha squared."

Strangely, the result is somewhat reminiscent of the printing codes that you used to have to insert into your text back in the 1960s to achieve a similar effect.

All is not lost, however, because it is here that XML is already beginning to prove the value of its extensibility. In April 1995, shortly after the WWW conference in Darmstadt, Germany, at which the proposal for HTML Math was dropped, a group of interested parties formed to discuss the problem further. Over the following years, the informal group grew into a formal W3C working group, attracting members from such renowned sources as the American Mathematical Society and Elsevier Science Publishers. Finally, in May 1997, the group published a working draft of the specification of an XML application called the Mathematical Markup Language (MathML).

Of course, as with so much involved with XML, there is still a lot of ground to be covered and a lot more work to be completed, but the working group already has an agenda in mind. June, July, and August of 1997 will see three planned revisions, with a formal recommendation being made in September 1997, and a second working draft being made in May 1998. Beyond that date, only the group members can guess at what the timetable will be.

Presentation and Content

MathML represents a very interesting variation on a theme that has pervaded the SGML world since the very beginning: the seemingly conflicting interests of presentation-based and content-based markup. Presentation-based markup is primarily concerned with the appearance of the final result, and it has given rise to such HTML elements as the horizontal line <HR> and <BLINK>. Content-based markup, on the other hand, is far more interested in identifying the information content of a document so that interesting things can be done with it, such as render it audibly for the sight-impaired, or even (in the case of MathML) submit it to a computer algebra system that can plot or solve the equation for you.

Perhaps recognizing that a picture really is worth a thousand words, MathML intends to incorporate both presentation-based and content-based markup schemes. Consider the simple binomial equation of $x(x + 4) = 1$. Multiplying out the brackets, this can be written using purely presentation codes as follows:

```
<MROW>
    <MROW>
        <MSUP>
            <MI>x</MI>
            <MN>2</MN>
        </MSUP>
        <MO>+</MO>
        <MROW>
            <MN>4</MN>
            <MO>&InvisibleTimes;</MO>
            <MI>x</MI>
        </MROW>
        <MO>-</MO>
        <MN>1</MN>
    </MROW>
    <MO>=</MO>
    <MN>0</MN>
</MROW>
```

Here the codes merely describe the appearance of the symbols on the page.

Now compare this with the same equation marked up with content-based codes:

```
<EXPR>
    <EXPR>
        <EXPR>
            <MI>x</MI>
            <POWER>
                <MN>2</MN>
        </EXPR>
        <PLUS/>
        <EXPR>
            <MN>4</MN>
            <TIMES>
                <MI>x</MI>
        </EXPR>
        <MINUS/>
            <MN>1</MN>
    </EXPR>
    <E/>
    <MN>0</MN>
</EXPR>
```

The two sets of markup give completely different views of the same objects: one as a set of pretty meaningless symbols that are positioned in relation to each other, where terms such as superscript (element <MSUP>) and subscript (element <MSUB>) have predominated, and another where the code represents a semantically meaningful statement consisting of expressions (element <EXPR>).

These two views of markup are, however, not irreconcilable and both have their place. Presentation markup is ideally suited for display and even provides a means for an expression to make sense when it is read out loud. In contrast, content markup represents the mathematical meaning of an expression in such a way that the statements can be understood.

Recognizing the need for both types of markup, MathML has taken a unique step and introduced a sort of "super element"—the <SEMANTIC> element. This element has two *children*. The first child is the presentation markup, and the second child is semantic markup. Within MathML, the semantic markup would of course be a set of MathML content tags, but this is not a requirement. The content of the semantic markup could be a computer algebra expression, or it could even be computer program source code (in C or even Java).

In its present incomplete form, XML has already given MathML a powerful means for specifying the structure and syntax of mathematics. More than this, XML has provided a flexible, extensible means to cater to current needs while keeping options open for an unpredictable future. At some point in the future, you can expect, or at least hope, that WWW browsers will be able to interpret and properly render MathML codes. Until this happens, the MathML application cannot call itself finished. The kind of powerful processing that the MathML working group already has in its dreams cannot yet be accomplished in any browsers that are available or planned. It could even be argued that the browsers available now cannot accommodate this sort of processing because they are too presentation-centered. Java (and possibly JavaScript) probably will provide the mechanisms that really do justice to all the promise of MathML. Until then, you must wait for the XML style and document object model standard developments to provide the basis for what will become a very exciting future for mathematics publishing. (Chapter 17, "Resolution of the XML Specification," looks at the steps needed to complete the definition of the XML specification.)

HL7

The Health Level 7 (HL7, named after the seven layers that make the ISO standard network model) group was founded in 1987 at the Hospital of the University of Pennsylvania, USA, to develop standards for the electronic interchange of clinical, financial, and administrative information between independent medical computer systems (hospitals, clinical laboratories, medical insurers, pharmaceutical companies, and so on). The outcome of many years of hard work and dedication from this volunteer group is the HL7 standard (now in version 3), which includes the following definitions:

- The overall structure for all information interfaces, including a generalized query interface
- Patient admission, discharge, transfer, and registration interfaces
- Order entry interfaces
- Patient accounting (billing) system interfaces
- Clinical observation data interfaces (for data such as laboratory results that are sent as identifiable data elements rather than as display-oriented text)
- A generalized interface for synchronizing common reference files (master files)
- Medical information management system standards

- Standards for patient and resource scheduling interfaces
- Standards for messages concerning the referral of patients between two institutions
- Standards for patient care messages that support the communication of problem-oriented records

Looking at the preceding list, it should be quite apparent how information-intensive the health care industry is. Your whole medical history—information possibly vital to your survival in the event of an accident—is floating around somewhere in every hospital, in every physician's surgery, in your pharmacist's accounting system, in a thousand different places in a hundred different forms. Therefore, it is perhaps a little surprising that there was no formal evidence of any interest in the use of SGML until as late as April 1996. Since then, however, the HL7 SGML Special Interest Group (SIG) appears to have made up a lot of ground and has taken a very active and prominent role in promoting the adoption of SGML (and more recently XML) and in the creation of a standard for the use of SGML in all domains of health care.

Although the SIG appears to always favor the use of "full" SGML, it is obvious that the group has not failed to take a sideways look at what has been happening on the World Wide Web and how successful HTML has been. In an almost parallel effort commissioned by the British National Health Service, a study was conducted into the application of SGML and HTML for electronic patient records. The draft report published by the SIG (in June 1997), as evidence of this attention, makes it quite clear that the DTD that the group is developing for HL7 version 3.0 messages is compliant with both SGML and XML.

The work of the HL7 SGML SIG has lately been gaining momentum. Recent legislation passed by the Unites States Congress (the 1996 Health Insurance and Portability and Accountability Act, HIPAA), the increasing transfer of the burden of health care from hospital to home care settings, and the deep financial difficulties being experienced by many hospital and health care agencies have given the movement impetus. HIPAA legislation has since been passed that requires the Secretary of the Department of Health and Human Services to select a standard by February 1999 for automated medical claims processing, and it has fueled the intention to develop an XML application to be called the Health Care Markup Language (HCML).

Although it is unclear precisely what form these developments will take, undoubtedly XML will have an important role to play. In the foreseeable future, a patient will be admitted into the hospital, and the staff will log into the hospital's Web site and access the patient's records using a Web-based software package that lets you view and handle the information fragments as *objects*. Drag one over to the database icon to load the information into the database; drag another to an e-mail icon to send a notice of discharge to the patient's general practitioner. Drag the accounting information to another icon and have it compose and send the accounts and claims for reimbursement to the patient's medical insurance provider. With the richness that XML can give to the identification of data and the processing power that Java can apply to leverage applications like this, even this scenario could be overtaken by events.

Electronic Datasheets

The electronics industry—especially in the area of semiconductors—represents a very specialized but extremely competitive market. An electronics engineer faced with a design problem might be faced with an impossible task of finding the right component needed to make the circuit complete. The component manufacturers, for their part, have devoted an unbelievable amount of time, effort, resources, and funds to their problem of finding the best means to distribute their data to these engineers as quickly, cheaply, and efficiently as possible.

The so-called Pinnacles Initiative was a first step in the move toward producing this information. (It is published in the form of loose-leaf *datasheets* and as bound volumes of *databooks,* which contain the same datasheets grouped according to application or component type and printed on a different size of paper.) It's worth pointing out that a very large number of datasheets are concerned; the complete set published by Philips, for example, represents several meters of shelf space. Originally, each manufacturer had its own way of representing the data, and all manufacturers shared the same problems of publishing the material before it became outdated. In 1993, realizing the underlying problems that not each electronics giant could solve on its own, Hitachi, Intel, National Semiconductor, Philips Semiconductors, and Texas Instruments formed the Pinnacles Group to define a common standard called the Pinnacles Component Information Standard (PCIS).

The heart of PCIS is an SGML DTD. It took the group very little time to select SGML as the modeling and interface format (vendor and platform independence were decisive factors) but several years to develop the DTD. After the data started to become available in this format, however, things really started to take off.

The richness of the chosen SGML format and the fact that it was a common format suddenly made it possible for engineers to search the books for specific parameters. It was only a matter of months before the first electronic databooks started to appear on the Web.

In 1996, the Pinnacles Group placed itself under the organizational umbrella of the CAD Framework Initiative (CFI), and people started to think about what else they could accomplish with this wonderful new initiative. The result was the Electronic Component Information Exchange Project (ECIX). Somehow it seemed ironic that so much effort had been expended in transferring the semiconductor information into a usable electronic form, but so much else was left to manage with old-fashioned paper methods, and this in an industry that would shut down tomorrow if it were deprived of its computers! The end result was the start of an ambitious project to create an electronic databook, one that could provide data directly to be used in electronic design applications and in simulation software to create behavioral and functional models. And if it could be done for semiconductors, why stop there? It could surely be done for *all* electronic components.

At first glance, the dream didn't seem quite as simple as it looked. The PCIS DTD successfully defined the structure of datasheet and databook documents (sections, section titles, text paragraphs, lists, and so on), but no two companies have as yet agreed on what to call these generic divisions. One company might have a section titled "pin description," another might prefer "pin functions," and yet another might use "pinning" instead. So, the project is now hard at work on the next step—a common dictionary for all of these items, called the Component Information Dictionary Standard (CIDS).

So where is this long story leading us, and where does XML come into this? The simple answer is "in the future." Similar to so many stories concerning XML, while this application was taking shape, the Internet happened, or to be more precise, the Web arrived. Although the original vision for PICS had been CD-ROM distribution, the Internet was a natural alternative, and SGML-to-HTML conversion was, and is, a relatively simple task to automate. However, HTML format was simply too limited to be useful (which is another recurrent theme in the "XML story"). SGML, HTML, and Java together were feasible, though. Norbert Mikula, then a little-known undergraduate student and now earning some acclaim as the author of the NXP XML parser (covered in Chapter 16's list of XML software), produced a very workable "proof of concept" for Philips Semiconductors. Norbert's Electronic Databook (called the PSC-EDB) used SGML, DSSSL, and Java with a great deal of success.

The PSC-EDB was only partially successful in overcoming some of the built-in restrictions of Java. Java was designed to be *safe*, meaning it cannot normally be used from within a Web browser to do anything potentially damaging (such as accessing local files) to the computer system on which its programs (applets) are running. Furthermore, Java left one major issue open. The most important part of a component datasheet is unquestionably the parameter information it contains (voltages, timing characteristics, and so on). Although PICS sorted out the structure of the information, CIDS is working on the terminology problem. But yet another obstacle must be overcome, and it is here, finally, that XML enters the picture!

So far, I've drawn a picture of complete chaos in the electronics industry, as if each company was doing exactly as it pleased without caring about—or even looking at—what other companies did. It seems that the only way electronics companies can work together is by forming massive committees and groups and spending years in discussions. Not so. Basically, much room is left for being different. Or is it? Again, nearly all the companies produced the same type of information, but it was all in different formats (such as tables, figures, or just text).

The answer was to go one level deeper. Each piece of data, called a *characteristic*, is further broken down into a value, a parameter name (such as voltage), a parameter symbol (such as V), and a parameter description (which is surprisingly important because each new type of component seems to bring a completely new set of parameters with it). Each of these characteristics can then be further identified according to types such as electrical or mechanical information, the products to which it applies, and so on. When the information is fully identified, it can be stored *outside* the datasheet. Using a concept called *reflection*, the data required at a certain point in the datasheet can then be referenced at the point at which it is to appear. All the author has to do is provide the context that determines how the data will appear (such as the surrounding table and all its columns and rows, or the rest of the sentence) and then reference the data that is to be included. However, in addition to the context providing the framework to make the data readable for a human being, the same mechanism can be used to make the same data processable by machines (in a CAD tool, by a database, and so on).

We are still in the early days for CIDS. The specification is nowhere near complete, and the ECIX project has a long way to go before it can even start implementation, but it is seriously considering XML (and is even rumored to have made the choice). XML's powerful addressing mechanisms (combining many of the strengths of both the TEI and HTML), its powerful linking mechanisms (combining the power of HyTime while escaping much of its complexity), its closeness to "full" SGML, its extensibility, and its close fit with machine processing (without necessarily being committed to Java), will undoubtedly provide the means to turn this grand vision into reality. And we are going to see it happen!

OpenTag

There was a time, not so long ago, when everyone had to admit to using predominantly American software, in the English language. Over the past eight or nine years, however, non-English–speaking users have been far more insistent on having a version in their own language. The translation industry and the software *localization* industry have therefore been experiencing golden years.

The effort that goes into translating manuals and localizing software is no trivial task—sometimes representing a task even larger than that of creating the original software and documentation. To make matters even more complicated, translation is never a matter of just one language; usually it's 10 or 11 languages at the same time! If that isn't enough, the professional translator then has to take into account a wide range of possible delivery formats, including FrameMaker MIF, Microsoft RTF, Interleaf IAF, and last but not least, plain ASCII. (ASCII is usually extracted from Windows resource, `.rc`, files—the files that a programmer uses to define the text appearing in the windows, menus, and dialog boxes that make up the user interface for Microsoft Windows applications.) For examples of the these formats in the context of translation, take a look at the comparisons that the OpenTag Initiative has placed on its Web site (for the address, see Appendix B).

It isn't as though every software package is different, though. Just imagine how often (assuming you're an MS-Windows user) you've seen a File menu that contains entries such as Open, Save, Print, and Exit. It doesn't take much imagination to realize that these words must come up time and time again, and it didn't take long before specialized software packages came on the market that offered a sort of "translator's memory." If a phrase came up a second time (either for the current job or from an earlier one), a database would be checked, and the previous translation for that language would be offered as a suggestion. (Not every software company uses the same terminology. Microsoft has a massive set of glossaries publicly available via the Internet for most of the leading world languages, and Microsoft is known to be very particular about its terminology.)

To handle the wide range of formats, many of the packages available on the market took a natural step forward and implemented a method of text extraction. Most of the formats mentioned earlier have a basic core of plain ASCII text in which you can, with patience, identify the actual text that you would see. Just as with HTML, if you can work around the codes, you can still find the text. However, a major difference with HTML is that the formats used by translators and localizers are extremely sensitive to mistakes. One slip in a Microsoft Windows resource file and the software quite possibly could never work again, forcing you to retrace your steps and, in the worst case, start over from scratch. (This happens far more often than a lot of translators would like to admit!) The software packages in general professional use are able to scan the formats they are offered, place markers at the points where they find text that needs translating, extract that text (ignoring any internal codes), and offer it to the translator as simple text. The translator can then translate the texts or, more often, distribute them to a whole team of colleagues for translation. When the texts are finished, they can be submitted to the software package, which then plugs them back into the file where they came from and leaves the internal codes intact.

In theory, it's a wonderful scheme. In practice, it actually works pretty well. Unfortunately, the software packages involved are expensive (which is a problem because many translators work on a freelance basis or are self-employed), and the packages are not compatible with each other. (Often, the packages use an internal coding mechanism that is almost as complex as the format they are supposed to be assisting you with.) When you have committed to one software package, you are basically locked in to that software package forever.

In February 1997, the American translation and localization company started a movement called the OpenTag Initiative in an attempt to break open this closed loop by establishing an open data encoding method to support the localization process in general, and to permit the robust interchange of data between the parties involved.

At the center of the OpenTag Initiative is an XML DTD, demonstrating the inherent flexibility that XML has inherited from SGML. But this DTD has a real twist. The point is that for this application, even the HTML DTD (weak as it is) is simply too complex. The OpenTag XML DTD does not need to describe information or model a complex structure; all it has to do is identify information and its location. The full XML DTD (version 5, May 14, 1997) easily fits on two sheets of paper (which is less than 200 lines including comments) and consists of a meager 26 elements, nine of which are empty (including the top, root element, which is an XML requirement even though it serves little real purpose) and a maximum of only six attributes.

In support of the DTD, an MS-DOS and a Java parser have already been developed (and are available free via the Internet), and customization files have been produced for most of the major software packages (IBM TranslationManager/2, Trados Translators Workbench, ILE LocaliX, and Atril DéjàVu).

So how does the OpenTag Initiative think it can get away with so little? Quite simply, by keeping it simple! More than 75 percent of the information contained in a file (an RTF file from a Microsoft Windows Help file or even an HTML page) is concerned with the formatting of the information (the physical appearance). Of course, this is of absolutely no interest to the translator, who only wants to change the text. The following is a simple example, a translation of a very basic HTML sentence from English into Dutch, French, and German:

```
HTML English: XML is <STRONG>undoubtably</STRONG> the future.
OpenTag English: XML is <G n="1">undoubtably</G> the future.
OpenTag Dutch: XML is <G n="1">zonder twijfel</G> de toekomst.
OpenTag French: XML est <G n="1">sans doute </G> l'avenir.
OpenTag German: XML is <G n="1">ohne Zweifel</G> der Zukunft.
```

If someone decides to change the markup at a later stage from <STRONG> to <EM>, it won't make much difference because the OpenTag markup is really only positional, as you see here:

```
HTML English: XML is <EM>undoubtably</EM> the future.
OpenTag English: XML is <G n="1">undoubtably</G> the future.
OpenTag Dutch: XML is <G n="1">zonder twijfel</G> de toekomst.
OpenTag French: XML est <G n="1">sans doute </G> l'avenir.
OpenTag German: XML is <G n="1">ohne Zweifel</G> der Zukunft.
```

Of course, this is a very trivial example, but it at least illustrates the intention. By using a very simple tagset, you can extract information from a document regardless of the original format (rather than convert it, as is normally the case in SGML applications), you can use the extracted information in a common neutral format, and then you can merge it back into the source document in the original format.

The OpenTag Initiative is very much in its infancy and a lot of work still needs to be done, but it opens up some extremely interesting future possibilities for XML (some of which are discussed later in this chapter in the section "Looking to the Future"). The amazing thing is that amidst all the hue and cry about HTML being too small, lacking power, lacking richness, being less desirable when SGML can do so much more, and many other less polite things, here is an application that actually benefits from having *less*!

Topic Navigation Maps

You've just looked at the OpenTag Initiative and how it is contriving to do more with less. In this section, the last of our grand tour of existing XML applications, you learn about the other end of the spectrum. Topic Map Navigation is, in all honesty, an extremely complex XML application, one that pushes even SGML far beyond its normal limits. To explain it here in all its richness would require several books and a fair understanding of not just SGML but also HyTime. However, because Topic Map Navigation uses XML's mechanisms to describe links, and it links XML documents, Topic Map Navigation does qualify as a true XML application (in fact, it might qualify as the first true XML extended-link application), and I will try to limit the discussion to that context. Be warned that it won't be easy. But by only skimming the surface of the technical detail, you should be able to at least get a taste of what Topic Navigation Maps could mean for the future of library science.

> Note: Officially designated as *ISO/IEC CD 13250, Information Processing–SGML Applications–Topic Navigation Maps,* topic maps currently exist only in concept form, even though there are some excellent proofs of concept. (The proceedings of SGML Europe 97 were produced in topic map form using HTML on a CD-ROM, and the EnLIGHTeN software package, from the French company of HighText, is a topic map tool without equal.) This means that a lot of detail still needs to be worked out before a draft standard can be submitted in 1998, and much is liable to change.

So what are topic maps? It's probably easier to start by looking at the problem that topic maps are meant to solve. Imagine that you have a vast quantity of information. Now double that quantity, double it again, and think *big*. Don't be shy; I'm talking about collections possibly as big as the whole Library of Congress. Putting all this source information into electronic form—or, better, into a structured electronic form such as SGML or XML—turns each of the documents into a sort of database. Suddenly you are able to electronically catalog, index, abstract, summarize, and ultimately link all this information together. You are able to *navigate* this information.

Along come the librarians, the catalogers, the indexers, and the glossary writers, and it looks like we will actually be able to make masses of data truly accessible as has never been done before. Wrong! The number of relationships between topics in a collection of books is literally infinite. Worse, there is no common agreement on the number and nature of the topics, and no consensus on the nature of the links between them. Indexes are often one-off affairs, tied to a particular document and context; when indexes are expanded into the context of multiple document *master indexes*, they quickly become vague and inconsistent. The larger they become, the worse they become, as more people are required to cooperate. Add a new book to the collection (or even a new field of knowledge such as genetic engineering), and existing indexes become instantly obsolete. But little if any thought is given to making such indexes maintainable, so there's a good chance that you have to restart the indexing each time from scratch.

Topic maps provide a formal, machine-executable way to create and maintain information by classifying the information in documents into topics and, taking it one step further, classifying the topics themselves with relation to each other.

This is all well and good but all pretty academic so far. How does it work in practice? Brace yourself because this bit gets technical. Topic maps rely on one essential feature of XML (and HyTime)—the capability to link two objects by means of an external link description (an *independent link*, called an *ilink* in HyTime, and an *extended link* in XML). A set of linked objects is called a topic. (Remember that—unlike HTML, for example—links can include multiple sources and multiple targets.) Why not just call it a link? Links between objects, such as index entries, are location identifiers where the link simply describes the location of a piece of information. Topics are far more powerful than this. They can also describe the semantics of the link, such as the way a glossary entry points to a location that is considered to be the definition of something. Topic maps provide a means to add an element (called the *semantic assignment*) to all the related objects and their anchors (the topics) and assign them a role, a description, or something significant that means that they can be merged with other topics, linked to other topics, maintained, and machine generated.

Taking this to the next level of abstraction, these topics—or a particular architecture of topics that was designed for a particular document or a specific field of knowledge—can be represented as a set of topics and a set of topic relationships, together called a topic map.

So why the fuss? Put in the simplest of terms, topic maps exploit the fact that in XML (and HyTime) the links between objects can be kept outside the documents themselves. When you describe the nature of these links, or at least identify them as topics, a relation can then be defined between the topics themselves—which is the topic map. You can have any number of topic maps for any set of documents, and topics can be included in any number of topic maps. Because everything is external to the documents themselves, topics can be made and modified at the whim of the reader to suit any purpose, no matter how transient. Even better, there is no restriction on the nature or significance of the relationship, and each reader can combine topics and other topic maps in a way that suits his or her particular needs at that time.

Before leaving the subject of topic maps, one last facet should be examined. Topic Map Navigation will exploit all of XML's linking mechanisms. (In fact, it will probably exploit many if not all of HyTime's far more powerful addressing and locating mechanisms, but this is something that still must be decided on.) It will be possible to link *any* kind of electronic information, whether it's SGML, non-SGML, XML, non-XML, structured, or non-structured.

Looking to the Future

It's been a long journey, but this grand tour of XML applications has taken you from the simplest (OpenTag) to the most complex imaginable (Topic Map Navigation). It has covered commercial ground (Channel Definition Format), and it has covered scientific territory (Math Markup Language). No tour like this can ever be complete, though, because new applications for XML are being thought up and announced all the time (and this is even before the introduction of any real support in the way of tools).

Before you hang up your traveling shoes, I should do one thing to make this tour complete. Let's take a final glimpse at the crystal ball of the future and try to anticipate some of the other applications that probably will be announced over the next year or two. However, whereas someone once said that a week in politics is a long time, a year in the Internet world is a century of normal life, and it is absolutely impossible to look very far ahead. So, to round out this tour, let's make a quick examination of two applications that are not yet XML applications but probably will become them. Each of these applications is a classic example of two of the most important features that will make XML a force to be reckoned with: HDML for handheld devices where a specialized version of HTML is needed, and DDTP for support services where the richness of SGML is needed but without the complexity. XML will flourish in these areas where SGML is too complex or simply too bulky, and where HTML is too limited.

Handheld Devices

When someone talks about "being on the Internet," a picture automatically springs to mind of the person sitting at a computer screen or perhaps a television screen. However, this image is slowly drifting away from reality as more so-called handheld devices arrive on the market. Most of us have seen some kind of pocket agenda, and we've at least heard of these new pocket-sized computers (*Personal Digital Assistants*, *PDAs*, to use the imaginative term thought up by their manufacturers). These are one type of handheld device, but they are only the tip of the iceberg. Nokia already has one telephone on the market that can send and receive e-mail, send and receive faxes, and even browse Web pages. Although sophisticated machines such as Nokia's telephone sport a standard (if very small) keyboard, with the increasing adoption of Java (which was also meant to be able to run on domestic electronic appliances), it becomes quite easy to imagine a fairly cheap and simple telephone (or even a pager) being used for surfing the Web.

Typical handheld devices can be characterized as having a small display area, limited input capabilities, a very limited bandwidth (the amount of data they can handle at once), and limited computing resources (memory, processing power, and so on). (These devices don't really even need to be handheld as such. This could just as easily apply for voice-operated devices, or specially adapted devices for the sight-impaired or the physically disabled.)

In the Handheld Device Markup Language (HDML) specification of April 1997 (version 2.0), the American company Unwired Planet puts forward a proposal for a markup language that is similar in many ways to HTML but is much more attuned to this kind of device. The specification also proposes a supporting environment for interpreting this language, called a *user agent*.

The markup language itself is extremely simple. It uses 16 or so elements and manages to describe the basic interaction between a user and a system using menus, menu choices, and tasks and pages (called *cards*). It even manages to include basic text formatting (wrap, bold, centering, tabs, and so on). Most of the work of displaying cards and acting on menu choices is done by the user agent, which acts on a very extensive list of element attributes (which the specification calls *options*).

If it was implemented, HDML would most certainly work and would probably do a very good job. However, the specification, at least at the moment, does represent just one company's idea with seemingly little or no outside support yet. Despite all the hard work and careful thought that has gone into formulating the specification, it can surely be only a matter of time before HDML is rewritten as an XML DTD and the user agent is implemented as a Java applet.

Software Support

Computer customer support (software and hardware) has experienced a phenomenal growth over the past few years. Today, it is almost unthinkable for a software company not to have a *help desk*, and computer companies have come to appreciate this kind of customer support as a central part of their business that is essential to their survival. However, for many companies, the expense, resource drain, and specialized skills demanded by a full-scale support organization are well beyond their capabilities, forcing them to contract out these activities to specialist bureaus and agencies. On the other hand, the giants who can afford to provide this kind of support have increasingly been made to face up to the fact that the majority of problems causing someone to seek this kind of assistance are not restricted to their products alone, but are more often the result of the difficulty of making several products from different companies work together properly. Add to this the fact that computer products (both hardware and software) are becoming so complex that they are beyond the possible understanding of any one individual, and then complicate matters even further by accelerating the speed at which products are released onto the market, and it is impossible for a support engineer to keep up. The result is an environment in which the exchange of information is rapidly becoming essential to survival.

Since 1992, some of the major players faced with these problems (including some giants such as Microsoft, IBM, Novell, Lotus, Silicon Graphics, Hewlett-Packard, and Adobe) have been participating in an alliance called the *Customer Support Consortium*. The main task of this alliance is to define a standard (called the *Solution Exchange Standard*) by which the member companies can "share customer knowledge and problem resolution information" by "capturing, reusing, and exchanging solutions to user problems."

Surely it will come as no surprise that an SGML DTD forms a central part of the Solution Exchange Standard, because nearly all the companies use different software to manage support calls (some using simple text retrieval tools, and some using extremely sophisticated *case-based reasoning tools*). Companies can use an SGML DTD (called the *Digital Document Transfer Protocol*, or *DDTP*) to identify the important information contained in incident reports, diagnoses, and ultimate problem resolutions, plus any annotations, in a way that can be made meaningful to customers, resellers, customer service providers, hardware vendors, and software publishers via automated electronic document exchange.

At the end of 1996 and during the early part of 1997, the first software packages supporting the standard started to appear on the market. Typical of this software is the SolutionPublisher, published by a company called Primus from Seattle, Washington. SolutionPublisher is a Web-based package that simulates a typical dialog between a user and a support engineer to collate a usable problem description. This description is then matched against existing solution data, or if a solution cannot be found, a properly formed description is e-mailed to a human support engineer who can take things from there.

It is notable that Primus opted for HTML as its format for SolutionPublisher. Although it is possible for us to only guess why they chose not to implement the full SGML DTD, the answers cannot be far from the many reasons I have already mentioned for SGML to not be adopted (such as its complexity, its bulk, and its cost). HTML will inevitably prove itself to be far too limited, far too rigid, and far too generic to survive for very long in this application. This is an application where XML can be expected to make its entry very soon. SGML, on the other hand, is well up to the task, but the fact that user support is very quickly focusing on the Internet as its prime medium for communication is also another good reason why XML will almost certainly be adopted at some time in the future.

Summary

In this chapter, you've made a quite extensive grand tour of a wide range of XML applications—from the simplest (OpenTag) to the most complex imaginable (Topic Map Navigation). You've seen what commerce plans to do with XML (with the Channel Definition Format), and you've seen one example of a scientific application (Math Markup Language). It would be pointless to even try to suggest that this tour has been nearly complete. New XML applications are being conceived all the time, and each new application sparks some new idea in someone else's head, giving rise to yet another new application. You can be sure that as XML makes it way into mainstream software packages, it will more than live up to its promise of being extensible.

Differences Between SGML and XML

by Simon North

Rumor has it that the SGML community has always been jealous of the success that HTML has experienced on the World Wide Web. Rumor also has it that when a replacement for HTML started to look like a serious possibility, the SGML community decided it had to act quickly or be left out in the cold. As a member of the general SGML community, I too have fought my share of battles trying to win wider acceptance for SGML. I am not, however, the least bit jealous of HTML's success, and I actually do welcome XML. It may not be *full* SGML, but it's close, and close is better than nothing.

In developing XML, the XML Editorial Review Board had the unenviable task of dissecting SGML to produce a functional core. Every single sentence in the quite formidable SGML standard passed review. If no one could prove that they really could not survive without a particular feature, it went!

In this appendix, you learn about the differences between XML and SGML from the viewpoint of XML as a subset of SGML. This means I take XML as the starting point and examine what differences XML imposes that SGML doesn't impose. It would help if you already have at least a basic familiarity with SGML, but it isn't essential because I try to explain the significance of each feature in SGML or give you an example of how it is used in SGML.

XML as a Subset of SGML

Before I get into the details of the differences between XML and SGML, you really should keep one point in mind throughout the discussion.

HTML is an *application* of SGML, and XML is a *subset* of SGML.

This is a very important distinction because although nearly all of the tools developed for use with SGML can easily be used for HTML, few if any existing SGML tools can be used for XML. For example, a full-SGML validating parser cannot validate SGML documents for conformance with XML unless it is modified to support XML.

Like any other SGML application, HTML is defined by a fixed SGML declaration and a DTD. (In fact, there are several HTML DTDs, reflecting various proprietary HTML extensions such as Netscape's <BLINK> element and Microsoft's <MARQUEE> element.) Unless you are at least a little SGML-aware, it's quite possible that you never have seen an HTML DTD; you might simply never have needed to see one. The success of HTML on the World Wide Web can be ascribed, at least in part, to the fact that the SGML side of HTML is almost completely hidden by everything being hard-wired in the Web browser. However, give an SGML editor a copy of an HTML DTD to work with, and it can happily be used to create HTML files. (As an example, SoftQuad manages to publish an excellent SGML editor in Author/Editor, and a pretty good HTML editor in HoTMetaL Pro.)

XML also uses a fixed SGML declaration, and it can have an SGML DTD. But, unlike HTML, XML imposes certain restrictions on the use of the SGML language and these restrictions cannot be expressed in an SGML declaration.

SGML is a *metalanguage*, a language for defining languages (DTDs) that define SGML applications (generally, but not exclusively, the structure of documents). Through the mechanism of an SGML declaration, SGML also has the power to redefine itself. It is possible, for example, to even redefine the markup characters so that instead of marking up elements using `<ELEMENT>`, you could mark them up using `:ELEMENT:`.

XML is also a metalanguage; it is a language for defining XML DTDs for SGML applications. In order for XML to work, like HTML, it must have a specific SGML declaration. This declaration defines the XML character set, the syntax, and the SGML features that are either supported or explicitly forbidden. It is possible to change the SGML declaration for HTML. The price is that a Web browser might not be able to interpret any of your HTML files, but an SGML editor has no problems with the changes at all. In contrast to HTML (or any other SGML application), it is forbidden for XML to have an explicit SGML declaration. The language that XML is specified to be is the language as it must always be. You cannot change it in any way.

SGML Extensions

Because XML is a subset of SGML, it would be natural to assume that XML is far less powerful than SGML and that you can do a lot less with it. Up to a point this is true and, as you will see later in this appendix, XML does impose a fair number of restrictions on the use of the standard SGML syntax, but not necessarily at the cost of performance.

XML should not be simply regarded as a "crippled" version of SGML. In addition to restricting some of SGML's features, XML also adds some powerful new features to SGML and can be thought of as a fine-tuning of SGML to make it more suitable for use on the Internet (and the World Wide Web, in particular).

In Chapter 17, "Resolution of the XML Specification," you learned about the effect that XML has had on SGML and how some of XML's features are being incorporated into the SGML standard through a Technical Corrigendum (TC) called the *TC for WebSGML Adaptations*. Much of the Web Adaptations TC will most likely be incorporated into the main body of the SGML standard when it is revised and is of no direct interest to anyone solely interested in XML. However, one change to the base (1986) version of the SGML standard is of immediate interest—the so-called Extended Naming Rules annex, which is an integral part of XML because it is optional in SGML but compulsory in XML.

Note: You do not need to understand the extended naming rules to be able to follow the rest of this appendix. If you think discussions about SGML declarations are simply too technical, skip the next section and go straight to the detailed discussion of the differences.

Extended Naming Rules

In its original form, the SGML standard was very heavily weighted in favor of the use of the "standard" western alphabet, which is otherwise known as the ASCII character set. In retrospect, this was a mistake on the part of the developers of SGML. The European languages (with their accented characters) could be accommodated by allowing the use of additional SGML entities taken from the ISO standards (such as ISO Latin 1). However, while the use of external entities allowed the content of SGML instances (documents) to use non-Latin characters, it didn't allow these characters to be used for element tagging itself (in the SGML DTD).

This accidental enforcement of the use of ASCII was actually in conflict with one of the basic principles of SGML itself. (Clause 0.2, subclause e, states "There must be no national language bias.") In December 1996, a Technical Corrigendum called the *TC for Extended Naming Rules* was therefore published to correct this situation.

The Extended Naming Rules corrigendum added a normative Annex J to the SGML standard. This annex extends the syntax of the SGML declaration to allow the definition of extended character sets and the use of character sets that do not make a distinction between uppercase and lowercase characters.

Annex J is an *optional* extension of SGML, and an SGML system does not need to be able to support the Extended Naming Rules for it to qualify as a "conforming" SGML system. However, the implementation of the changes called for by this Annex are compulsory in XML, and the changes are included in XML's SGML declaration and must be supported by any XML tools. (As you remember from the discussion on XML as a subset of SGML, there is a specific SGML declaration for XML that cannot be changed.)

Detailed Differences

I have covered some of the fundamental differences between XML and SGML. Now it's time to look at the detailed differences.

Document Type Definition

Probably the most striking difference between XML and SGML is the fact that an XML document (an *XML instance* in official SGML terms) does not need a Document Type Definition (DTD) if it is well-formed. An SGML instance, in contrast, must always have a DTD (and nearly always an SGML declaration as well, unless you are willing to accept the default concrete syntax).

The requirement for an SGML instance to have a DTD will of course change with the adoption of the WebSGML Adaptations (which were explained in Chapter 17), but for now it is a hard and fast rule that there must always be a DTD for an SGML instance.

SGML doesn't yet have a concept of well-formedness, even though some of the requirements of well-formedness are good coding practice because they make the markup easier to read and understand (for a human as well as for a computer). A particular difference is that SGML does not require you to always have a single element that serves as the *root*. In fact, it is even possible (if a bit far-fetched) for an SGML instance to not contain any tags at all! It could be empty, or it could contain text and rely on various SGML features such as tag minimization and short references—both of which are illegal in XML but allowed in SGML. (See the "Element Declarations" section of this chapter for an explanation of tag minimization, and see the "Other Forbidden SGML Declarations" section for an explanation of short references.)

Comments

In SGML it is quite acceptable to scatter comments all over a DTD and all over your documents. Although this practice makes it very easy to, for example, add high quality comments to a DTD, it makes it very difficult for a parser to determine what is a comment and what isn't, as you can see from this example:

```
<!-- this example comes from the HTML 3.2 spec. -->
<!ATTLIST tr -- table row --
%cell.halign; -- horizontal alignment in cells --
%cell.valign; -- vertical alignment in cells --
>
```

To keep things simple (because it is a design rule that an XML parser has to be quick and easy to write), XML imposes the following important restrictions on what you can do with comments (which are permitted in SGML):

- Comment declarations must be properly delimited with the <!-- and --> strings, and there can be no spaces within these delimiters.
- Comments cannot be placed inside markup declarations.
- You cannot jump out of comments and back into them with -- and --.
- Comments cannot be nested inside each other.

Element Declarations

It is probably in the declaration of elements that XML imposes the most restrictions when it is compared to SGML. Again, it is worth remembering that most of these restrictions really were necessary in order to keep XML software simple, easy to write, and by implication, inexpensive and fast. Some of the SGML features will be seriously missed by people familiar with SGML; the only possible consolation is the knowledge that they have been sacrificed for a good reason.

These are the restrictions that XML imposes on SGML's element declarations:

- The *and connector* (&) is forbidden in XML. In SGML, this symbol allows you to declare the content of an element and specify that all the elements must appear, but leave the order of appearance open, as in this example:

  ```
  <!ELEMENT record - o (name & address & title)>
  ```

  This example says that a <record> must contain a <name>, an <address>, and a <title>, but they can appear in any order.

- Element declarations cannot be grouped together into *name groups*. In SGML this is a very useful shorthand way to make a single element content or attribute list apply to multiple elements, as in the following legal SGML example (which is illegal in XML):

  ```
  <!ELEMENT (chapter, appendix, part) - - (title, intro?, body+)>
  ```

- CDATA (*character data*, data in which any markup other than an end tag will be ignored) and RCDATA (*replaceable character data*, data in which character references and general entities will be recognized but any markup other than an end tag will be ignored) cannot be declared as the content of elements. In SGML, you could declare an element like this:

```
<!ELEMENT code - - CDATA>
```

This is particularly useful for items such as tables of contents. In this example, after the <CODE> element start tag has been seen by the SGML parser, any other element start tags will be ignored until a valid end tag open delimiter </ is seen. The direct result of this is that any text inside an XML element will be parsed when the document is validated. In SGML, by using CDATA and RCDATA element content declarations, you can force the parser to selectively ignore pieces of text. You can, of course, still "hide" the markup by using a CDATA marked section. (See the "Marked Sections" section, later in this chapter, for details.)

■ Element inclusions are not allowed. In SGML, an element inclusion allows to you specify that an element can appear anywhere in the current element or in any of the elements that are contained in it, without including the element in the *content model*. Inclusions are often used for items such as index markers and footnotes that can appear anywhere in a document:

```
<!ELEMENT book - - (front, body, back?) +(indexmarker)>
```

■ Element exclusions are not allowed. In SGML, exclusions are almost the reverse of inclusions. They allow you to specify that an element cannot be used while the current element is still open. They are often used to prevent elements from being embedded inside each other (such as tables within tables, and so on):

```
<!ELEMENT footnote - - (#PCDATA ¦ %text;)* -(footnote)>
```

■ Element declaration minimization parameters are not allowed. (In XML, both element start and end tags must always be used.) In SGML, an element declaration must have two characters included after the element name (or name group), provided the SGML declaration has OMITTAG YES in it, as it does in the *reference concrete syntax*. The first character specifies whether the start tag can be omitted (o for yes, - for no), and the second specifies whether the end tag can be omitted (o for yes, - for no). The subject of tag omission is quite complex because even though an element declaration might specify that a start or end tag can be omitted, you really can omit an element tag only if the presence of the tag can *unambiguously* be implied from the model of the element in which it is embedded. End tag omission is most often used in SGML with empty elements (such as graphics entities), where all you want to do is identify the location of the element:

```
<!ELEMENT artwork - o EMPTY>
```

A familiar example of end tag omission for HTML authors is the <P> element whose declaration in the HTML 3.2 (Wilbur) DTD is as follows:

```
<!ELEMENT P - o (%text)*>
```

This means that the </P> tag can be omitted, and you won't see very many in the majority of HTML pages on the Web.

■ Mixed content declarations must be optional repeatable OR groups (elements joined by *or connectors*, ¦), and they always must have the #PCDATA (parsed character data) content as the first element, like this:

```
<!ELEMENT P (#PCDATA ¦ PARA ¦ CLOSING)*>
```

In SGML, an element model that can contain only other elements is said to contain *element content* only; if it allows data as well as elements, the model is said to contain *mixed content.* Mixed content in elements can cause a lot of problems in SGML applications. Tabs, spaces, record ends, and other separator characters are normally ignored within elements. Elements are declared as having mixed content with a *sequence connector* (,) as in this example:

```
<!ELEMENT a - o (b, #PCDATA) >
<!ELEMENT b o o (#PCDATA) >
```

In this case, if the text

```
<a> <b>this is element b</b> within text</a>
```

was entered, the SGML parser would see the spaces between the start of the <a> element and the start of the <b> element and treat them as PCDATA, or rather as a <b> element with both the start tag and the end tag omitted. When it suddenly encounters the start of the <b> element, you get an error because, according to the content model, the embedded element can occur only once. Similar problems can occur in SGML with the *and connector* (&) and mixed content elements, but this connector is forbidden in XML. This problem cannot occur in XML because of these restrictions and because it is forbidden in XML to omit element start and end tags.

> Note: XML has its own quite specific rules for dealing with white space. Unlike SGML (which discards spaces that are not part of element content), XML has an XML-SPACE attribute that allows you to specify whether spaces should be kept or not (with *not* being the default). The attribute can, of course, only be specified in a DTD; if the XML is processed without a DTD, all the spaces are passed to the application.
>
> This white space handling behavior will also be retrofitted to SGML in the form of a white space in content rule (WSCON) feature in the SGML declaration.

Attributes

As you've just seen, there are quite a few restrictions in XML on what you are able to do in SGML with elements, and they have some far-reaching implications. With attributes, which describe the properties of an element, there are fortunately far fewer restrictions, but these restrictions are quite radical and possibly will cause even more tears to be shed among SGML purists.

XML's restrictions on attributes are as follows:

■ References to external entities in attribute values are forbidden.

■ Attribute default values must always be enclosed in quotes. In SGML, this is necessary only when an attribute value contains a *delimiter* (a space, a tab, or some other separating character).

■ The following SGML attribute types are forbidden in XML:

- NAME and NAMES: The attribute value is a valid SGML name or list of names.

- NUMBER and NUMBERS: The attribute value is a number or list of numbers.

- NUTOKEN and NUTOKENS: The attribute value is a name token or list of name tokens. (A name token is just like a name except that it can have digits or other valid name characters as the first character as well as normal name characters.)

- #CURRENT: If not specified, the attribute value will be the same as the last value used.

- #CONREF: The attribute value is a recognized element ID reference value (the unique identifier of an element), or the element contains the exact wording for a cross-reference. In SGML this is particularly useful for referring to subdocuments.

Marked Sections

Marked sections allow you to have multiple versions of a document in the same SGML or XML file. The text for specific versions is put in marked sections, and text common to all versions is not:

```
<![ %A; [text for version A]]>
<![ %B; [text for version B]]>
```

By defining the correct values to the A and B entities, you can process just the version you want:

```
<!ENTITY % A "IGNORE" >
<!ENTITY % B "INCLUDE" >
```

In SGML, you also can use a marked section with the CDATA to identify text that is not to be parsed:

```
<![CDATA[
<p>This &entity; is hidden
]]>
```

The RCDATA keyword identifies text that can contain character and entity references, but all other delimiters will be ignored:

```
<![RCDATA[
<p>This &entity; will be seen,
but the element markup won't.
]]>
```

The TEMP keyword is used to flag a section as temporary for easy identification:

```
<![TEMP[check spelling here]]>
```

In XML, only CDATA marked sections are permitted in the document *instance*; use of the other keywords and the use of parameter entities (as shown in the example) are forbidden. All of these types of marked sections can, however, be used in the XML DTD.

An extra restriction on the syntax of marked sections is that in XML no spaces are allowed in the marked section markup. The following code is illegal:

```
<! [ CDATA [ text ] ] > is illegal in XML, <![CDATA[ text ]]>
```

Internal Entities

Internal entities (entities whose replacement text appears in the declaration of the entity, which are also known as *text entities*) must obey the following restrictions in XML. These restrictions do not apply in SGML:

- SDATA declarations are forbidden. In SGML, SDATA (*specific character data*) is used to identify data that has some meaning to the processing system on which the SGML application is running. Here is an example:

```
<!ENTITY f12 SDATA "?rf si;&;?fr" -- a photosetter command -->
```

- CDATA (character data) entity declarations are forbidden. (See "Marked Sections" for an explanation.)

- Bracketed text in internal entity declarations is forbidden. In SGML, putting the entity declaration in brackets is a so-called "convenience" that allows you to include markup (even incomplete markup) in the entity text. This is forbidden in XML simply because it requires too much processing to determine how to deal with markup entered in this way.

- Attribute value specifications are forbidden in internal ENTITY declarations. In XML, internal entities are, by definition, text entities. They contain text that will be inserted in place of the entity reference when the XML document is processed. In SGML, you are not bound by this rule, and you can do some pretty sophisticated things using attribute value specifications in entities, including inserting marked sections (using the MS keyword) and inserting markup (using the STARTTAG, ENDTAG, and MD keywords).

- You cannot declare a default general entity value. In SGML, there is a special entity declaration, using the #DEFAULT keyword, that allows you to specify a replacement text that will be used whenever a general entity reference is seen whose name is not recognized as one of the currently declared entities:

```
<!ENTITY #DEFAULT "&RE;&RS;Entity text not found&RE;>
```

External Entities

External entities (any entity that is not an internal entity) must obey the following restrictions in XML. These restrictions do not apply in SGML:

- External entities can be declared in two different ways. They can be declared by means of a SYSTEM keyword followed by a *system identifier* (which is an identifier that means something to the system, such as a URL or a directory path and a filename). This is not different from

SGML. External entities also can be declared using the PUBLIC keyword followed by a *public identifier.* In SGML, this would be enough, but in XML it is not. In XML, the public identifier must be followed by a system identifier as well. The XML processor can use the public identifier to resolve the reference; if it can't do this, it must use the public identifier.

Note: At the moment, there is no defined resolution mechanism in XML for public identifiers. A favorite candidate is the *SGML Open Catalog* system (affectionately known as "socat"), but the final choice has not yet been made.

- ■ SUBDOC entity declarations are forbidden. In SGML, this allows you to nest documents inside each other, each of which must be separately parsed before returning to the calling level.
- ■ SDATA (specific character data) entity declarations are forbidden. (See the section "Internal Entities" earlier in this chapter.)
- ■ CDATA (character data) entity declarations are forbidden. (See the "Internal Entities" section.)
- ■ Attribute value specifications are forbidden in external ENTITY declarations.
- ■ You cannot declare default entities. (See the "Internal Entities" section.)

Notations

Data attributes are forbidden on NOTATION declarations. In SGML you can further qualify the declaration with data attributes that are then passed as parameters to the program that controls the access to the data in that particular notation (for example, the order of the pixels in a raster file).

Other Forbidden SGML Declarations

In XML, the following SGML declarations also are forbidden:

- ■ SHORTREF declarations. In SGML, a *short reference* is a very powerful feature that allows you to use characters, or strings of characters, as a shorthand reference to an entity.

- USEMAP declarations. In SGML, this declaration can be used in the DTD to automatically enable short references whenever a specific element is encountered, or it can be used in the SGML instance to manually enable and disable short references.

- LINKTYPE declarations. In SGML, this declaration allows you to apply concurrent document structures (multiple DTDs) to an SGML instance and, with the LINK declaration (also forbidden in XML), to associate attributes with an element.

- LINK declarations. In SGML, this declaration allows you to automatically or manually associate processing-oriented attributes (for example, formatting attributes) with elements.

- USELINK declarations. In SGML, this declaration is used with the LINKTYPE and LINK declarations (both forbidden in XML) and allows you to specify context-sensitive processing.

- POSTLINK declarations. In SGML, this declaration is used with the LINKTYPE and LINK declarations (both forbidden in XML). Like USELINK, it allows you to specify context-sensitive processing.

- IDLINK declarations. In SGML, this declaration is used with the LINKTYPE and LINK declarations (both forbidden in XML) to associate processing specifications with an individual element (identified by its unique identifier attribute).

- SGML declarations. As discussed in the "XML as a Subset of SGML" section at the beginning of this appendix, XML has a standard SGML declaration that cannot be changed.

Predefined Entities

There are no predefined entities in SGML. The general entities that are predefined in well-formed XML documents that are processed without reference to a DTD (&, ', >, <, and ") would have to be explicitly declared in SGML (just as they should be declared in a valid XML document). This is normally done by including entity references to external entity files that contain sets of text entities (for example, ISOLat1 for accented Western European characters, ISOgrk1 for the Greek alphabet, and ISOtech for technical symbols).

XML Forgives You

So far, this description of the differences between XML and SGML seems to have been completely negative—nothing more than a long list of SGML features that you can't use in XML or you can use only in a limited form. It's all very well saying that they are all given up in a good cause, but that will hardly convince the SGML devotees.

There is hope. It isn't *all* bad! One of the more positive things about XML—which will certainly be a well-liked aspect among those who have had to develop SGML DTDs at any time in their lives—is that XML is far more forgiving about certain things than SGML. The following things would be regarded by SGML tools as serious errors; in XML, the XML parser (or the user) decides whether a warning message is displayed, but in XML these are not considered to be errors:

- Attributes can be defined and attribute lists can be declared for an element declared more than once in XML. The first attribute definition and attribute list declaration counts in XML, and all others are ignored. An XML processor can, but is not required to, issue a warning when a second definition of an attribute or a second attribute list declaration for an element is found, but it is not considered an error. In SGML, both of these would be treated as errors.

- Attributes can be defined for an element, but in XML the element need not be declared. Again, an XML processor can, but is not required to, issue a warning when this happens, but it is not an error. In SGML, this would be treated as an error.

As you can imagine, because XML is intended for use on the Web, and because its linking mechanisms allow you to pull other documents into the current document, this kind of tolerance is essential or the whole system would break very easily.

Note: The fact that XML is more tolerant than SGML does not, however, mean that it is as loose as HTML. Although the Web's premise of accepting anything but generating only good HTML pays lip service to validity in HTML coding, the practice is somewhat different—if the browser interprets it, it's OK. XML's approach to error handling might be called draconian in contrast to HTML, but it is a very pragmatic all-or-nothing approach. For the

> sake of processing simplicity and speed, an XML document may claim to be valid and will be processed accordingly. If it then fails a validity check, it will be treated as invalid with absolutely no attempt being made to skip the offending part and pick up the thread of validity at some later point.

Uppercase Conversion of Attribute Values

One last difference between XML and SGML must be mentioned.

The values of ID, IDREF, IDREFS, NMTOKEN, NMTOKENS, enumerated, or notation type attribute values are converted to uppercase before they are passed to the application by the XML processor. (This is to accommodate languages that have no clear uppercase/lowercase preference, as European languages do.) In SGML, the reverse is done; the values are converted to lowercase.

This difference will probably rarely be noticed by normal mortals like you and me, but it can make a major difference to SGML processing software.

Congratulations if you made it this far! You now have reached the end of a complete description of all the differences between XML and SGML. (The list is as complete as possible, bearing in mind that the XML specification is still only in a draft form, but there is of course no guarantee that things won't change.) I haven't mentioned absolutely everything because some things (such as the special end tag <IMG align="left" src="graphic2.gif"/> for an empty element and white space handling) have already been covered in considerable detail in the main body of this book. Some other differences not mentioned have yet to be resolved (name space problems), and some (such as extended pointers and other XML linking mechanisms) might seem like major differences but were actually already possible within "standard" SGML, so they don't even qualify for a mention.

The differences between XML and SGML might not seem like much at first glance. (In the XML language specification, just one page is devoted to the differences between SGML and XML.) However, after reading through this appendix, you will start to appreciate the fact that some of the differences have very far-reaching implications. XML is a wonderful language, and it represents an incredible improvement on HTML, but somehow it still pales a little when it's put up against SGML. This is not to belittle XML, nor to advocate the use of SGML. It is merely the quiet voice of someone with an SGML background who welcomes XML but, at the same time, is only beginning to realize what will be missed, and who has started to appreciate some of the richer, more exotic features of SGML. As an old Joni Mitchell song says, "you don't know what you've got 'til it's gone."

Bibliography

by Simon North

XML is concerned most with the distribution of information over the Internet. It is therefore somewhat inevitable that the majority of information about XML is also available on the Internet and, more particularly, on the World Wide Web. To assemble the listings included here, I have spent many hours scouring the Web, but even then it is impossible to avoid missing some. To try to be as thorough as possible and avoid giving you locations that could be already out of date by the time you read this, I have tried to include major locations that include pointers to exact locations.

Of course, for people who still like to see the dead-tree editions (and that might even include you, because you are reading this book!), I have also included a selection of some of the most useful books.

Books

Because XML is so new, it can hardly be surprising that there are as yet very few books about it. I have therefore chosen a very few selected SGML books that may also be of interest or assistance to someone predominantly interested in XML and only interested in SGML aspects as they affect XML.

I have intentionally not included any books on HTML. There are simply too many books on the subject and often far better sources of information on the Web.

- *The SGML Handbook*, Charles F. Goldfarb, 1990, Oxford University Press (ISBN 0-19-853737-1): This is probably the most definitive book on the SGML standard, and it is written by someone who really ought to know. Be warned, though, that this is not light reading, but, thanks to its excellent index, it makes a very good technical reference.

- *Practical SGML*, Eric van Herwijnen, 1994, Kluwer Academic Publishers (ISBN 0-7923-9434-8): This is probably the best and the most accessible introduction to SGML that exists.

- *SGML on the Web: Small Steps Beyond HTML*, Murray, Maloney, and Yuri Rubinski, 1997, Prentice Hall PTR (ISBN 0-13-519984-0): Apart from being interesting historically and a tribute to the sad loss of Yuri Rubinski, this book gives some interesting insights into the reasons for using SGML, rather than HTML, on the Web. The book includes a copy of SoftQuad's Panorama SGML browser/plug-in.

- *Developing SGML DTDs: From Text to Model to Markup*, Jeanne El Anduloussi and Eve Maler, 1996, Prentice Hall PTR (ISBN 0-13-309881-8): Although it is focused entirely on SGML, this is one of very few books that adequately covers the subject of DTD development. It will also be of interest to anyone interested in developing serious XML DTDs.

- *The SGML FAQ Book: Understanding the Foundation of HTML and XML*, Steven J. Derose, announced for June 1997, Kluwer Academic Publishers (ISBN 0-7923-9943-9).

- *HTML and SGML Explained*, Martin Bryan, expected 1997, Addison-Wesley Developers Press (ISBN 0-201-40394-3).

- *ABCD...SGML: A User's Guide to Structured Information*, Liora Alschuler, 1995, International Thomson Computer Press (ISBN 1-850-32197-3).

Online Resources

If only two addresses remain in your memory after scanning through this appendix, I hope it will be the following two because they are probably the most complete reference sites for anything connected with SGML and XML. Here are the two addresses:

■ *The SGML Bibliography*: Robin Cover has been collecting bibliographic data on SGML and related topics since 1986. Cover claims that the online, searchable listings are merely a subset of the database, but even so, the online listings appear to cover nearly every kind of print media. This site is a must and can be reached at `http://www.sil.org/sgml/biblio.html`.

■ *The Whirlwind Guide to SGML Tools and Vendors*: Steve Pepper started compiling this guide in 1992, back in the days when doing so was easy in your spare time. The rapidly expanding market has forced him to become somewhat more selective in his entries, but it is still one of the definitive sources, and can be reached at `http://www.falch.no/people/pepper/sgmltool/`.

Articles

Some of the articles on XML can often seem more like advertisements than serious attempts to inform, but there are still quite a few that are worth reading. The following is a selection of some of the best:

■ *The Case for XML, and Others*: Dianne Kennedy is an SGML consultant and writer of some repute. She has written several well-informed and highly informative articles about XML matters that can be accessed online at `http://www.mcs.net/~dken/xml.htm`.

■ *Multidimensional Files: There's a Bright Future Beyond HTML*: This is a very good article covering not just XML but CDF and the Document Object Model as well. You can access it online at `http://webreview.com/97/05/16/feature/xmldim.html`.

■ *XML: Adding Intelligence to Your Business-Critical Documents*: This white paper from Grif discusses the place for XML in intranets. It can be reached at `http://www.grif.fr/newsref/xml.htm`.

- *Some Thoughts and Software on XML*: Bert Bos provides this very short article containing some public thoughts about XML and links to some software. You can reach it at `http://www.w3.org/XML/notes.html`.

- *XML: A Professional Alternative to HTML*: Aimed at HTML authors, this quite technical article by Ingo Macherius gives a fairly thorough picture of XML as an HTML replacement. You can access it online at `http://www.heise.de/ix/artikel/E/1997/06/106/artikel.html`.

- *Microsoft Press Release on Channel Definition Format*: It is somewhat brief but gives an impressive list of all the parties supporting CDF. You can reach it at `http://www.microsoft.com/corpinfo/press/1997/mar97/cdfrpr.htm`.

- *Webcasting in Microsoft Internet Explorer 4.0 White Paper*: This is a fairly good layman's explanation of CDF. You can reach it at `http://www.microsoft.com/ie/ie40/press/push.htm`.

- *An MCF Tutorial*: Worried that the MCF proposal might seem too technical, Tim Bray tries to clarify matters with this retitled rewrite, which can be reached at `http://www.textuality.com/mcf/MCF-tutorial.html`.

- *Building Blocks, Turning the Web Into a Data Source, April 21, 1997*: This is a brief description of how XML (and WebMethod's server software) can bridge the gap between HTML and databases. You can access it online at `http://tni.webmethods.com/news/stories/turning.html`.

- *XML, Java, and the Future of the Web*: This is Jon Bosak's milestone article, originally written in October 1996, and it has been greatly updated since then. You can access it at `http://sunsite.unc.edu/pub/sun-info/standards/xml/why/xmlapps.htm`.

- *CAPV—Document Software Strategies: Gilbane Report*: This publishing industry's view can be reached at `http://www.capv.com/dss/gilbane/report.html`.

- *XML Ready for Prime Time?*: Martin Bryan's conversational review of the very first European XML conference held in London on April 22, 1997 can be accessed at `http://www2.echo.lu/oii/en/xml.html`.

- *XML White Paper*: This is Microsoft's policy on XML, but it still is an excellent description of what XML is and how it works. It can be accessed at `http://www.microsoft.com/standards/xml/xmlwhite.htm`.

■ *PushConcepts—Microsoft*: This useful explanation of the concepts behind CDF can be reached at `http://pushconcepts.com/microsoft.htm`.

■ *An Introduction to Structured Documents*: This is Peter Murray-Rust's extremely readable discussion of the reasons for using XML and CML. It can be accessed at `http://www.sil.org/sgml/murrayRustECHET.html`.

■ *XML for Structured Data*: This is a very interesting open discussion about the use of XML for representing structured data. It can be reached at `http://207.201.154.232/murray/specs/xml-sd.html`.

Applications

These are the Web sites containing the descriptions of the XML applications I knew at the time I wrote this. Most of these applications are also discussed in Chapter 18, "Potential Applications of XML."

■ *Welcome to the OpenTag™ Site*: This Open Tag solution for translation and localization can be reached at `http://www.opentag.org/`.

■ *Web Collections Using XML Submission*: This official W3C submission can be accessed at `http://www.w3.org/pub/WWW/TR/NOTE-XMLsubmit.html`.

■ *CDF, Internet Explorer 4.0, and Third-Party Support*: This shows how CDF and Internet Explorer 4.0 fit together. You can access it at `http://www.microsoft.com/ie/ie40/content`.

■ *Dynamic HTML*: This location contains many useful documents on Microsoft's interpretation of Dynamic HTML and pointers to a wide variety of other sources. You can reach it at `http://www.microsoft.com/workshop/author/dhtml/`.

■ *Unwired Planet—HDML Proposal*: The official W3C proposal can be accessed at `http://www.uplanet.com/pub/hdml_w3c/hdml_proposal.html`.

■ *HDI LifeRaft Selects—Revolutionizing the Support Services Industry*: This is XML for help desk and software support information exchange. You can access it at `http://www.helpdeskinst.com/members/96j_alr1.htm`.

■ *HL7 SGML SIG*: This covers everything associated with HL7 and can be found at `http://www.mcis.duke.edu/standards/HL7/committees/sgml/`.

- *HTML Math Overview*: This definitive site for MathML can be found at `http://www.w3.org/pub/WWW/MarkUp/Math/`.

- *Topic Navigation Map FAQ*: This includes the most often asked questions about topic maps. You can reach it at `http://www.sgml.u-net.com/tnm-faq.htm`.

- *Open Financial Exchange Specification*: XML for the exchange of financial information can be accessed at `http://www.microsoft.com/finserv/ofxdnld.htm`.

- *Sun's On-line (XML) Docs*: This is Sun's answerbook documentation stored in XML and converted dynamically into HTML for publication. You can reach it at `http://docs.sun.com/`.

- *Electronic Databooks Proof of Concept*: This is Norbert Mikula's presentation on the subject of electronic datasheets to the Third Annual (Belux) Conference on the Practical Use of SGML. You can access it at `http://www.sgmlbelux.de/96/mikula.html`.

Standards

ISO standards are copyrighted documents and because they represent a major source of income for ISO, it is understandable that copies are not too easy to find in the public domain. For paper copies of the definitive versions of these standards, you should contact your local national standards organization (all national bodies are authorized to sell copies of ISO and other international standards documents). However, drafts of these standards are readily circulated via the Internet. The following are the locations of some of the most important standards documents available online:

- *Submissions to W3C*: All new proposals to the W3C are listed at `http://www.w3.org/pub/WWW/Submission/`.

- *Extensible Markup Language Version 1.0 Part I: Syntax*: The definitive W3C source can be reached at `http://www.w3.org/pub/WWW/TR/WD-xml-lang.html`.

- *Extensible Markup Language (XML): Part 2. Linking*: The definitive W3C source can be accessed at `http://www.textuality.com/sgml-erb/WD-xml-link.html`.

- *Extensible Hyper Linkage Version 1.0 Henry's Redraft Partial*: This version of the draft (of mainly historical interest) can be accessed at `http://www.sil.org/sgml/new-xml-link970211.html`.

- *XAPI-J: Standardized XML API in Java*: This is Datachannel's focus for discussion on the standard. You can reach it at `http://www.datachannel.com/channelworld/xml/dev/`.

- *SBN Specs & Standards: XML Parser*: Microsoft's attempt to define a standard can be reached at `http://www.microsoft.com/sitebuilder/standards/xml/`.

- *XML-Style* (draft): This very early draft is unfortunately only in PostScript format, but it is better than nothing. You can access it at `http://sunsite.unc.edu/pub/sun-info/standards/dsssl/xs/xs970522.ps.zip`.

- *Document Object Model (DOM)*: This is the definitive W3C source. It can be found at `http://www.w3.org/MarkUp/DOM/`.

- *DOM Requirements*: The W3C requirements document can be reached at `http://www.w3.org/pub/WWW/MarkUp/DOM/drafts/requirements.html`.

- *Draft Specification on Channel Definition Format*: This is Microsoft's official standard proposal. You can reach it at `http://www.microsoft.com/standards/cdf.htm`.

- *Unwired Planet—HDML Language Specification*: The official specification in HTML format can be reached at `http://www.uplanet.com/pub/hdml_w3c/hdml20-3.html`.

- *Mathematical Markup Language (MathML)*: This definitive W3C source can be accessed at `http://www.w3.org/pub/WWW/TR/WD-math/`.

- *Meta Content Framework Using XML*: This is R.V. Guha and Tim Bray's proposal to the W3C and can be accessed at `http://www.textuality.com/sgml-erb/w3c-mcf.html`.

- *Open Financial Exchange Specification*: This is Microsoft's official specification. You can reach it at `http://www.microsoft.com/finserv/ofxdnld.htm`.

- *PICS-NG Metadata Model and Label Syntax*: This is the official working draft from the W3C working group. It can be seen at `http://207.201.154.232/murray/specs/WD-pics-ng-metadata-970514.html`.

- *Web Collections—IBM revision*: The official document at the W3C site can be accessed only by members. This copy is open to the public at `http://www-ee.technion.ac.il/W3C/WebCollection.html`.

- *CD ...: SGML Applications—Topic Navigation Maps, WG8 N1860:* This is the draft of what might become the official ISO standard and is still in a very early stage (even the number hasn't been settled yet). You can reach it at `http://www.ornl.gov/sgml/wg8/document/1860.htm`.

- *Web Interface Definition Language (WIDL):* This is a very brief but informative description of WebMethod's XML application. You can access it at `http://www.sil.org/sgml/xml.html#widl`.

- *HyTime Working Group FTP Archive:* This is the official working group's site for the interchange of files. You can get it at `ftp://infosrv1.ctd.ornl.gov/pub/sgml/WG8/HyTime/TC/`.

- *HyTime: ISO 10744 Hypermedia/Time-based Structuring Language:* This is a public copy of the official standard. You can find it at `http://dmsl.cs.uml.edu/standards/hytime.html`.

- *ISO/IEC 10744 HyTime (Second Edition):* This is Eliot Kimber's (Dr. Macro) unofficial, but as good as definitive, copy of the latest revision of the standard. You can reach it at `http://www.drmacro.com/hythtml/is10744r.html`.

- *Unicode Home Page:* This is the official unicode site and can be reached at `http://www.unicode.org/`.

Information Sources

The following sites contain information of a general nature about SGML and XML:

- *SGML and XML Resources:* This is a very useful set of links and pointers. You can access it at `http://www.arbortext.com/linksgml.html`.

- *What is XML?:* The GCA are the main organizers of SGML and XML conferences around the world. This site has some useful pointers and can be reached at `http://www.gca.org/conf/xml/xml_what.htm`.

- *Commonly Asked Questions about the Extensible Markup Language:* This is maintained on behalf of the W3C and is the definitive site for a lot of those nagging questions that aren't answered by the official documents. You can access it at `http://www.ucc.ie/xml/`.

- *XML (W3C Site):* This is more or less the focus for all XML activity. You can reach it at `http://www.w3.org/pub/WWW/XML/`.

- *XML (Robin Cover's Site)*: This SGML Web site is an Aladdin's cave of useful information and pointers to XML information. It can be reached at `http://www.sil.org/sgml/xml.html`.

- *XML: The Extensible Markup Language—James K. Tauber's Site*: This very useful source of information can be accessed at `http://www.jtauber.com/xml/`.

- *XML Developers' Mailing List*: This is a public mailing list for extremely technical discussions about the development of XML and XML software. The following site keeps hyperlinked archives of all the messages sent to the list: `http://www.lists.ic.ac.uk/hypermail/xml-dev/`.

- *Distributed Objects Mailing List*: This is a public mailing list for extremely technical discussions about the development of distributed object software. This site keeps hyperlinked archives of all the messages sent to the list. You can see it at `http://www.infospheres.caltech.edu/mailing_lists/dist-obj/`.

Software Packages

The following software packages are packages that are known to support XML now (most of this software is discussed in Chapter 16):

- *Chris Stevenson's Java Applets*: These Java Applets for processing XML can be reached at `http://www.users.on.net/zhcchz/java.html`.

- *Chrystal Software Astoria*: This is XML document management software. You can access it at `http://www.chrystal.com/xml.htm`.

- *Balise Home Page*: This is SGML and XML middleware. You can get it at `http://www.balise.berger-levrault.fr/`.

- *DSC*: This DSSSL syntax checking software can be reached at `http://www.ltg.ed.ac.uk/~ht/dsc-blurb.html`.

- *DSSSLTK*: This DSSSL toolkit is available at `http://www.copsol.com/products/index.html`.

- *GRIF S.A.*: The Symposia HTML/XML editor and browser can be reached at `http://www.grif.fr/`.

- *Jade*: This is James Clark's DSSSL engine. You can get it at `http://www.jclark.com/jade`.

- *Scientific Information Components using Java/XML*: The Jumbo XML/CML viewer Java application can be accessed at `http://ala.vsms.nottingham.ac.uk/vsms/java/jumbo/index.html`.

- *Lark*: Tim Bray's non-validating parser written in Java can be seen at `http://www.textuality.com/Lark/`.

- *LTG software: LT XML tools and developers' API*: This is the Language Technology Group's C++ and Java processing software for XML. You can see it at `http://www.ltg.ed.ac.uk/software/xml/`.

- *MSXML*: This is Microsoft's XML parser written in Java. You can access it at `http://www.microsoft.com/standards/xml/xmlparse.htm`.

- *NXP*: Norbert Mikula's XML parser is written in Java and can be reached at `http://www.edu.uni-klu.ac.at/~nmikula/NXP`.

- *Tcl Support for XML*: This Tcl toolkit for processing XML documents can be accessed at `http://tcltk.anu.edu.au/XML/`.

- *Stilo WebWriter*: This is an HTML/XML editor. You can get it at `http://www.pimc.com/WebWriter/download.html`.

- *webMethods—Automate the Web*: This WWW server software for XML can be accessed at `http://www.webmethods.com/home.html`.

- *Copernican Solutions Incorporated—XML Developer's Toolkit (XDK)*: You can see this XML middleware at `http://www.copsol.com/products/xdk/index.html`.

- *Sean Russell's XML Package*: This XML parser is written in Java. You can reach it at `http://jersey.uoregon.edu/ser/software/`.

Software Companies

The companies listed here either already produce software that supports XML, have already announced software packages that support XML, or can be expected to release software that supports XML in the very near future (most of the software in the following list is discussed in Chapter 16):

- *AIS Berger-Levrault*: This company makes SGML and XML processing and database software. You can reach them at `http://www.balise.berger-levrault.fr/`.

- *ArborText Inc.*: They make SGML and XML editors, formatters, and conversion software. They can be reached at `http://www.arbortext.com/`.

- *Chrystal Software Inc.*: This document and component management software company can be reached at `http://www.chrystal.com/`.

- *Copernican Solutions Incorporated*: XML, DSSSL, and SGML software is produced here. You can reach them at `http://www.copsol.com/`.

- *Grif S.A.*: This manufacturer of SGML and XML editors, browsers, and formatters can be accessed at `http://www.grif.fr/`.

- *High Text*: These Topic Navigation Map experts and SGML and HyTime consultants can be reached at `http://www.hightext.com/`.

- *Inso Corporation*: This manufacturer of SGML and XML conversion and browsing software can be reached at `http://www.inso.com/`.

- *Language Technology Group*: You can reach these makers of DSSSL and XML processing software at `http://www.ltg.ed.ac.uk/`.

- *Microsoft Corporation*: You can reach this manufacturer of XML (and other) software at `http://www.microsoft.com/`.

- *SoftQuad Home Page*: These makers of SGML editors and browsers can be accessed at `http://www.sq.com/`.

- *STILO Technology Ltd.*: These makers of SGML, HTML, and XML editors can be reached at `http://www.stilo.com`.

- *webMethods*: This is a manufacturer of WWW server software for XML. You can reach them at `http://www.webmethods.com/home.html`.

DSSSL

Pointers to the parts of DSSSL that are directly relevant to XML (such as the XS specification) can be found among the main lists of XML sites. The following addresses are for those with wider interests; the first is historical (a copy of the original DSSSL-O draft) and the others are for those who want to follow the development of the DSSSL specification (you will need to refer to this if you want to understand the XS specification):

- *DSSSL Online Application Profile*: This is the 1996.08.16 draft of the standard for the predecessor to XS. You can see it at `http://sunsite.unc.edu/pub/sun-info/standards/dsssl/dssslo/do960816.htm`.

- *A Tutorial on DSSSL*: This is one of the best (and one of the few) existing tutorials on DSSSL. You can access it at `http://csg.uwaterloo.ca/~dmg/dsssl/tutorial/tutorial.html`.

- *Introduction to DSSSL*: Paul Prescod's very able introduction to DSSSL's style language can be reached at `http://itrc.uwaterloo.ca:80/~papresco/dsssl/tutorial.html`.

- *DSSSList—The DSSSL Users' Mailing List*: This is a public mailing list for the highly technical discussion of matters concerned with DSSSL. You can reach it at `http://www.mulberrytech.com/dsssl/dssslist/`.

SGML

There are literally thousands of Web sites containing information concerning SGML. The following is an extremely select list of the most useful sites:

- *SGML Open Home Page*: This is the organization for SGML vendors and other companies. You can see it at `http://www.sgmlopen.org/`.

- *SGML FTP Archive*: Erik Naggum in Norway has been archiving the comp.text.sgml Usenet group for several years. The complete archive, containing more than 11,000 Usenet postings, can be found at `ftp://ftp.ifi.uio.no/pub/SGML`.

- *The SGML University*: This very useful repository for SGML bits and pieces can be found at `http://www.sgml.com/`.

- *The SGML Web Page*: This is probably the best existing online source for SGML information. You can access it at `http://www.sil.org/sgml/`.

- *ISO/IEC JTC1/SC18/WG8 Home Page*: This is the semi-official site for the ISO working group on SGML. You can reach it at `http://www.ornl.gov/sgml/WG8/wg8home.htm`.

- *Charles F. Goldfarb's Web Site*: Because Charles is one of the inventors of SGML, this is one of the definitive sources for news and information on the subject. You can find it at `http://www.sgmlsource.com/`.

- *SGML on the Web*: This is a useful collection of pointers to Web sites that publish in SGML. You can reach it at `http://www.ncsa.uiuc.edu/WebSGML/WebSGML.html`.

- *W3C SGML Working Group Mailing List*: This is the public mailing list for the W3C SGML working group. The messages are archived at `http://lists.w3.org/Archives/Public/w3c-sgml-wg/`.

You should note that the Web addresses given here can change at any time. Although I personally have checked all of these addresses, and many have proved to be stable for a period of several years, I cannot absolutely guarantee that they are correct and, if so, for how long.

Glossary

> Note: Where a concept is described in the current draft (June 30, 1997) of the XML-Lang or XML-Link specification, its definition in this glossary is followed by a reference to the appropriate section of that draft.

application: The piece of software on behalf of which an XML processor processes XML documents. (XML-Lang 1.) More colloquially, a usage of the generic XML framework for a particular purpose, with its own DTD, linking conventions, and style sheets.

attribute: A name-value pair that is associated with an element. Attribute values can be specified in the element's start-tag, or default values can be inherited from the DTD. (XML-Lang 3.)

attribute declaration: A declaration in the DTD specifying an attribute's name, type, and default value. (XML-Lang 3.3.)

attribute-list declaration: In the DTD, a list of attribute declarations for a particular element type. (XML-Lang 3.3.)

CDATA section: A part of an XML document in which markup (apart from that indicating the end of the CDATA section) is not interpreted as such, but is passed to the application as is. (XML-Lang 2.7.)

character: An atomic unit of text represented by a bit string. (XML-Lang 2.3.)

character data: The actual text of an XML document, as opposed to the markup of the document. (XML-Lang 2.4.)

character reference: An escape code for a single Unicode character that quotes the numerical value of its bit string. (XML-Lang 4.2.)

comment: A piece of markup within an XML document containing text that is not to be considered part of the document. (XML-Lang 2.5.)

conditional section: In the DTD, a set of markup that can be included in, or excluded from, the logical structure of the DTD, depending on the keyword at its start. (XML-Lang 3.4.)

content model: In the DTD, a description of what might occur within instances of a given element type. (XML-Lang 3.2.1.)

document: See *XML document.*

document element: The single element that contains all the other elements and character data that comprise an XML document. (XML-Lang 2.2.)

document type declaration: A declaration at the start of an XML document that specifies where the external DTD subset can be found and includes the internal DTD subset. (XML-Lang 2.9.)

document type definition: See *DTD*.

DSSSL: Document Style Semantics and Specification Language. An International Standard, ISO/IEC 10179:1996, which defines a transformation language and a style language for the processing of valid SGML documents.

DTD: A set of rules governing the element types that are allowed within an XML document and rules specifying the allowed content and attributes of each element type. The DTD also declares all the external entities referenced within the document and the notations that can be used. See also *external DTD subset*. (XML-Lang 2.9.)

element: A logical unit of information within an XML document. (XML-Lang 3.)

element construction rule: An instruction in an XS style sheet specifying which flow objects are to be constructed when a particular element type is encountered.

element content: In the DTD, a content model that allows other elements only inside instances of a given element type. (Compare *mixed content*.) (XML-Lang 3.2.1.)

element type: A particular type of element, such as "paragraph." An element's type is indicated by the Name that occurs in its start-tag and end-tag. (XML-Lang 3.1.)

empty element: An element containing no subelements or character data. (XML-Lang 3.1.)

encoding declaration: A declaration of the character encoding scheme used for a particular text entity. (XML-Lang 4.3.3.)

end-tag: A tag that marks the end of an element, such as `</section>`. (XML-Lang 3.1.)

entity: Any data that can be treated as a unit. Often used to refer to an external file that holds parts of an XML document, or to non-XML resources such as images. (XML-Lang 4.)

entity declaration: Part of the DTD. Declares a name for the entity and associates it with a replacement string or externally stored data identified by a URL. (XML-Lang 4.3.)

entity reference: A reference within the text of an XML document to a previously declared entity, signifying that a copy of the entity is to be included at this point. (XML-Lang 4.2.)

extended link: A link that can involve any number of resources and is not required to be co-located with any of them. (XML-Link 3.4.)

Extensible Markup Language: See *XML*.

external binary entity: A non-XML resource, such as an image file, referred to from within an XML document. (XML-Lang 4.3.2.)

external DTD subset: The part of the DTD that is held in a separate resource addressed by a URL. The external DTD subset is often referred to as the *DTD* of a class of documents. See also *DTD*. (XML-Lang 2.9.)

external text entity: A resource (often, a file) containing XML character data and markup that is referred to from within an XML document. (XML-Lang 4.3.2.)

flow object: A formatting feature, such as a paragraph or a table cell, into which the content of an XML document is flowed under the control of an XS style sheet.

flow object tree: The complete set of flow objects into which an XML document is converted by an XS style sheet.

generic identifier: The name assigned to an element type.

GI: See *generic identifier*.

grove: A representation of an XML document in which each node represents a property of the document.

HTML: Hypertext Markup Language. An encoding scheme for displaying and hyperlinking pages of information on the World Wide Web. HTML is, formally speaking, an application of SGML.

inline link: See *simple link.*

internal DTD subset: The part of the DTD that is declared within the XML document itself, before the first start-tag. (XML-Lang 2.9.)

internal entity: An entity whose value is given in its entity declaration in the DTD. (XML-Lang 4.3.1.)

locator: A character string that identifies a resource participating in a link. (XML-Link 1.3, 5.1.)

logical structure: The declarations, elements, character references, processing instructions, and so on that make up an XML document. These are all indicated by explicit markup. (XML-Lang 3.)

markup: Information that is intermingled with the text of an XML document to indicate its logical and physical structure. (XML-Lang 2.4.)

mixed content: In the DTD, a content model that allows character data, optionally interspersed with subelements. (Compare *element content.*) (XML-Lang 3.2.2.)

Name: Within an XML DTD, consists of a letter or underscore followed by zero or more name characters. (XML-Lang 1.5.)

name character: A letter, digit, hyphen, underscore, full stop, or one of a set of special characters specified in the XML standard. (XML-Lang 1.5.)

Name token: Any mixture of name characters. (XML-Lang 1.5.)

non-validating XML processor: An XML processor that checks whether XML documents are well-formed but not whether they are valid. (XML-Lang 5.)

notation: The format in which an external binary entity is held, such as a BMP image or an MPEG video. (XML-Lang 4.6.)

out-of-line link: A link that does not serve as one of its own resources. (XML-Link 1.3, 3.5.)

parameter entity: A text entity used within the DTD or used to control processing of conditional sections. (XML-Lang 4.2.)

physical structure: The arrangement of physical storage units (entities) in which an XML document is held. (XML-Lang 4.1.)

PI: See *processing instruction.*

processing instruction: A piece of markup that gives information or instructions to software that will process an XML document. They do not form part of the document's character data. (XML-Lang 2.6.)

prolog: The part of an XML document, including the XML declaration and DTD, that precedes the actual document element. (XML-Lang 2.9.)

required markup declaration: An indication, by the author of an XML document, to the parts of the DTD an XML processor needs to read to interpret the document correctly. (XML-Lang 2.10.)

resource: Any addressable unit of information that can participate in a link. Includes complete XML documents, elements (or spans of elements) within them, and chunks of text. (XML-Link 1.3.)

root element: See *document element.*

SGML: Standard Generalized Markup Language. An International Standard (ISO 8879:1986) that describes a generalized markup scheme for representing the logical structure of documents in a system-independent and platform-independent manner.

simple link: An inline link, such as the familiar `<A HREF="X">` tag in HTML, that links a specific point in an XML document to some target resource. (XML-Link 3.3.)

Standard Generalized Markup Language: See *SGML.*

start-tag: A tag that marks the start of an element, such as `<section>`. (XML-Lang 3.1.)

style sheet: A set of instructions specifying how each structural object within a document is to be formatted.

traversal: Use of a link to access the resource at the other (or another) end of that link. (XML-Link 1.3.)

valid XML document: An XML document that conforms to all rules expressed in its DTD. (XML-Lang 2.9.)

W3C: World Wide Web Consortium.

well-formed XML document: An XML document that consists of a single element containing correctly nested subelements. All entity references within the document must refer to entities that have been declared in the DTD, or be one of a small set of default entities. (XML-Lang 2.2.)

XML: Extensible Markup Language. A profile, or simplified subset, of SGML. Supports generalized markup on the World Wide Web.

XML declaration: A processing instruction at the start of an XML document, which asserts that the document is XML. (XML-Lang 2.9.)

XML document: An XML document consists of an optional XML declaration, followed by an optional document type declaration, followed by a document element. (XML-Lang 2.)

XML processor: A program that reads XML documents, checks whether they are valid and well-formed, and makes their contents available to XML applications. (XML-Lang 1.)

XPointer: A syntax for identifying the element, range of elements, or text within an XML document that is the target resource of a link. (XML-Link 6.)

XS: The XML style sheet language.

Index

M

A VIACOM SERVICE

The Information SuperLibrary™

Bookstore

Search

What's New

Reference

Software

Newsletter

Company Overviews

Yellow Pages

Internet Starter Kit

HTML Workshop

Win a Free T-Shirt!

Macmillan Computer Publishing

Site Map

Talk to Us

CHECK OUT THE BOOKS IN THIS LIBRARY.

You'll find thousands of shareware files and over 1600 computer books designed for both technowizards and technophobes. You can browse through 700 sample chapters, get the latest news on the Net, and find just about anything using our massive search directories.

All Macmillan Computer Publishing books are available at your local bookstore.

We're open 24-hours a day, 365 days a year.

You don't need a card.

We don't charge fines.

And you can be as **LOUD** as you want.

The Information SuperLibrary

http://www.mcp.com/mcp/   ftp.mcp.com

MACMILLAN COMPUTER PUBLISHING USA

A VIACOM COMPANY

Technical ---┐
                └--- **Support:**

If you need assistance with the information in this book or with a CD/Disk accompanying the book, please access the Knowledge Base on our Web site at **http://www.superlibrary.com/general/support**. Our most Frequently Asked Questions are answered there. If you do not find the answer to your questions on our Web site, you may contact Macmillan Technical Support **(317) 581-3833** or e-mail us at **support@mcp.com**.

HTML 4 Unleashed

—Rick Darnell, Michael Larson, et al.

HTML 4 Unleashed is a comprehensive guide and reference to the foundation language of the World Wide Web, and it provides an exhaustive resource devoted to the language of Web development. The Web's explosive growth continues to foster an expanding market of Web authors ranging from casual home hobbyists to the professional Web developer. *HTML 4 Unleashed* provides these readers the information they need in order to grow with an ever-changing technology. This book covers all the latest proprietary extensions, including Microsoft's Active HTML and Netscape's JavaScript Stylesheets, and it includes information on integrating HTML with other technologies such as Java and ActiveX. *HTML 4 Unleashed* details new HTML technologies such as the experimental "Cougar" specification, cascading style sheets, and Extensible Markup Language (XML). The book's CD-ROM contains a wide variety of HTML development tools, a collection of examples from the authors, and two electronic books in HTML format.

$49.99 USA/$70.95 CAN   Accomplished–Expert   1-57521-299-4

Teach Yourself Web Publishing with HTML 4 in 14 Days, Second Professional Reference Edition

—Laura Lemay & Arman Danesh

Teach Yourself Web Publishing with HTML 4 in 14 Days, Second Professional Reference Edition is a thoroughly revised version of the best-selling book that started the whole HTML/Web publishing phenomenon. It is easy enough for the beginner, yet comprehensive enough that even experienced Web authors will find it indispensable for reference. This book includes 16 more chapters than the softcover edition, plus a 300-page HTML reference section. It also covers the new "Cougar" specification for the next version of HTML and the new Netscape and Microsoft technologies such as style sheets, absolute positioning, and dynamic HTML. The book's CD-ROM includes an electronic version of the reference section, plus additional Web publishing tools for Windows and Macintosh platforms.

$59.99 USA/$84.95 CAN   New–Casual–Accomplished   1-57521-305-2

Teach Yourself Web Publishing with HTML 4 in a Week, Fourth Edition

—Laura LeMay

Teach Yourself Web Publishing with HTML 4 in a Week, Fourth Edition is a thoroughly revised version of the shorter beginner's softcover edition of the best-selling book that started the whole HTML/Web publishing craze. This book now covers the new HTML "Cougar" specification, plus the Netscape Communicator and Microsoft Internet Explorer 4 environments, as well as style sheets, Dynamic HTML, and XML. It teaches Web publishing in a clear, step-by-step manner with lots of practical examples of Web pages, and it is still the best HTML tutorial on the market.

$29.99 US/$42.95 CAN   New–Casual   1-57521-336-2

Teach Yourself Dynamic HTML in a Week

—Bruce Campbell & Rick Darnell

Teach Yourself Dynamic HTML in a Week gives you detailed instructions on how to use Dynamic HTML and Web scripting languages to create Web pages and Web applications that change in response to user actions. The book includes a thorough tutorial on all the technologies collectively referred to as Dynamic HTML. It also includes coverage of both the Microsoft Internet Explorer 4 and Netscape Communicator technologies, and it teaches the new Dynamic HTML tags and concepts such as the Document Object Model in a clear, step-by-step manner with lots of practical examples.

$29.99 US/$42.95 CAN   Casual–Advanced   1-57521-335-4

Add to Your Sams.net Library Today
with the Best Books for Internet Technologies

ISBN	Quantity	Description of Item	Unit Cost	Total Cost
1-57521-299-4		HTML 4 Unleashed	$49.99	
1-57521-305-2		Teach Yourself Web Publishing with HTML 4 in 14 Days, Professional Reference Edition	$59.99	
1-57521-336-2		Teach Yourself Web Publishing with HTML 4 in a Week, 4E	$29.99	
1-57521-335-4		Teach Yourself Dynamic HTML in a Week	$29.99	
		Shipping and Handling: See information below.		
		TOTAL		

Shipping and Handling: $4.00 for the first book, and $1.75 for each additional book. If you need to have it NOW, we can shi product to you in 24 hours for an additional charge of approximately $18.00, and you will receive your item overnight or i two days. Overseas shipping and handling adds $2.00. Prices subject to change. Call between 9:00 a.m. and 5:00 p.m. EST f availability and pricing information on latest editions.

201 W. 103rd Street, Indianapolis, Indiana 46290

1-800-428-5331 — Orders   1-800-835-3202 — FAX   1-800-858-7674 — Customer Servic

Book ISBN 1-57521-334-6